OUTFC

TAKE TWO

My journey to expose and oppose the cruel mistreatment of animals and a factual account of 'sporting' activities in our countryside

By
Mike Huskisson

For Barbara,

Mike Huskisson.

Published by
Animal Welfare Information Service
PO Box 8, Halesworth, Suffolk, IP19 0JL
www.acigawis.org.uk

Outfoxed (ISBN 0 9509284 02) was first published in Great Britain by Michael Huskisson Associates in November 1983.

This revised and updated version is published by the Animal Welfare Information Service in November 2015.

© Copyright Mike Huskisson 2015

The right of Mike Huskisson to be identified as the author of this work has been asserted in accordance with the Copyright, Designs and Patents Act 1988.

ISBN 978-0-9933822-0-8

Printed and bound in Great Britain by Clays Ltd, St Ives plc

DEDICATED TO SUE AND MY FAMILY.

THEIR LOVE, TOLERANCE AND SUPPORT
HAVE BEEN BEYOND EQUAL.

CONTENTS

Page

CHAPTER ONE Up close to a hunt..8

CHAPTER TWO Learning how a hunt works..........................12

CHAPTER THREE Direct action to save lives........................28

MY ANTI-HUNTING DIARY...42

CHAPTER FOUR Beyond the legal front line....................... 50

CHAPTER FIVE Prison life...67

CHAPTER SIX Life after jail..71

CHAPTER SEVEN Deer hunting...81

CHAPTER EIGHT Fox hunting..117

CHAPTER NINE Hare hunting and hare coursing..................157

CHAPTER TEN Mink hunting...177

EPILOGUE..216

GLOSSARY OF SOME HUNTING TERMS........................225

DIARY OF UNDERCOVER INVESTIGATIONS..................228

INDEX.. 233

PREFACE TO REVISED EDITION

For years I put off writing a revised and updated version of this book simply because I had too much further investigation work to do. However the passage of time and the realisation that records and films fade, coupled with repeated requests for the original book, have prompted this new edition.

I have corrected some grammatical or spelling errors in the original. I have elaborated and explained outdated terms where necessary. I have added a diary listing my early work as a hunt saboteur — where I learned exactly how hunting works. Most importantly I have added an index. There are some other new parts and extra photographs. For all these changes I have tried so far as is possible to retain the immediacy and anger of the original text that was written a matter of mere months after my original investigations.

Of course all that is written about here — fox, deer, hare and mink hunting, and hare coursing was banned by law on the grounds of cruelty by the Hunting Act 2004. At the time of writing (2015) this law is widely flouted but it remains the law and there is hope that one day a Government will respond to the overwhelming demands of our nation and strengthen the Act and ensure that it is enforced.

This original text was written in the summer of 1983. As hunting was all fully legal then I have retained the use of the present tense. I have tried to follow the hunting convention whereby unless or until it is shown otherwise all hunted foxes are male and hunted hares are female. For hunted deer their sex is obvious — apart from young calves. For mink hunting I followed the fox hunting convention and assumed that hunted mink are male.

My words of over 30 years ago describe investigation work carried out in a totally different world, in technical terms, from today. We had no mobile phones. If you needed to make an urgent phone call you had to find a phone box, secondly have coins to hand, and then probably search further for a phone box that worked.

We had no video cameras. Our movie cameras were Super-8mm cine cameras. Each film recorded just a few minutes. You also needed good light to film. Few cameras came with sound and for this project I chose a camera with the best optical quality rather than a lesser quality lens with sound. We could only have dreamed of using the concealed body cameras, drones, and remote self-contained cameras that are available to investigators today. The latter can be concealed in woods. They go to sleep until triggered by a passing person when they wake up, film for a few minutes and then return to sleep mode.

There were no digital still cameras in 1981 — no ability to take countless images a day, or many a second, at various ISO (film speed) settings from 200 to 8000 plus. In little light you selected a wide-open aperture on your lens, a very slow shutter speed and steadied your camera but if that was not enough you could not take the picture.

I used a 35mm film camera where each film allowed 36 exposures. You used a film of set ISO (200, 400 or 800) and had little opportunity to change it mid-roll. Today if you can see it you can picture it. That would have been a real asset all those years ago. In addition my Nikon F2, the top professional camera of the day, had no autofocus and no auto-exposure. You had to twist focus the lens. Getting the exposure right was a matter of adjusting a swinging needle by altering aperture or shutter speed. None of this could be done quickly. At the end of a hunt there was often very little time, particularly with a stag at bay. Finally, there was no immediate checking of your photographs. In those days you had to take your finished film to a chemist or photographic shop for processing, or even worse post it away and wait a week for it to be returned.

We had no satnavs to aid navigation in cars. You simply had to be able to read a map, pick out and recognise landmarks and learn your way around our countryside. We had no hand-held Global Positioning System (GPS) devices that can give you your exact location on the ground. Again you had to be able to read a map.

Time has inevitably taken some of the people named in this book: from our side Bob August, Mary Beith, Richard Course, John Hicks and Sue Smith to name but five great campaigners. Some from the hunting side have passed on. Some have also changed sides. Some have changed back again, with at least one going in each direction.

When I wrote the original text in the summer of 1983 I would never have thought that in the hunting season just ended (2014/15) I would have been witnessing exactly the same cruelty to our wildlife — and certainly not a full ten years after the so-called hunting 'ban'.

It is fair to point out that much of this book is denied by the hunting world. Hunters were outraged after the original *Outfoxed* was published. They damned me as a contemptible criminal and cursed the fact that many from various hunts unwittingly befriended me and guided me to the very core of hunting. Spokesmen for hunting accused me of lying, exaggerating, or setting up incidents.

Over the years hunters have perfected a whole repertoire of excuses to explain anything untoward that happens in the hunting fields. It never happened or it was faked. If it did happen it was set up or they were not there. If they were there they saw nothing. If they did see anything it was an accident. If it was not an accident then whoever did it was unknown to the hunt. If they were known then swift and severe disciplinary action has been taken.

I stand by my original words. I described what I saw and heard. I provoked nothing. I photographed and filmed what I could. I am neither a professional writer nor a professional photographer but I hope that I am able to convey some idea as to how animals are really treated in our world. Yes, the hunting described here was all a long while ago now but at the interface between hound and quarry little has changed.   Mike Huskisson, Suffolk, England. September 2015

ACKNOWLEDGEMENTS FOR OUTFOXED

I extend thanks first and foremost to Richard Course, at the time Executive Director of the League Against Cruel Sports (LACS), for accepting that, having paid my debt to society, I still had a legitimate and useful role to play in the fight against cruelty. Without his far sightedness in recommending this project and my employment to the League's Executive Committee the evidence contained in this book would have remained concealed from the general public.

I am most grateful to the Executive Committee and staff of the LACS for their assistance, support and encouragement throughout the two year undercover operation, and since. Special thanks are extended to Maureen Lawless for her assistance in preparing and editing the manuscript, to Liz Jordan for her excellent typing, and to Cee Wetton and Ken Sheridan for permission to reproduce their cartoons.

Lastly of course I express my appreciation to Ian Coghill, Arlin Rickard, Terry Beeney and the many others amongst the hunting set who showed me the truth.

ACNOWLEDGEMENTS FOR OUTFOXED TAKE TWO

In addition to the above I thank Mark Quested for re-typing the original text and Dave and Cee Wetton for checking the hunt sabotage part. I thank Joe Hashman for his great help with proof-reading and creating the index, Kevin Hill for help with the text and Ed Maynard for assistance with the photographs. Over the years I have worked with many colleagues, few of whom are named here but I thank all for their support and assistance. I also thank the supporters of the Animal Cruelty Investigation Group and Animal Welfare Information Service whose generous donations have made this publication possible.

Finally this would never have happened without the support, advice and encouragement of my family to whom I am eternally grateful.

CHAPTER ONE
Up close to a hunt

Light rain was falling as I fought my way along a muddy track and through deep undergrowth.

Ahead of me, people swept forward screaming and shouting. Behind, motorbikes and Land Rovers bumped and roared their way through the mud. Screeching to a halt, their occupants ran past me as I slipped and slithered over a pile of wet logs, shielding my camera as I fell.

Through the dense pine wood, several hundred yards from the River Exe, an exhausted young stag had stumbled only seconds before. Four hours and many miles of desperate chase had taken its inevitable toll. Now he was defenceless.

Escape to the river was blocked by car and motorbike followers. Behind was an approaching fan of riders. All the participants had arrived. The scene was set for the bloody, barbaric end of a stag hunt.

Hounds were all around him, snapping and biting at his flanks. As he twisted, head down to fend one off, so another of the pack of forty would move in. Bewildered, the stag was stationary, at bay beneath the green pine canopy.

I was carried along in the headlong, ghoulish rush, as hunt followers dived to grab him and wrestled him to the ground. The proud beast keeled over as more and more people piled on top until he collapsed flat on his side.

"*Grab his antlers. Grab him, pull him down. Let them at him,*" the cries rang out, as the hounds tried to move in.

My hands, numbed with cold, twisted and turned the camera controls. Menacing glances switched from the focussed lens to my British Field Sports Society (BFSS) [forerunner to the Countryside Alliance] badge on the lapel of my green Barbour jacket, then to my face and their owners, by tacit agreement, shuffled silently around, shielding the gruesome spectacle from the outside world.

Under the dense foliage on a late spring evening there was no light anyway; a lens aperture of f1.4 and a shutter speed of eighth of a second on my Nikon F2 is no combination for action photography. I concealed my camera, and squeezed through the closed ranks, determined at least, to see for myself.

Four muscular hands gripped the stag's short antlers and pressed his head into the soft pine mould soil. The young beast blinked, wide eyed and helpless and panted the primeval fear of all creatures who stare death in the face.

Rough work boots and tweed covered knees held his body steady, as hands deterred the hounds from their wilder excesses.

"*Where's the bloody gun?*" a shout went up, but there was no hunt supporter with a gun nearby. Perhaps feeling twinges of remorse some willing people ran off searching for one of the hunt's executioners.

Others, young and old, male and female, crowded round to watch, laughing and joking at the creature's misery. They lit up cigarettes or had the last tots from their battered hip flasks.

The seconds ticked into minutes. The stag panted on, but there was no escape. Over five minutes elapsed before a delighted red-coated gentleman rode up with a small calibre pistol.

The crowd parted to give him access and I inched forward in his wake. After a few taunts as to where the muzzle of the pistol was placed on the stag's exposed head, a merciful shot rang out. The stag shuddered and was still.

The drawn out, staccato notes from the hunting horn blown by the Huntsman, signalling the kill, echoed across the deep, murky hillside as if taunting the nation of so called animal lovers.

It was April 1982 and I, a member and employee of the League Against Cruel Sports (LACS) had stood and watched as the Tiverton Staghounds made another kill. The LACS had been set up in 1924 with the express aim of ending all such cruel sports.

Why was I standing there watching? What was I doing?

To understand it is necessary to turn the clock back almost a year.

*****

Cold April air bit sharply at my face as I stepped out of the building into a late London afternoon. The door behind me closed on the top secret meeting I had just attended.

The place: the LACS Headquarters in Union Street just south of the Thames, where a plot had been hatched that was aimed at destroying the sport of some of the most powerful people in Britain, including the Royal Family – hunting.

For the next two years only a handful of people were to know the truth of my assignment, even fewer to actually know my real name.

Officially, I was to be employed as Mike Wilkins, Press Officer for the LACS, dealing with inquiries from the press and publicising the sheer brutality of hunting.

To the hunt, whenever I met them socially, I was Michael Wright, an avid follower and supporter of all field sports.

Only my family and close friends knew I was Mike Huskisson, ex-public schoolboy with a degree in Zoology/Ecology from University College London, a teaching qualification and a prison record.

At that fateful meeting on April 25th 1981 I was given two specific tasks and told to use any name I liked other than my own.

I was instructed to destroy the credibility of hunts by research and analysis. To show the public through the letters columns of newspapers and magazines how all arguments in favour of hunting were false and illogical.

My second task was perhaps more valuable and certainly more dangerous – to slip undercover and penetrate the secretive world of hunting and expose the gruesome truth. To use my cameras to collect indisputable evidence to show the British public that hunting was cruel, barbaric and should be banned by law.

The LACS already had a long, successful record of deploying its staff and supporters to gather evidence of the cruelty inherent in bloodsports by pretending to be hunt supporters.

The *Daily Mirror* May 31st 1962 reported under the caption: "*The Quiet Man Took Pictures As A Fox Was Torn To Pieces*" describing how LACS member Raymond Rowley, wearing a hunt supporters' club badge, photographed as a fox was killed after being marked to ground in a drain by the Hertfordshire Hunt. At a subsequent court case Mr Petre Crowder MP, a member of the Puckeridge Hunt, appeared for the defence and criticised Mr Rowley for adopting the disguise of a hunt supporter.

Raymond Rowley was a dedicated and determined investigator. Some five years later the *Daily Mirror* on February 10th 1967 printed an article under the heading: "*Found — A Spy At Horror Sport's Big Day.*" This described how Raymond Rowley, by then Chairman of the LACS, had attended the Waterloo Cup hare coursing event pretending to be a supporter of hare coursing and had taken photographs using a camera cunningly disguised as a pair of binoculars.

He was spotted a mere five minutes before the day-long meeting was due to end and was ejected. Raymond announced that the many photographs he took would be sent to Eric Heffer, the Liverpool MP whose Anti-Coursing Bill was due a second reading in the House of Commons.

Raymond Rowley continued his undercover work to expose such cruelty throughout the early 1970s, particularly against stag hunting. Around 1980 the LACS employed another investigator — Mike O'Reilly. This young former hunt saboteur worked undercover within various fox hunts using a cine film camera with sound to expose the truth about the pastime, in particular the terrierwork. In May 1980 Mike courageously filmed as Chris Wood, Whipper-in for the Holderness Foxhounds dug out four fox cubs from an earth near Birmingham. These cubs were taken back to the hunt kennels and put into an artificial earth near a railway line (*Cruel Sports* number 12, Spring 1984).

Could the world of hunting be caught yet again by another undercover investigator in 1981? Maybe, if another form of hunting was the primary target. The earliest LACS investigators had turned up at events on the day adopting a variety of disguises, later ones devoted more time to developing their cover stories. My task was to target stag hunting initially. I planned to just turn up at a meet as a hunting tourist — to gain the entry point, the trust from hunters that was needed — but then to develop a whole alias as a keen hunter with an interest in all forms of hunting. I was to use a false name and a safe address to allow me to correspond with hunters; to go to their social events and get really close to them to understand how they thought as well as how they played. The goal was to prove the truth about hunting that lurked beneath the glamorous façade.

It was a task close to my heart and one for which I was well equipped. Throughout the previous decade I had learned the ways of the hunt and sabotaged them. My interests not only extended to putting an end to the cruel abuse of the hunted, be they otters, mink, deer, hares or foxes; but to abuse against any animal.

I had been sabotaging a variety of hunts for over 10 years. In 1975 I broke into the Imperial Chemical Industries (ICI) toxicological research laboratory in Cheshire to save two of the smoking beagles and was arrested, charged and subsequently bound-over for my part in the plot.

I had also taken part in the 1977 desecration of John Peel's grave in Cumbria, a mecca for the hunting fraternity. For this I served a nine month prison sentence, part of the time in one of Britain's maximum security prisons — Durham.

So, there was no question that I had all the qualities of determination to infiltrate the inner sanctums of the various hunts and the knowledge to pass as a dedicated follower of hounds.

I even came from the right background. Indeed, I had relatives who hunted, so if there had been any early influence at all it should have been to participate myself.

11

CHAPTER TWO
Learning how a hunt works

The son of an army officer who had been evacuated from the beaches at Dunkirk during the Second World War, served in the Western deserts of North Africa and rose through the ranks, I was born in 1953. With Dad in the military my childhood was a world of short stays, distant moves and in time a boarding school education.

From an early age I learned to empathise with our fellow creatures. Dad had a three year army posting to Cyprus from 1959-1962. Amongst much happiness I remember some disturbing incidents involving animals.

We lived on the edge of a fenced camp near Limassol and it seems there were problems with feral cats. Periodically there would be attempts to hunt these down and I recall a group of soldiers coming after one that was seen in our garden. They chased her and one soldier leaned over our fence and threw a bladed implement at her. The cat was hit but only injured so the army squad, with me in their wake, crossed the fence to follow her trail of dripping blood. It led all the way to the base of an old hollowed out olive tree. I was held back then to spare me from seeing the final act and later told that the cat and her kittens were all killed.

Another time my parents talked about some neighbours that had acquired a new puppy. This was an adorable black Labrador/Retriever cross named Smudge. Apparently the husband had seen a young Cypriot lad throw a sack from a bridge into a river. Seeing the sack moving he had retrieved it and found this young puppy inside that he gave a home to. I was haunted for some considerable time by thoughts as to what it would be like trapped in such circumstances.

Mum also spoke about seeing young lads outside our camp hanging an Alsatian dog from a tree. She rushed out to try and stop them but was too late.

Such early events taught me firstly that there was a dark side to the interaction between humans and animals and secondly that you could take direct action to try and stop the cruelty.

I knew little about hunting until my father left the services in 1967, returned to England and bought a house in the small quaint village of Abbotsley near Cambridge.

From the late 1960s onwards I took an interest in protecting our wildlife and environment. I supported the group campaigning against the Canadian seal cull. I raised money for the World Wildlife Fund by envelope collections door to door. Knocking on one door, the householder gave me support but also advised that as well as seeking to protect wildlife in Africa I should take a look at the suffering of wildlife here in the UK. He described the cruel nature of fox, hare and stag hunting.

It was impossible for me to avoid fox hunting as the local pack, the Cambridgeshire Foxhounds, had two meets in the vicinity. One was at the pub overlooking the village green and the other at a large farm on the outskirts.

I held no strong feelings then either way about hunting. Like most people I was benevolent towards wildlife. I felt that we owed a duty of care towards the creatures that share this planet with us. That animals should not be killed unless all alternatives had been tried first and if they are killed it should be in the most humane way possible.

With a much-loved uncle who had a passion for horses and rode to hounds (for the riding) any family influence would have been in favour of hunting — but I was keen to find out for myself. What was the reality of the traditional colourful images seen in so many rural pubs? Huntsmen in their bright pink coats mounted on beautifully turned out horses, ladies in black jackets and smart headgear, all partaking of a stirrup cup as the lovely hounds sniffed around eagerly awaiting the off. Was it all just a glamorous façade?

It was when I came into closer contact with the hunting fraternity on social excursions to the pub with my parents that I felt the first stirrings of revulsion. I did little to hide my sympathy with and regard for animals. Neither did I hide my support for the underdog in any competition or conflict. This meant that in the case of foxhunting, for all its undoubted glamour, I innately sided with the fox.

The hunting types I encountered interpreted such feelings in a young man as signs of weakness, an effeminate nature. They loved to draw me into arguments about hunting and delighted in baiting me to see my reaction. Inevitably they carried things too far as they recounted the full gory details of how they had dug out foxes and clubbed them to death. The more they goaded me with their lurid tales the greater my sympathy grew for the fox. But were these hunters merely bragging foolishly to anger me? I decided to see for myself.

I began to follow the Cambridgeshire Foxhounds whenever possible, using my pushbike to keep up. I soon noticed that fox hunters are very two-faced. They have a public face and a private one. I saw and heard people, when out of public sight, really delight in inflicting suffering. When I asked the hunt supporters with my nagging innocence why they enjoyed killing animals they always reacted angrily.

Acknowledging whose side I was on I soon determined not to remain a bystander but to take an active part in thwarting the hunters and helping the quarry. At that time I knew nothing about the existence of any organisations such as the Hunt Saboteurs Association (HSA) or the LACS. My decision to act was a purely personal one.

Although unaware of it our local foxes now had at least one ally. I saw the contest simply. Whenever I could attend it was the hunters against the pair of us.

I read up in military history books on the best techniques to use to fool hounds that hunted by scent. During the Second World War the French Resistance had used dried blood and cocaine to put German tracker dogs off their scent. Such tactics seemed a bit extreme for our tiny village in the calm of rural England. Clearly I needed to find a substitute. After discussions with friends and teachers at my school I found a solution that was much easier to obtain — aniseed oil.

I saved feverishly, bought up all of the local chemist's stock of aniseed and planned phase one of my campaign against the cruelties of the Cambridgeshire Foxhounds. The evening before their meet in Abbotsley on Saturday 25th March 1972 I went out with a bundle of rags heavily soaked in aniseed oil. Trailing them round and round the meet I led off down the side of an adjacent field. Dragging my decoy, I ran up one field, zig-zagged round another and ran on before circling back to my starting point.

If my plan worked the hounds would be running rings around themselves, going nowhere and harming nothing. To strengthen the false trail I cut up the rags and retraced my steps, dropping small pieces at 25 yard intervals.

That day the hunt was singularly unsuccessful, in fact it descended into utter chaos. With the benefit of hindsight I appreciate now that my actions can have had little influence and if they affected anything it would only have been at the start. However at the time I felt that I had achieved a great deal, had won my first battle and was looking to repeat the success.

Soon after this there was a storm of publicity in the media about the activities of the HSA. The HSA had been founded less than ten years before in December 1963 in Brixham, Devon by 22-year-old journalist John Prestidge. The idea of intervening directly to save the lives of hunted animals proved attractive, particularly to youngsters. Groups soon sprang up across the country and it was not long before a national committee was formed to run the fledgling organisation.

At Northampton, near to me, there was a particularly active HSA group led by Rorke Garfield, a tough and fearless former paratrooper, whose exploits really impressed. His well-publicised clashes with hunts involved the use of smoke canisters, thunder-flashes and hunting horns to reduce the hunt to a complete shambles and allow the quarry to escape.

In September 1972 I went to University College, London to read Zoology, specialising in Ecology and took student accommodation at Ifor Evans Hall of Residence in Camden Town.

I quickly joined the University Officer Training Corps more out of an interest in the outward bound style of activities than from any desire to kill people. In November that year I also joined the HSA determined to continue to do my best for hunted animals.

A couple of incidents at University reinforced my resolve to work for animal welfare. I had chosen Ecology to avoid dissecting animals but even so we had some disturbing lectures. One involved an academic turning up with a menagerie of small animals and birds all of which he had harmed in some way by cutting or removing some parts of their brains. He wanted to show their various handicaps but urged us to close all the windows as, he jokingly recounted, on a previous occasion a blinded pigeon had flown out of an open window and been lost. Most students laughed but not me, it was not my kind of science.

On another occasion I joined a party of fellow students on a visit to an agricultural research station. We were told about all the harm that rabbits caused and the various attempts to control the rabbit population. One scientist boasted that his role was to try and overcome any natural immunity that rabbits might develop to myxomatosis (first found in the UK in 1953) by improving and upgrading the myxoma virus. I had seen far too many rabbits suffering from myxomatosis and viewed it as the most appalling cruelty visited by man on animal.

Like most idealistic young men of that era, just after the sixties, I sought to take an active, adventurous role in a cause. We were from a generation that perhaps naively just wanted to make the world a better place. Human welfare, the obligatory Che Guevara poster on the wall, and rightful condemnation of the war in Vietnam was very much the in thing amongst my fellow students. Realising that there were many fighting to improve the lot of humans I decided to concentrate on the more helpless species who share this planet with us.

At that time, long before the wonders of the Internet brought us web sites and Facebook, making contact with the direct action animal welfare groups was difficult. I had previously seen an advertisement for the HSA in the back of the satirical magazine *Private Eye* but lost the relevant issue. In the end I sought the help of my local reference library at Camden. I was given the telephone number of the LACS.

I rang and spoke to Mark Davies who was at the time Secretary of the League and was later a member of the Executive Committee. He was really helpful and gave me the telephone number of Iain McNay a Committee member of the HSA.

From the start I enthusiastically pledged my body and soul to the HSA. Years later I learned that I was immediately marked down as 'Mike the Nutter'! My first organised 'sab' was against the Mendip Farmers Foxhounds meeting at Clapton, near Midsomer Norton, on Saturday December 9th 1972.

I was told to rendezvous with a van load of fellow hunt saboteurs at Ealing Broadway underground station at 5.00a.m. Ealing at that time of the morning was singularly inaccessible from my Hall of Residence in Camden Town. All the more so considering that I had no transport whatsoever and like all students then I was near penniless. The only way for me to make the rendezvous was to set out at 2.00a.m. and walk. I gladly did so taking the view that after that supreme effort it could only get easier!

I remember little of that first day of hunt sabotage as part of an organised group except at one point having to cross a flooded track. We ended up wading up to our knees and had to endure wearing soaking wet jeans for the rest of the day. Hunt sabotage was clearly no fun. At that first 'sab' I met Dave and Cee Wetton the key organisers for the HSA. Both became lifelong friends — and both are still actively protecting our wildlife. Dave Wetton had joined the HSA in April 1964 at the age of 20.

From early on I was attracted by the camaraderie — the companionship of like-minded people from all ages and all walks of life who shared the belief that by their own actions they could make a real difference for wildlife. We could and did save lives. There was nothing to beat the sight of the hunted animal slipping away quietly to safety at the end of the day — rather than ending up ripped to shreds. We were all motivated by compassion rather than by any need to wage a class war. Anyone seeking such a conflict would have found it easier (and safer) to disrupt the likes of the Henley Royal Regatta.

Christmas 1972 I spent at my home in Abbotsley. Naturally I was keen to try out newly learned sabotage techniques against my local pack. I phoned Dave Wetton seeking to make contact with keen sympathisers near me who could help. I was given the phone number of Ronnie Lee. A mild-mannered young man, he was later to become one of the founder members of the Band of Mercy and the Animal

Liberation Front (ALF) and a driving force for the whole Animal Rights movement worldwide. But at the time he was a trainee solicitor.

I eagerly arranged my first organised 'sab' against the meet of the Cambridgeshire Foxhounds at Boxworth, a small village to the north-east of Abbotsley, on December 23rd. Ronnie collected me from my home and showed me how to mix the pungent smelling but harmless 'sab special' that is so successful at masking the scent of a fleeing fox. I had alerted the local papers claiming that there would be a dramatic attempt to thwart the Cambridgeshire hunt. The reporters that turned up were visibly disappointed to find five dishevelled looking individuals pouring dirty liquids in gateways.

It would doubtless have made a better story if we had thrown paint or bricks at the hunt followers but that would not have helped the fox. As it was we trailed after the hunt around the fields. We sprayed wherever possible, bogged ourselves in the mud and ended up thoroughly soaked. Our only consolation was that we felt we had achieved something.

After this start I drifted into the basic HSA routine of planning all week for action on Saturdays. The HSA was organised on a group structure with small active units of volunteers dotted about the country. They also had close links with satellite groups such as Save Our Stags that was set up by Ian Pedler to protect the red deer in the West Country. Another West Country group was the Campaign for the Relief of Wildlife.

The usual idea was for new hunt saboteurs to join their local group. As I lived in London like Dave and Cee Wetton, the driving forces behind the HSA at the time, I was in close contact with them and became affiliated to what was in effect the headquarters group — the London group. We became akin to flying pickets travelling all over the country to bolster local groups, offering advice and exchanging ideas. The London group was also responsible for the routine organisational activities of the HSA.

Hunt disruption takes many forms with two examples being open and covert sabotage. Open sabotage involves groups of recognisable sabs preventing the hunt from killing by obvious and direct interference. The aim is to mislead the hounds by laying false trails, by masking the scent of the quarry, by giving false holloas (shouting to pretend you have seen the fox when really you have not) and by blowing the hunting horn to confuse and mislead the hounds.

We employed covert techniques when we were few in number or when the hunt we were up against was known to be particularly violent. Then we would simply slip into the woods dressed as hunt supporters and surreptitiously lay false trails and spray to conceal the real ones. I rapidly learned to converse with hunt supporters to gather intelligence about the hunt and to behave and act as a genuine hunt supporter at the appropriate time. Often at the end of the day, unless we had been giving false calls on the hunting horn, the hunters had no idea that sabs were even with them! Effective sabotage without conflict with the supporters was regarded as by far the best result for us.

For the benefit of the media it became a common HSA policy to demonstrate peacefully at the hunt meets with banners and placards bearing slogans like: "*Watch out Sadists about!*" or "*Warning! Pink Perverts at large*". These were usually effective at encouraging local people to give vent to their deeply felt but seldom expressed disapproval of the hunt. "*Good on yer!*" they would shout.

This did not please the hunters and our peaceful protests would often end with our banners being torn down and the bearers being hit. Incapable of offering any coherent arguments the hunting set would frequently resort to violence and intimidation. They damned sabs as dirty unwashed Kremlin-financed students hell-bent on wrecking the British way of life. When the hunting brigade issued a call to arms to their rural comrades to resist such an 'invasion' it was not surprising that there was no shortage of burly, muscular volunteers, particularly from the rural pubs.

I sampled this kind of opposition on January 13th 1973 when I joined fellow sabs at the meet of the Whaddon Chase Foxhounds at Shenley Brook End near Bletchley, Bucks. A tank-like, bullet headed, country 'gentleman' warned us that if we attempted to disrupt 'his' hunt our cars would be tipped into ditches and we would be put six feet under!

Against such threats, although terrified, we had no choice but to carry on — albeit that we spent most of the day checking who or what was behind us. At one point the hunted fox crossed the road right in front of our vehicle. We stopped, jumped out and sprayed the whole area to mask his scent. Then we heard the rumbling storm of approaching hunt followers.

The hounds arrived and stopped, baffled. We sped off, laughing, and out of a somewhat childish bravado gave two-fingered gestures of non-respect to the pursuing hunt thugs who were uttering the direst threats. We immediately regretted this when a horse-box appeared round the corner ahead of us almost blocking the road.

The pursuing supporters, labouring to retain their flat caps and wellingtons as they ran, now saw and seized their chance. They shouted to the driver of the horse-box urging him to swing across the road and block our escape. Revving our engine to drown out these instructions we bumped up onto the grass verge and managed to squeeze past and escape, just.

Operating with groups of experienced sabs, in particular those from the London HQ group, I soon mastered the basic arts of sabotage. I learned at first-hand how a hunt works. Additionally I was forced by necessity to operate on my own on many occasions. This inevitably led me into undercover work. For this my own mobility was essential and in the autumn of 1972, just before I went to University, I purchased a motorbike. I had never ridden a motorbike before but as for training things were different in those days. I just turned up at the shop; paid my money for a 250cc motorbike; was shown how the throttle, brakes, gears and indicators worked; put the L-plates on and rode off into the chaotic Cambridge traffic. It was a wonder that I survived.

One favourite sabotage tactic involved visiting the scheduled meet hours before hounds arrived and liberally dousing the area with 'sab special', a harmless concoction of chemicals. The idea was to dull the sensitivity of the hounds noses as they milled about at the meet, a bit like asking a piano tuner to work at the end of an airport runway.

I did this at one pub where the Cambridgeshire Foxhounds were due to meet three hours later. The astonished landlord queried why I was watering his car park. I explained that I was from the University and was testing the ability of a highly nutritious plant food to produce plants that could break through concrete. I sped off leaving him more than a little bemused. I had rapidly learned that it mattered little how fatuous any explanation was; what counted was that it be given with honest conviction.

We did have some amusing interactions with hunt supporting pub landlords. On one occasion hounds met outside an establishment and saboteurs loudly voiced their opposition. The hunt moved off. Later in the morning some saboteurs returned to the pub to buy crisps or peanuts, use the toilet and look for any hunt meet cards on display. The landlord barred the way with the query: "*You are not friends of those anti-hunt people are you?*" To this Dave Wetton replied: "*We are not friends with them — we are them.*" We were all told to "*bugger off!*"

Hunting methods differ depending on the choice of quarry, fox, deer, hare etc. For open sabotage in groups it is enough to know the rudiments of what is going on. That will not suffice for undercover work. For that it is necessary to know every aspect of the chosen type of hunting. I learned techniques that would set me in good stead for my later career.

Hounds hunt the scent left by foxes therefore false scent trails and the masking of real scents are of vital importance. The pack are controlled and wielded by the Huntsman using his voice and horn. The riders and onlookers are there to have fun but they can make a significant contribution to the success of the hunt by revealing the whereabouts of the fleeing quarry.

I soon realised that undercover sabotage offered unlimited opportunities to confuse the hunt and therefore these tactics appealed to me far more than the open more confrontational methods.

From my traditional student uniform of tatty flared jeans and sweatshirt I converted to the uniform of our hunting opposition. Now it was flat tweed cap, waxed Barbour jacket and Hunter style wellies. So attired I became adept at blending in with hunt supporters. I chatted with the followers and readily opened and closed gates for the riders. I found myself accepted and in time made more and more inroads thereby gaining a greater understanding of how hunting really works. Most hunt followers were content to stay in their cars sipping coffee and chatting to their fellows or to passing riders. I declined such socialising and always aimed to be with the hounds whilst the hunt was running, up with and chatting to the really dedicated followers. I learned so much from these experienced hunters.

Keeping up with the hounds usually necessitated running miles over ploughed fields and ending up plastered with mud; battling through thick undergrowth and wading through streams. In short wherever the hounds went I followed. It was tiring but fruitful. From that close-in viewpoint I could see the hounds being directed by the hunt staff. I learned to calculate where the fox would most likely make his run and was able to make an informed decision as to how best to thwart the hunt.

When drawing a copse or small wood the Huntsman will put his hounds into the wood to flush their quarry out but before doing so he will position chosen riders at vantage points around the wood. Should the fox make a break from the wood these riders on point duty give a loud call, a cross between a shout and a scream known as a 'holloa', to summon the hunt staff. If the Huntsman elects to hunt that fox he then blows his horn to call up the hounds.

I must have been fairly convincing in my undercover role. On occasion the trusted riders on point duty, bored with waiting in solitude often under the discomfiture of howling gales or torrential rain, would ask me to stand in for them thereby enabling them to ride off and chat with the other riders. I would readily oblige.

Left in this valued position I would often see the fox break out of the wood. If I thought no-one else would see him I had the option either to say nothing or if I thought he was going to be spotted soon I could run to a point away from his real line, holloa like mad and claim that the fox ran in another direction.

The risk of being caught out whilst performing such tactics was slight. The greatest danger came from the foot followers that might be lurking in the undergrowth rather than the more visible riders. Several times I was accused of holloaing where there was no fox or ignoring an escaping fox.

I found it best then to offer profuse apologies and maintain that I was only doing my best to help. Anyone could make a mistake I would say explaining along the lines: "*Okay it must have been a hare or a small deer but I thought it was a fox*". If they were adamant that I had ignored the hunted fox I would resolutely maintain that the fox in question was not actually the hunted fox and that to holloa him would be to wreck the hunt. It is a cardinal sin for genuine hunt supporters to call hounds off the hunted fox and switch them to another fresh one.

Like most people I thought of fox hunting as simply a matter of a contest between fox versus hounds and riders. In those early days although I had heard stories I knew little at first hand of the extra element in the equation — the hunt terriermen. Terrier work is the most barbaric, cruel and totally unsporting aspect of fox hunting.

The idea of foxes being chased and eventually caught by hounds and ripped to pieces is abhorrent enough. That pales into insignificance though when compared to the cruelties all too often dished out by the terriermen before and after the above-ground chase.

When an exhausted fox goes to ground, finding sanctuary in an underground earth or pipe, the hunters seldom give sporting salute to a quarry who has outwitted them and give him best. More often they guard the spot and summon the terriermen to either bolt him for further hunting or dig him out and kill him.

The terriermen's standard equipment consists of picks, spades, iron bars, and terriers: Jack Russell, Lakeland, Patterdale, Border or whatever cross-breed between them. The terrier(s) will be sent down to battle with the fox. To all intents and purposes an underground dog fight will ensue in the dark tunnels. The fox may bolt or, particularly if she is a vixen defending her cubs, may stand and fight with the near inevitable result of being dug out and killed.

Even when the hunt has a fox trapped underground it is still possible for an undercover saboteur to intervene, to foil their plans and save the fox's life. I had been out with one hunt all day playing the part of the stupid supporter and being a hindrance whenever possible. Late in the afternoon the hounds marked an exhausted fox to ground. The hunt staff leapt off their horses and I followed to observe them feverishly blocking all the exits from the earth to prevent the fox escaping.

The Huntsman blew his horn until his face matched the colour of his jacket trying to summon the terrierman but to no avail. "*Shall I go and get him?*" I helpfully volunteered. Welcoming the help the Huntsman sent me off. Dutifully I disappeared running over the brow of the hill. Sadly for him I am still looking!

On January 27th 1973 I was out with the East Essex Foxhounds again in the undercover role. The hounds marked a fox to ground in an earth in a wood. I battled through the undergrowth to the site and found the Huntsman proudly standing over the blocked earth I tried to repeat the tactic of 'going for help'. This time I was told "*No.*" For a moment I thought he suspected me. Then he added "*It will be quicker if I go. You stay here and guard the earth.*"

He could not have made a better decision. As he galloped off into the distance I feverishly unblocked all the entrances to the earth before running swiftly in the opposite direction. Much as I would have liked to have lingered to see the fox escape it was necessary to go. As long as the fox could smell me outside the earth he would not have ventured out. That he did escape was confirmed to me later by irate supporters. Thankfully they were unaware that I was the culprit responsible for ruining their fun.

Many hunters appeared genuinely perplexed as to why we worked so hard to oppose them. They often shouted that we were merely jealous of their wealth, that it was all a class issue. But for us the wealth or otherwise of our opponents was an irrelevance. It was the cruelty that they delighted in that we loathed. And I soon learned that whilst it took money to own and ride a horse the poorest of the poor could easily help with the terrier work. The only real perception of class in this conflict came from the hunters themselves as they looked down on us from their horses.

I soon appreciated that the ability to mimick the hunting horn would be a particularly useful trick to acquire. The horn is used by the Huntsman to direct his pack, summon and inform the riders, call up the terriermen and signal a kill to supporters.

In the summer of 1973 I bought a quality (Swaine and Adeney) hunting horn and despite having no musical ability whatsoever set about learning how to blow it. Blowing a hunting horn is devilishly hard; it has no reed. It took me six months and a lot of patient advice from my close friend Dave Wetton, a proven expert, to master even the rudiments but it was worth the effort. Practicing at home disgusted neighbours so I realised that the one place where I could blow to my heart's content was at hunts.

I practiced openly when out with groups of sabs. I had anticipated opposition but instead the hunters roared with laughter as all too often my lung-bursting attempts ended in pathetic stuttering, spluttering, raspberries. Their laughter and taunts merely spurred me to greater efforts.

In time I gained a small measure of expertise and thereby acquired another useful weapon to deploy when operating undercover. Only the Huntsman carrying the horn and those near him could know for certain that my calls were not genuine. On many occasions the mounted field arrived in response to my horn calls expecting to find the Huntsman but instead found only 'empty' woodland.

Foxhounds — like all pack hounds — hunt by scent not sight. Only at the very end of a hunt, when their victim is in clear sight, do they course their prey. Foxhounds are bred not for the speed that might produce a quick kill but rather for the stamina that guarantees lengthy hunts and therefore the lengthy gallops that followers seek and pay for.

Because they hunt by scent hounds run with their noses to the ground. Once they lift their heads they lose the scent. We found it a good sabotage tactic to distract the hounds into lifting their heads by horn blowing or holloaing. Whistles and whip-cracking can also be used.

Hounds are also prone to rioting (hunting non-target quarry) and it can occur for several reasons. Like all dogs they can become victims of boredom. If foxhounds are taken from covert to covert and always draw a blank they may become restless. If a hare, rabbit or deer pops up they may chase them in a riot just for the heck of it.

Rioting can also occur near the end of a hunt due to overexcitement. Hard pressed tiring foxes frequently run through a field of farm livestock or into gardens in a desperate attempt to lose their scent. With hunt followers holloaing and screaming like dervishes and the Huntsman blowing his horn it can be all too much for the hounds. If they encounter pets such as cats, dogs, or rabbits, or farm chickens they may riot and chase and kill them.

Hounds can also riot over busy roads and railway lines causing chaos, accidents and injuries or even fatalities to themselves. They have also been known to interfere with air travel as this press report confirms:-

"FOX HUNT HOLDS UP AIRLINER

As a jet airliner approached to land at Gatwick airport yesterday members of Surrey Union hunt careered after a fox crossing the airport. Air control spotted the danger and warned the incoming plane. The aircraft circled. Meanwhile the fox slipped across the runway to escape and the hunt turned away. Col Barry Girling, hunt secretary, said later: "We didn't get too close."

Told that a jet had been delayed Col. Girling said: "Country sports were here before jets, old boy.""

(News report, *Sunday Telegraph*, February 4th 1973 [Col. Girling was Hunt Secretary from 1964-84])

To try and prevent rioting the hounds are trained to stop when certain horn calls are blown. Similar calls are used to stop hounds when they are heading towards danger such as a railway line or main road or to prevent them changing quarry (i.e. stop them from switching from an exhausted fox to a fresh one.)

We found it very effective to use the hunting horn to stop hounds from hunting the fox. Of course such horn blowing must be done responsibly. In essence the saboteur is taking the pack, at times a brutally effective killing machine, out of the control of the hunt staff. Horn battles could ensue between the Huntsman and the saboteurs and the hounds would run from one to the other backwards and forwards and sometimes end up so confused that they declined to hunt anything. On occasion confused hounds could just sit down and throw their heads back to howl in frustration.

As an example of how dangerous a pack of hounds could be, and not just to their chosen quarry, in 1967, with no saboteurs present, the Vale of Clettwr Foxhounds ran riot amidst a flock of sheep. In a short time twenty six lambs were killed and many others injured. Here is the press report:-

"Hounds go wild, eat sheep alive

Four lambs were eaten alive after a pack of hounds taking part in a fox hunt went wild among his flock, a West Wales farmer told a Lampeter court yesterday. Altogether 26 lambs were massacred.

The master and huntsman of the Vale of Clettwr Hunt, farmer Mr. Trefor Owen Jones (38), of Dancapel, Bancyffordd, Llandyssul, was fined £5 and £10 10s. advocate's fee after pleading not guilty to being in charge of dogs which worried sheep on farmland at Drefach

Llanybyther......
Mr. Lloyd told the magistrates that on March 11 he had about 286
young lambs on his 150 acre farm.
About midday his sheep started bleating and running up towards the
farm. He saw a pack of fox hounds hunting on land adjoining his
farm. Mr. Lloyd said, "While I was watching the dogs some riders
came down a nearby lane at full gallop like a pack of Indians.
I was very distressed to find a pack of hounds out at that time of year
and I was concerned about the young lambs. I called to the master to
call the dogs away from my land but they didn't take any notice of me
and kept urging the dogs on." said Mr. Lloyd.....
He said he had again asked the master, Jones, to keep away from the
sheep but Jones replied that his were a registered pack and had a
right to go anywhere." (Western Mail news report May 27th 1967)

Hunt saboteurs are always mindful of the need to safeguard the welfare of the pack. Hounds are as innocent as the animals they chase and must never be drawn into danger. Accordingly HSA rules instruct that the horn should never be blown from a location that might lead hounds over main roads or railway lines, or anywhere where they might chase, injure, or kill pets or livestock. A saboteur provoked hound riot should involve the hounds baying like mad but chasing nothing.

Hounds could easily riot of their own accord. They most commonly riot by chasing deer that apparently leave a scent that is very sweet for hounds. At such times saboteurs were often the first on hand to safeguard hounds that crossed busy roads. This could involve stopping the traffic to shield the hounds or restraining the hounds with improvised leads.

Other tactics deployed against the hunt were the use of padlocks and barbed wire. These could be used to delay the progress of the hunt by closing and securing gates. Padlocks and chains were the most effective but expensive as of course both were lost. A cheaper method was to secure gates shut by barbed wire twisted round and round tightly using pliers. The rider would have to dismount to undo this and the time that took could make the difference between life and death for the hunted animal.

I am sure the Huntsman of the Cambridgeshire Foxhounds long remembered the Boxing Day meet in 1973 when he found every gate on his first draw safely — and for him frustratingly — secured. The subsequent delay to his progress can only have helped the foxes.

Other weapons in the saboteur's armoury were fireworks such as air-bombs and rook-scarers. Both could be highly effective so long as they were used with care to avoid panicking any horses. This was before the modern gas-powered bird scarers. The equivalents for this era were called rook-scarers that were commonly used on farms. They were nothing more than a string of firework bangers tied to a long rope spaced to go off every 20 minutes or so to scare birds away from crops. They were noisy but harmless.

We strung up rook-scarers and set off air-bombs in woodlands for two purposes: to drive foxes and other wildlife out of the way of hounds; secondly to simulate the sound of shooting. Many times after such tactics were used I've heard the Huntsman curse "*Some bastard is shooting in there.*" Invariably he pulled the hounds out believing, wrongly of course, that the hounds might be hit by stray pellets.

Electronics experts such as the HSA Chairman, John Meddows, developed and deployed ultrasonic devices (like electronic dog whistles) to disrupt the link between a Huntsman and his hounds. This was another peaceful but effective way of saving lives.

In the face of such effective sabotage tactics hunters began to employ counter measures. One method was to become secretive and elusive. Hunt organisers were aware that saboteurs learned of their meets from their advertisements in the likes of *Horse and Hound*, *Shooting Times* and local papers. Some hunts ceased such advertising but that created another problem for their side — even their own supporters did not know their whereabouts. And there was zero prospect of recruiting new supporters.

Other hunts such as the Enfield Chace Foxhounds based just north of London adopted different tactics. At the meet they would be openly friendly to sabs then as soon as the hounds moved off they disappeared at breakneck speed. Keeping within woodland wherever possible they left no straggling riders to betray their whereabouts. As we combed the countryside searching for them it was a case of the hunters becoming the hunted.

The other most obvious counter attack available to hunters was sheer violence. Violence was already commonplace at the meets when sabs held banner demonstrations. As sabotage became more effective and the hunters more irate, attacks on saboteurs and their property during the hunts occurred with increasing frequency and viciousness.

The question of how hunt saboteurs were financed became an obsession to the hunters and their media allies. We were damned as 'unemployed, unwashed layabouts' and variously accused of being financed by the USSR and then later by Colonel Gaddafi and Linda McCartney. This was untrue of course but it is possible to see how irate hunters misinterpreted the facts. Saboteurs usually shared a vehicle or grouped together to hire a vehicle.

At the end of the day it was common practice for each saboteur to make a contribution towards petrol or hire costs and I guess that to malevolent minds seeing money gathered and given to the drivers could be misinterpreted as 'payment'. The reality was that saboteurs would spend large sums of their own money and give freely of their own time each hunting season to protect our wildlife.

There was of course an element of irony in hunt followers who could follow hounds 2,3,4, or even 5 days a week accusing saboteurs who are limited to following on their days off (usually a Saturday) of being unemployed or lazy. Hunt saboteurs were also, even from the early days, mostly vegetarian or vegan as they care passionately to protect all life.

CHAPTER THREE
Direct action to save lives

Hunt saboteurs call themselves sabs and when sabs attend a hunt they call it 'sabbing' that hunt. Throughout the early 1970s I sabbed as many hunts as possible ranging the length and breadth of Britain.

Our activities against hunting generated a great deal of media interest. One day in March 1975 we even had the author Jilly Cooper accompany us for the day to see how hunt saboteurs worked. She was delighted to witness some effective hunt sabotage involving the use of masking scents and hunting horns.

Often I accompanied the headquarters group of the HSA. At other times I operated on my own using initially my motorbike and then in time my car and working in the undercover role. If one hunt was cancelled due to the weather I would try for another nearby.

After an early concentration on fox hunts I paid attention to the other bloodsports — hare hunting with beagles, harriers or bassets, hare coursing, deer hunting in the West Country and in the summer otter hunting, which was later replaced by mink and coypu hunting.

Beagling — (hare hunting), takes place with the huntsmen and supporters following on foot. We sabotaged them quite openly by spraying to mask the scent of the fleeing hares, laying false trails, giving false holloas and by blowing hunting horns. This necessarily entailed larger groups of saboteurs running amongst the hounds and hunt supporters — a move which usually ended in the frustrated hunters resorting to physical violence against those trying to protect hares.

In response to any threat hares have a characteristic defence mechanism of running at speed in great circles. As they tire their circles become smaller and smaller until, at the very end when exhausted, they break off the circle and run in a straight line.

Once, out with the South Herts Beagles, the hounds closed up on the hare after an hour of chasing her. Turning, the hare passed by us, pushed through a hedgerow and laboured across a muddy field. The pack was strung out and in full cry in close pursuit. There was no escape and when all the lead hounds met her there was a pitiful squealing and screaming, then it was all over. We dived into the melee to try and help the hare. We knew we were too late and that it would do no good, but we felt we had to try.

The hunt supporters roared with laughter at our frantic but futile efforts. The hare was torn limb from limb, dowsing the hounds with her warm blood. Grabbing the remains the Huntsman thrust them in our faces, goading us and mocking our failure.

Hares did not just have hunters to fear. Another 'sporting' section of the community indulged in hare coursing. This was a rural pastime so antiquated and barbaric that many in the 1970s mistakenly believed that along with cock-fighting and bear-baiting it had already been banned. Encouraged by the LACS there had been many attempts in Parliament to ban hare coursing by Private Members Bills. One had even been supported by Margaret Thatcher MP. All had failed. The great influence the hunting fraternity exert on the Conservative party is confirmed by this letter from Conservative Marcus Kimball MP, the Chairman of the British Field Sports Society, to Humphrey Atkins MP, the Tory Chief Whip, dated February 12th 1975 (just a day after Margaret Thatcher was elected to lead the Conservative party):-

"Dear Humphrey

I am reluctant to add to your problems at the moment but I am extremely uncertain about one aspect of Margaret as our leader. My personal view is very minor and I would never do anything to undermine the Conservative party.

I must consider the 1.6 million members and associates of the Field Sports Society. We have had for many years a "special relationship" with the Conservative party at constituency level, the House of Commons, and within your office. We had support from Ted [Heath] *and active encouragement in our tactical battles and help in a major way from Willie* [Whitelaw] *and you under Ted continued this support.*

Before the 1970 election Margaret voted for the abolition of coursing and made it clear to me that she felt our vote on that night was an error. We appreciate that this was on the eve of a general election.

We now face a very different situation — country sports are to be legislated against one by one year after year.

I hope Margaret will allow our special relationship to continue and will agree to stand by any tactical successes we may achieve in either House.

An undertaking on those important matters would make it much easier for me to continue as always, to obey and receive your whip.

Yours ever   Marcus.
(Quoted in HOWL magazine No 12 Spring 1979)

Another letter later the same month revealed a sinister plot by hunters to 'get at' Margaret Thatcher through her sister (Muriel Cullen).

The coursing of hares is one of the most clinical, stage-managed and cold blooded of all bloodsports. In its best known form, static coursing, a line of beaters sweep across the open fields walking in organised lines to drive the hares before them towards an open field, selected as the arena. The beaters shout, bang sticks on the ground or wave sticks with makeshift flags attached.

Although many hares may be driven forwards, great care is taken by manoeuvring or checking the beating line to ensure that only one hare at a time runs onto the field. The dogs can only course a single hare. Once the unsuspecting and perhaps already tiring hare hits the open ground, she is chased on past a 'hide', often a pole and canvas construction or a screen of straw bales camouflaged by greenery. Behind this screen lurks a man known as the 'slipper', who holds in check two greyhounds straining at their leashes.

His job is to align both dogs to sight the hare and then gauge the required start the hare is to be given — which according to the hare coursing rule book, should be 80 yards (about 73 metres) — before releasing the greyhounds.

It is then a straight test of power, speed and agility, between the hare and the two greyhounds. The hare, being no match for the greyhounds' straight line speed, has only one means of escape – to turn sharply at the last instant, leaving them running on. The greyhounds then shudder to a halt, sight the hare again, chase after her, catch her up and force her to turn again.

Without doubt Nature's perfect running machine, the hare can turn about in her own body length at full speed.

As she zig-zags across the field, the scene may be repeated over and over as the greyhounds quickly catch up with her, forcing her to turn and twist again. The two dogs wear bright distinctive collars, one wears red the other white, so that the mounted and usually red-coated judge, galloping alongside, can award points to whichever dog turns the hare first. The dog with the most points wins. The judge waves an appropriately coloured handkerchief (red or white) to indicate the winner. In contrast with hunting with packs of hounds the greyhounds clearly have the speed advantage but the stamina advantage lies with the hare. If she can survive a few turns her pursuers will tire and she can escape.

If the hare slips, makes a mistake, or perhaps has been driven over wet muddy fields that cause her feet to be balled up with soil, or perhaps if she is heavily pregnant, she can be caught. Coursing authorities claim that any kill is of no consequence in the contest. It may be true that no extra points are awarded for it, but coursing supporters appear keen to proclaim their lust for blood as they raucously cheer every kill.

I attended my first hare coursing sabotage at the early morning meet of the Oxfordshire Coursing Club at Stanton Harcourt west of Oxford on February 2nd 1974.

At that time such disruption was a dangerous activity for the saboteurs. It entailed invading the coursing field and using marine smoke canisters, fireworks and gas-powered foghorns to scare the hares away. Later sabotage tactics were refined to include beating over the whole area hours before the meet to drive the hares out of the fields and away to safety.

Observing that first meeting, about one in three hares were caught. Many suffered a horrific death.

Hare coursers seeking to justify their pastime to a sceptical public claimed that few hares were killed in coursing and any that were killed were killed instantly. One only had to watch and listen to know the truth. When it came to the kill the greyhounds do not run alongside the hare and give her a 'nip to the back of the neck'. They have to strain every sinew to catch the hare and if they succeed they grab the first piece of her they can. Often one dog has the back legs, the other the head and a tug-of-war ensues — with the hare the living squealing rope between the two dogs.

Watching a harmless hare being literally pulled apart is sickening. The hare screams pitifully, even more heart-rending as it sounds just like the plaintive cries of a young child.

'Pickers up' rush onto the field to intervene. If they can catch the tussling trio they will release the hare and break her neck but the dogs can be difficult to catch.

An even more prolonged agony and a common one for the hare, is when one dog wins this final tussle and makes off in triumph with the live hare struggling in its mouth.

That first day I saw several triumphant dogs run from the coursing field; each with a hare dangling from their jaws, alive and screaming, hotly pursued by the respective owners of the dogs and by other supporters.

Needless to say, as in all other forms of hunting, hare coursers loathe outsiders with cameras recording what happens. As Lord Kenyon, Honorary Secretary of the premier event the annual Waterloo Cup Coursing, succinctly put it: *"We have a rule forbidding photographs of coursing. The ban was imposed to prevent these anti-bloodsport people from getting ammunition to use against us."*

At another meeting of the Oxfordshire Coursing Club, at Shilton west of Witney on December 6th 1975 I discovered that even a single protester can be effective. A planned major demonstration by sabs had to be cancelled. Disappointed but undeterred I went along alone, planning to simply observe.

After watching two hares being torn by the greyhounds I was so incensed that I marched onto the field alone and sat down in the middle. At first the coursers, thinking I had made some ghastly error, approached me politely and said: "*Look 'ere mate, you mustn't sit there.*"

When I retorted: "*I'm on the side of the hare!*" their mood changed drastically to one of threats and abuse against me. A strong deputation came over to 'sort me out' (and surely would have done) but I was saved by the timely arrival of a police inspector.

Whereas, at the previous demonstration sabs had been swiftly evicted by the police, this totally impartial officer pointed out to the irate coursers that I had every right to make a peaceful protest — and he stayed with me to make sure everything remained peaceful.

The coursers cursed, but eventually admitted defeat. But it was only in that single field. They simply moved on to another field and successfully stopped me from following. I had to leave the hares to their fate.

The sabotage of the main hare coursing event, the Waterloo Cup held each year in late February or early March near Liverpool, commenced with an aerial attack. In 1975 the HSA paid for a helicopter to circle overhead for nearly an hour scaring the hares away for miles around. This coincided with a peaceful banner demonstration on the ground. The press loved the visual imagery.

The following year we resorted to the more usual tactics and on Friday February 13th I was one of seven people arrested when, after four hares had been killed, we ran onto the field to try and stop the slaughter. We succeeded for a short while. Subsequently we appeared at Ormskirk Magistrates Court on July 4th 1976 and were bound over to keep the peace for 12 months in the sum of £25.

In 1977 the Waterloo Cup was particularly brutal. On the second day no fewer than 27 hares were killed out of 56 coursed and as proof that it is not only the hares that suffer, one greyhound was put down after a hard run resulted in a broken leg.

Not surprisingly when 130 sabs turned up on the third day (February 11th) they were determined to end this cruelty. 70 ran on to the coursing field known as the Withins. They were hotly pursued by police officers. In what the press gleefully described as the "*Battle of*

Waterloo" (*The Sun* February 12th 1977) 38 sabs were arrested and charged and two reported for charge. Cognisant of my binding over I was forced to stay on the side-lines. Instead I took the opportunity to photograph the proceedings.

The resultant court case gave an indication of the measure of hunting influence on our legal system. Thirty-one protestors were found guilty of "action likely to cause a breach of the peace" and fined. The HSA was advised to appeal and application for legal aid was made in Preston Crown Court to Judge W.H. Openshaw. All the applications were turned down. Nevertheless, the solicitor acting for three defendants from Manchester offered to act for nothing. Their appeal was held at Preston Crown Court before Judge Dewhurst who upheld it without even bothering to hear any evidence on the part of the defence. Judge Openshaw was a member of the BFSS — a significant fact that he neglected to mention at the time.

I was learning all the time. In 1974 following a summer 'holiday' spent working seven days a week in the kitchens at my University Hall of Residence I earned enough to purchase a professional Nikon F2 camera and set about gathering the images of the cruelty that I witnessed.

Of all bloodsports, deer hunting with hounds was the one surrounded by the most mystique in the 1970s. Undoubtedly, it is the most bloody and barbaric; one where the quarry, once the pack has 'locked on' to the scent, has the least chance of escape.

With red deer hunted in Devon and Somerset and fallow deer in the New Forest, the roots of the pastime are Medieval; its followers clannish and insular. Supporters have fearsome reputations for violence towards opponents and the whole method of the chase and the kill is ritualistic and primeval.

Many hardened supporters of fox hunting are opposed to red deer hunting, yet it is still allowed to continue. [The hunting of fallow deer in the New Forest ended when the New Forest Buckhounds closed down in 1997. This followed intense pressure from hunt saboteurs and close scrutiny by hunt monitors including Joe Hashman and Peter White from Wildlife Action and Frankie Horan and Ken James from the New Forest Animal Protection Group filming their every move].

With the uncultivated habitat limited and farmers keen to maximise their profits there is a need to manage deer numbers. The one efficient and humane method of managing deer populations is by using chemical contraceptive methods. This has been done in other countries but in the UK killing is still seen as the preferred method. The most humane way of killing deer is by an expert, professional marksman using a high-powered rifle, a practice condemned strongly by deer hunting supporters. Any 'fun' there is gained only by the man with the gun, not by the huge crowd of followers that can enjoy a stag hunt.

In the West Country on and around Exmoor and the Quantocks the hunt usually ranges over an area of thirty miles from start to kill: a seven or eight hour chase which spares neither horses nor deer.

Stag hunting differs from the other hound sports in that selected deer are hunted. A hunt employee known as the 'harbourer' goes out the night before to locate the deer and select suitable stags for the chase — the fittest and strongest.

At the meet the following morning he reports to the Master and leads off to the deer. The most experienced hounds, known as 'tufters', are selected from the pack and sent in to find the chosen stag and start the chase.

As in the sabotage of hare coursing we found that one of the best tactics was to drive the quarry out of the area before the meet. For stag hunting that meant the previous night. The actual hunt covered such vast areas that scent masking and false trails were largely impracticable and useless. Once again the hunting horn and false holloas were most effective weapons for distracting the hounds and confusing the followers. At first the hunters came to every holloa, but they soon realised that they had saboteurs in their midst and were swift to take counter action.

Hunt supporters in Land Rovers and on motorbikes drove at us across moorland and along woodland tracks. They blocked our cars in the narrow Devon and Somerset lanes, preventing us from following. They threatened to overturn cars and to smash car windows.

Violence from hunters was only just under the surface. They were tightly knit, suspicious of strangers, unbelievably callous towards wildlife and they were not going to let us or anyone else spoil their 'sport'.

We never gave up nor gave in. Once the hounds have run a deer to exhaustion there is little hope of saving him. But we did have small triumphs. Like the day in September 1975 when the Devon and Somerset Staghounds chased a stag towards the large LACS sanctuary at St. Nicholas Priory near Dulverton.

We had tried all day to distract the hounds but by late afternoon the exhausted deer was struggling through woodland on one side of the River Barle, heading for the sanctuary with hounds in close pursuit.

Twenty of us arrived and dashed over, warning the hunt supporters not to follow us or they would be trespassing. On the river bank Raymond Rowley, Chairman of the LACS at the time, was also warning the hunt off. With his many years' experience he knew all about how such hunts operate. The hunt riders were lining the river bank trying to bar their victim from the safety of the League land. As we advanced across the river to form a beat-line to drive the deer to safety the riders gathered around to stop us.

Through all the mayhem of whip-cracking and shouting the stag reached the river and crossed over to the League's side but, instead of staying within the safety of the sanctuary, he ran off upstream. However, we kicked up such a commotion and caused so much confusion that even though the hounds followed we delayed them long enough to enable the stag to escape. They did not kill that day.

As we became more successful at disrupting hunts so it became noticeable that violence from hunt followers towards us escalated. This was no surprise.

Confrontations really came to a head with otter hunting — the oldest form of hound sport known in this country. It had an unbroken history dating back some 850 years to the time of Henry II.

Originally it was practised in the genuine, though woefully misguided, belief that the otter was a pest. Fishermen complained that otters were killing salmon and trout. With this excuse to kill the species it seemed a good idea to make a 'sport' of it as well.

Otter hunting was singularly brutal. The species could breed in any month of the year so there was always the chance that cubs or pregnant or nursing bitches could be hunted. Adult otters were tough and could run all day in front of hounds — hunts lasting all of 9½ hours were reported in the hunting literature. Furthermore, when eventually exhausted and cornered, otters could fight tenaciously. The hunters might then try to help their hounds by 'tailing' the otter. This term refers to grabbing the otter by his tail and holding him aloft for the hounds to savage.

As long ago as the nineteenth century naturalists realised that the otter population was dwindling and began to question whether killing them was necessary. Those who had studied the otter's habits discovered that far from causing harm, these creatures were very beneficial to fishing interests. Otters, like all predators, need to conserve energy and prefer to catch slow moving fish like pike and eels — both of whom consume large numbers of young salmon and trout.

Despite all the evidence hunters continued to pump out lurid stories of the damage otters could do, even going so far as accusing them of rolling in watercress beds! With their influence on the media, hunters convinced the nation that otters simply must be killed.

The truth was that otter hunting had assumed a vital place in the hunting calendar – filling the gap between the end of one fox hunting season in April and the beginning of the next in September. Otter hunting was simply the summer pastime for hound enthusiasts.

Although it was well known that otters were falling victim in large numbers to pollution — such as that caused by the insecticide Dichlorodiphenyltrichloroethane (DDT) — and were threatened by the increased use of waterways and the 'tidying up' of river banks, hunting otters continued unabated throughout the 1950s, 1960s and well into the 1970s.

By their own records the eleven otter hunts operating in England and Wales killed no less than 1,065 otters between 1958 and 1963. With increasing reports of the decline in otter numbers otter hunters agreed to stop hunting completely in some areas, to hunt but not kill otters in other areas and elsewhere to carry on hunting and killing as before. National newspapers rightly poured scorn on this 'act of mercy'. The *Sunday Times* in their editorial published on March 2nd 1969 under the heading "*Pity the Otter*" observed:

"The otter-hunters of Britain have agreed to suspend their activities, but for a curiously unappealing reason. This predatory sport, eliminating an animal which plays a very inoffensive role in the ecological cycle, has been afflicted with overkill. In many counties the otter is in danger of no longer being available to the hunter. This troubles otter-hunters with an eye to the future.

Perhaps more striking than their temporary self-denial is the reason advanced by otter-hunting interests against making the sacrifice permanent. If that were done, they say, the one reliable source of information on the state of the otter would be removed. Never, surely, has the wolf more deftly assumed the sheep's clothing, or the conservationist come in such thick disguise............ As a piece of argument, the otter-hunters' case should be embalmed as a model for casuists everywhere — along with their sport."

Where otter hunting continued unabated the killing continued. As late as 1971 the hunts still killed 23 otters, purely for fun. Each kill was doubtless recorded in triumph by another notch on the poles of avid hunters. Otter hunters had a long history of taking trophies from their victims. Aside from the obvious head and feet that could be mounted on wall plaques a much prized trophy was the penis bone from a dog otter that could be worn as a tie pin.

In opposition to this crime against nature the HSA staged a sit-in at the London headquarters of the BFSS on January 2nd 1974. We demanded an assurance from the BFSS that no more otters would be hunted and killed. Far from giving any such assurance the hunters taunted us with the boast that otters would be hunted until the last one was killed, stuffed and mounted on a wall plaque!

From the summer of 1973 onwards I joined other hunt saboteurs in the struggle to thwart otter hunts. We followed them whenever we could in the countryside and also pursued them when they paraded their hounds in front of the public. On the evening of Friday May 11th 1973 I joined with 20 fellow hunt saboteurs to protest against the parade of the Bucks and Courtenay Tracy Otterhounds at the Royal Windsor Horse Show in front of the Queen and Prince Philip. We paid our 70p entrance fees and went in with banners concealed beneath clothing. Many packs paraded — beagles, foxhounds and harriers as well as the otterhounds — but it was the latter that we concentrated on. We ran into the arena during their parade and unfurled banners bearing slogans such as "*Only Rotters Hunt Otters*" and "*Ban Otter Hunting*". The show ring commentator, the usually silky-toned Raymond Brooks-Ward, was decidedly tetchy.

A photographer jumped into the ring after us taking pictures. He asked me if we had smoke flares. When I confirmed that we had he told me that if I threw a flare up towards the Royal Box he would get pictures that could put our protest on the front pages of national papers. I declined his offer. I offered to take his photograph whilst he threw the smoke flare but he also declined.

It was not until 1978 in the face of bitter opposition from the hunting lobby within Parliament that the otter was given some protection. Even then hunting was not actually banned. This anomaly allowed mink and coypu hunting to continue as replacements — an unwelcome disturbance that could easily have driven the otter to extinction.

As an example of just how determined hunting interests were to protect otter hunting against any moves in Parliament to end the pastime here is the threat made at the time by the leading pro-hunt MP:-

"Let me warn you that if any attempt is made to add the Otter to the list of protected animals, my friends and I in Parliament will argue every clause in the Bill over and over again and add every other animal and extraneous reforms so that the proposal will

eventually be talked out." (Marcus Kimball, M.P. for Gainsborough [later Lord Kimball] and at the time Chairman of the BFSS talking at the Otter Conference held by the Joint Otter Group June 22nd 1977 reported in HOWL (magazine of the Hunt Saboteurs Association) No.9 Autumn 1977. Page 1)

Until 1978 we diligently sabotaged every otter hunt we could. It was not always a catalogue of violence and aggression. With a few hunters, usually the staff who we encountered right where the action is with the hounds, a grudging respect for each other's views developed. We recognised that professional Huntsmen had genuine expertise controlling their hounds and they accepted that we never tried to hurt their hounds — only to distract them. The violence came mainly from the hunt hangers on.

Otter hunts were the most secretive of all. They hardly ever advertised their meets so we were frequently involved in the most elaborate of ruses to discover their whereabouts. We would phone the hunt kennels, the Huntsman or Hunt Secretary and give them all manner of fanciful tales about wanting to see the hunt for the first time to try and ascertain the meets. We seldom succeeded and often had to follow known hunt supporters or scour areas where they had met the previous season (all hunters tended to be creatures of habit).

Sabotage was a matter of spraying the river banks ahead of the hounds to mask the scent of any otter and walking with the hunters along the river banks in case they bolted an otter from a refuge.

If nothing was found we all enjoyed a walk along the river bank but if the hounds did find a scent we distracted them by horn blowing and false holloas. On occasions other more drastic methods were employed. I recall one group of sabs who, witnessing an otter under merciless attack by hounds, waded into the river to try and help, but without success.

As otter hunts always followed the courses of rivers or streams, usually at a sedate pace, we were inevitably in close contact with the hunt staff and followers. There were some curious verbal exchanges. At one hunt a particularly large senior follower became completely exasperated over our efforts to protect wildlife. He said to me: "*I killed ten Germans in the last war and each one of them was a better man than you!*" I was baffled by this animosity. Did he really mean that for all his hatred of the Germans he hated me more, just because I was trying to protect otters?

As mentioned, a few hunt officials were affable but others loathed us and prided themselves with their reputations for violence. On several occasions, when greatly outnumbered, saboteurs would end up being beaten up and thrown into the river. Just occasionally hunt saboteurs would defend themselves but the premeditated violence was always one-sided. Two hunters amongst twenty sabs might hear ribald comments about their actions, looks or attire but they were perfectly safe. The same could not be said if two sabs found themselves amongst twenty hunt supporters.

The Border Counties Otterhounds were a particularly ruthless and violent bunch. They drew their support from the unsavoury ranks of fox hunt terriermen and badger-diggers, as well as hare coursing fanatics — in short the most vicious elements in the spectrum of bloodsports.

The local equivalent of hunt saboteurs in the area of this hunt, the Mid-Wales Wildlife Conservation Group, was very active and had persuaded many farmers and landowners to ban the hunt. They were also effective at putting their case to the media and had whipped up a great deal of public opposition to otter hunting.

On Saturday June 19th 1976 seven of them were peacefully following the Border Counties Otterhounds when they were set upon by twenty supporters of the hunt, anxious for revenge. Five conservationists were subjected to a violent ducking whilst two of their children looked on. (Years later when on undercover work with the Three Counties Minkhounds, a replacement pastime in the area whose supporters included former followers of the Border Counties Otterhounds, a supporter gleefully boasted to me about his presence at this incident and recounted how at least one saboteur had ceased breathing!) In addition one handicapped woman, walking with the aid of sticks and an elderly man were thrown down a 10ft bank into the river.

The response by the HSA was to hit back the following week by drafting sabs in from all over the country to that hunt in a major effort to prevent otters being killed. Ninety sabs turned up on Saturday June 26th at Llandinam near Newtown, Mid-Wales. But our security had lapsed. The hunters were forewarned and forearmed and had drafted in a mob of terriermen, gamekeepers, lurcher lads and anyone else keen to deal with antis.

The inevitable clash came on the edges of a nearby lake when the hounds spoke to the scent of an otter and the army of sabs, myself included, moved in to thwart the hunters and help wildlife.

Suddenly from the wooded slopes to our left some burly hunt followers, many armed with 4ft staves, broke out from the cover and charged at us bellowing with anger. It was like a scene from a Medieval battle and a totally unequal contest. On one side were the hunters — burly young men armed and looking for a fight. On our side the sabs double in numbers but all unarmed, pacifist by nature and two thirds women and children.

The hunters waded straight in. They hit conservationists about the head and shoulders with their staves and poles. The few sabs who did try to defend themselves were soon battered to the ground.

I was carrying my camera and quickly took a few images of the hunt violence before I was spotted. Knowing that I had evidence that could put them in court they cut off my escape. I was jumped on, punched to the ground, my glasses smashed and my camera wrenched from my grasp.

The hunters gave me the Devil's alternative: give them my film or have my expensive camera 'film and all' thrown in the lake. I had little alternative but to give them the precious film — and did so. A BBC TV cameraman was also warned that if he did not put his camera down it would be smashed. He complied.

By the time the battered and bleeding sabs made their way back to the road the local police had appeared on the scene. We were a sorry sight. Men and women alike had suffered. There were broken jaws and noses. Many had cuts, bleeding faces and bruises. Some were taken to hospital. It was no surprise that by contrast the hunt supporters were unscathed — apart from damaged knuckles and clothing stained by the blood of their victims. We expected the police to take some action but they were totally disinterested.

When asked if they were going to take statements the reply was: *"We're only local police, we don't want to get involved."*

The hunt not only won the fight on the day, they also won the battle in the press, as they were quick to claim that it was actually they who had been assaulted and they had merely defended themselves. Simon Murray-Wells, Master of the Border Counties Otterhounds, made his stance quite clear when he wrote: *"You will not stop our sport; you have not yet felt the edge of our anger."*

That day had a marked effect on my thinking and that of other saboteurs. The combination of merciless hunt violence, police indifference and sympathy shown by the media towards the otter hunters was a potent mix, driving young radicals with a fierce sense of injustice to further extremes.

If the hunt could use extreme violence without any repercussions, then the opposition would clearly have to come in more devious forms — and with no holds barred other than the avoidance of violence.

Our resolve to consider any measure in the fight against wanton cruelty was enhanced by our acquisition in 1976 of an internal bulletin from the Eastern Counties Otterhounds that included the following plea to followers from the Master of the hunt, Charles Corner: "*Help me to kill a few otters this season and I think that next year we will shake the pessimists by showing just how many there are about. We have been keeping a low profile for too many years now, and there is nothing quite like a pack of hounds that is catching otters, to show sport every day we go out. I am taking steps to bring this about, belated perhaps, but I realise that successful hunts don't just happen, they are made by their members and masters...............Good hunting*"

It was the Eastern Counties Otterhounds that the Queen had subscribed to up until 1965 (confirmed by letter from Buckingham Palace dated June 16th 1967).

For all the claims of Charles Corner it was obvious to ourselves and most others that otters were in serious decline. If we did nothing these delightful harmless creatures would be driven to extinction. Everything we had tried to date had failed. Failure seemed certain in Parliament. We had to explore more extreme actions to save lives.

MY ANTI-HUNTING DIARY
These are hunts and other events that I attended.
(On some days I tried to visit two or more hunts)

1972

March 25th: Cambridgeshire Foxhounds, Abbotsley.

December 9th: Mendip Farmers Foxhounds, Clapton, Somerset.

December 23rd: Cambridgeshire Foxhounds, Boxworth.

December 26th: Cambridgeshire Foxhounds, Caxton Gibbet.

December 28th: Cambridgeshire Foxhounds, Waresley park.

1973

January 13th: Whaddon Chase Foxhounds, Shenley Brook End, Bucks.

January 20th: Enfield Chace Foxhounds, *Bakers Arms*. Bayford, Herts.

January 27th: East Essex Foxhounds, Great Yeldham station.

March 10th: Enfield Chace Foxhounds, Lemsford Mills, Herts.

March 17th: Essex Union Foxhounds, Danbury.

April 28th: Bucks and Courtenay Tracy Otterhounds at King's Mill, Marnhull, Dorset.

May 11th: Bucks and Courtenay Tracy Otterhounds hound parade at Windsor Horse Show.

May 12th: Bucks and Courtenay Tracy Otterhounds at Evenlode, Gloucestershire.

May 26th: Eastern Counties Otterhounds at Drayton, Norfolk (hunting the river Wensum).

June 9th: Eastern Counties Otterhounds at *Shoulder of Mutton*, Aldham, Essex (hunting the river Colne).

July 21st: Bucks and Courtenay Tracy Otterhounds at Snelson, Lavendon, Bucks (meeting at the home of Hunt Master Richard Sanders to hunt the river Ouse).

September 12th: Cambridgeshire Foxhounds, Waresley. This was a cub hunt.

October 6th: North Bucks Beagles at Olney.

October 13th: Bucks and Courtenay Tracy Otterhounds at Fovant. We could not find them so went on to the New Forest Beagles at Thorney Hill.

October 20th: South Herts Beagles at Sharpenhoe.

October 27th: Devon & Somerset Staghounds at Comers Gate.

November 8th: We leafleted the Premier of the film *The Belstone Fox*.

November 10th: Whaddon Chase Foxhounds, Thornborough, Bucks.

November 13th: Southdown Foxhounds, Woodmancote, Sussex.

42

November 17th: Devon and Somerset Staghounds at Cuzzicombe Post.

November 24th: Puckeridge & Thurlow Foxhounds, Washall Green, Herts. Essex Foxhounds, Hatfield Broad Oak.

December 1st: Essex Farmers Foxhounds, Latchingdon. SNOWED OFF. East Essex Foxhounds, Wethersfield Place. SNOWED OFF.

December 8th: Essex Union Foxhounds, Margaretting.

December 17th: Puckeridge & Thurlow Foxhounds, Clothall Great Wood, Herts.

December 22nd: Puckeridge & Thurlow Foxhounds, Rickling Hall, Essex. Cambridgeshire Foxhounds, Barton.

December 24th: Cambridgeshire Foxhounds, Abbotsley.

December 26th: Cambridgeshire Foxhounds, Caxton Gibbet.

December 29th: Puckeridge & Thurlow Foxhounds, Cave Gate.

1974

January 2nd: Occupation of the offices of the BFSS in London.

January 11th: Saw and leafleted the film *The Belstone Fox*.

January 12th: Old Berkeley Beagles at *The Swan*, Great Kimble, Bucks.

January 19th: Oakley Foxhounds, Little Staughton, Beds.

January 24th: Cambridgeshire Foxhounds, Potton wood, Beds.

January 26th: Cambridgeshire Foxhounds, *The Fox*, Longstowe. Cambridgeshire Harriers at Longstanton.

January 31st: East Essex Foxhounds, Langford Grove Gates. There was at least one kill.

February 2nd: Oxfordshire Coursing Club at Stanton Harcourt.

February 16th: Puckeridge & Thurlow Foxhounds, Allens Green, Herts.

February 20th: Essex Foxhounds, Navestock Hall. At least one kill.

February 23rd: Eridge Foxhounds, Shover's Green, Wadhurst, Sussex.

March 2nd: Enfield Chace Foxhounds, *Red Lion*, Preston, Herts.

March 16th: Fitzwilliam (Milton) Foxhounds, Ashton Wold, Northants.

March 20th: Puckeridge & Thurlow Foxhounds, St. Aylotts Gate.

April 6th: Pytchley Woodland Foxhounds, Upper Lodge, Pipewell, Northants.

September 21st: Kendal & District Otterhounds at Penny Bridge, Greenodd, Cumbria (to hunt the river Crake) There were otters about.

October 6th: Met Dave and Cee Wetton, Richard Course and others at the *Plough*, Enfield for coach to Gainsborough to leaflet in Marcus Kimball's constituency.

October 16th: Essex Farmers Foxhounds, *Queens Head*, Bradwell. At least two foxes were killed.

October 19th: Puckeridge & Thurlow Foxhounds, Cave Gate. At least one fox was killed.

October 26th: Puckeridge & Thurlow Foxhounds, Walkern Hall. (Cancelled due to Swine Vesicular disease).

November 2nd: Cambridgeshire Foxhounds, Bellams, Longstowe; tried De Burgh Bassethounds at Street Farm, Western Colville but couldn't find them; Puckeridge & Thurlow Foxhounds, Brent Pelham Hall;

November 9th: Puckeridge & Thurlow Foxhounds, Anstey, Herts.

November 16th: Enfield Chace Foxhounds, *Woodman*, Wormley West End, Herts. Puckeridge & Thurlow Foxhounds, Allens Green (I could not find them — they had gone to Albury).

November 23rd: Enfield Chace Foxhounds, Nyn Park, Northaw, Herts.

December 21st: Fitzwilliam (Milton) Foxhounds, Windmill, Great Gidding, Cambs.

December 26th: Cambridgeshire Foxhounds, Caxton Gibbet. Unblocked twenty fox earths.

1975

January 11th: Puckeridge & Thurlow Foxhounds, Allens Green.

January 18th: Essex Foxhounds, Stagden Cross, Essex.

January 25th: East Essex Foxhounds, Leighs Lodge, Great Leighs.

February 1st: Essex Foxhounds, Lea Hall, Hatfield Heath. (Cancelled due to rain). I went on to the Essex Union Foxhounds, Ingrave Hall Farm, Ingrave. They had killed before I arrived.

February 8th: Chiddingfold, Leconfield & Cowdray Foxhounds, Gunter's Bridge, Petworth, West Sussex. They were hunting with the bitch pack. We had 26 sabs out. We held a banner demonstration at the meet that was filmed by the press. On to the Surrey and North Sussex Beagles at *The Swan*, Northchapel.

February 22nd: Fitzwilliam (Milton) Foxhounds, Miriams Corner, Ashton Wold.

March 1st: Enfield Chace Foxhounds, *Woodman*, North Mimms. Vale of Aylesbury Foxhounds, Golden Parsonage, Gaddesden Row.

March 8th: Enfield Chace Foxhounds, Knebworth House.

March 15th: Enfield Chace Foxhounds, *Grandison Arms*, Bramfield, Herts.

March 22nd: Chiddingfold, Leconfield & Cowdray Foxhounds, *Noah's Ark*, Lurgashall, West Sussex. I went with Iain McNay, the

HSA Press Officer. Iain arranged for Jilly Cooper to come along to see hunt saboteurs in action.

March 29th: Enfield Chace Foxhounds, Nyn Park, Northaw, Herts.

August 15th: Eastern Counties Otterhounds at *The Fox and Hounds*, Lyng, Norfolk.

August 16th: Eastern Counties Otterhounds at North Elmham, Norfolk.

September 6th: Bucks and Courtenay Tracy Otterhounds at Whelford Mill, Fairford, Gloucs.

September 13th: Devon & Somerset Staghounds.

October 4th: Oxfordshire Coursing Club at Woodstock.

October 11th: Eastern Counties Otterhounds at *The Bell Inn*, Cretingham, Suffolk. No sign of this hunt so we went on to the Sproughton Foot Beagles at Furneaux farm, Whatfield.

October 18th: Courtenay Tracy Otterhounds at Moreton Church, Dorset. This hunt did not turn up so we went on to the New Forest Beagles at Godshill.

October 25th: Cambridgeshire Foxhounds, Eversden Wood. The hunt cancelled their meet because the ground was hard and dry so I went on to the Trinity Foot Beagles at *Rose Inn*, Haslingfield.

November 1st: Vale of Aylesbury Foxhounds, Waterstock, Oxon. This was their opening meet. It was filmed by TV. We went on to the Christchurch and Farley Hill Beagles at *The Swan*, Islip.

November 8th: Puckeridge & Thurlow Foxhounds, Anstey House. At least one fox was killed, another saved. Went on to the Enfield Chace Foxhounds at the "*Woodman*", Wormley West End, Herts.

November 15th: Fitzwilliam (Milton) Foxhounds, Great Gidding, Cambs.

November 22nd: Old Surrey & Burstow Foxhounds near Hartfield, East Sussex.

November 29th: Joint meet of the Heythrop Foxhounds and the North Cotswold Foxhounds at Batsford, Gloucs. Nine hunt saboteurs out.

December 6th: Oxfordshire Coursing Club at Shilton. I stood on the coursing field then went on to the Warwickshire Foxhounds at Little Wolford.

December 20th: Tickham Foxhounds, Stalisfield Green, Kent. I was in a car with other hunt saboteurs when we were attacked by hunt supporters.

December 26th: Old Surrey & Burstow Foxhounds, Felbridge Hotel, East Grinstead, East Sussex.

1976

January 1st: Vale of Aylesbury Foxhounds, Thame. We held a banner demonstration at the meet.

January 10th: Puckeridge & Thurlow Foxhounds, Westmill, Herts. Cambridgeshire Harriers at South End house, Bassingbourn. Cambridgeshire Foxhounds, Little Barford.

January 17th: Essex Foxhounds, Chignal St. James. Essex Union Foxhounds, Apps Farm, Stock.

January 24th: Oxfordshire Coursing Club. We could not find them so we went on to the Heythrop Foxhounds at Bledington, Oxon.

January 31st: Southdown Foxhounds, *Cricketers*, Berwick, East Sussex. We took a road kill fox to the meet but the hounds were not interested in this. It was too cold for any horses. They started hunting on foot but we could not follow so we went on to the Brighton and Storrington Foot Beagles at the Old Kennels, Findon, West Sussex.

February 7th: Puckeridge & Thurlow Foxhounds, Benington.

February 13th: Waterloo Cup Hare Coursing at Altcar, Lancashire. I was arrested on the coursing field.

February 14th: West Norfolk Foxhounds, Grenstein farm, Mileham.

February 21st: Cambridgeshire Foxhounds, Hilton cross-roads. At least one fox was killed and another dug-out and bolted.

February 28th: Essex Union Foxhounds, Mountnessing church. Hounds rioted and despite our best efforts to prevent it one was killed on the railway line.

March 6th: Quorn Foxhounds, *Saracens Head*, Heath End. We had 130 hunt saboteurs out.

March 13th: Puckeridge & Thurlow Foxhounds, Therfield, Herts.

March 20th: Puckeridge & Thurlow Foxhounds, Little Chishill.

April 3rd: Mendip Farmers Foxhounds. Attended a lecture in Bristol the night before.

April 10th: Surrey Union Foxhounds, Woodcote farm, West Horsley.

June 5th: Eastern Counties Otterhounds at *The Inn*, Ingham, Suffolk, for Ampton Park. We lost them completely. Apparently the hunt was later reported as being at Hoxne, near Diss.

June 12th: Run-on to protest against the parade of the Chiddingfold, Leconfield & Cowdray Foxhounds at the South of England show at Ardingley, West Sussex.

June 26th: Border Counties Otterhounds at Llandinam, Powys. We suffered violent assaults by hunt supporters. One hunter took my film from me and threw it away.

July 24th: Run-on to protest against the parade of hounds at the Stow-on-the Wold show, Gloucs.

August 7th: Surrey Union Foxhounds, Ranmore church at 7.00a.m. This was a cub hunting meet.

August 14th: Essex Foxhounds, Woodside Green. This hunt was cancelled after an ALF attack on hunt vehicles the night before. I went on to an anti-fur demonstration in Brighton.

August 21st: Essex Foxhounds, Good Easter. Took slides of a fleeing cub.

August 25th: Essex Foxhounds, White Roding. One cub was killed after being chopped by hounds in a field of potatoes. I took photographs of the remains.

August 28th: Garth & South Berks. Foxhounds, Tolpiece Farm, Mattingley at 6.00a.m. Day ended at 10.15a.m. One cub was killed right near the end when it was trapped in a small wood. Robin Howard and myself tried our best to help.

August 30th: Oakley Foxhounds, Kempston wood, Beds. I was on my own. A cub was marked to ground. Dug-out with terriers and shot.

September 4th: Fitzwilliam (Milton) Foxhounds, Great Gidding, Cambs. At least two cubs were killed in a small covert. I went on to the Oakley Foxhounds at the Airfield gates, Chelveston, Northants.

September 11th: Puckeridge & Thurlow Foxhounds, Scales park.

September 18th: Fitzwilliam (Milton) Foxhounds, Sawtry gorse.

September 25th: Heythrop Foxhounds, Cornwell cross-roads, Oxon.

September 26th: Protest at Boscombe Church, Salisbury, Wilts. against service conducted by Reverend Robin Ray, Master and Huntsman of the Courtenay Tracy Otterhounds. We drove into Salisbury afterwards to deliver a letter of protest to the Bishop.

October 2nd: Duke of Beaufort's Foxhounds, the kennels, Badminton, Gloucs. This was a shocking day. They killed at least nine cubs. I left at 10.00a.m. to go on to the Curre Foxhounds who had met at Cobblers Plain, Monmouthshire. I chatted with some local villagers who were very anti-hunt.

October 9th: North Cotswold Foxhounds, Mickleton Hills farm. I photographed the hunt and hounds on the railway line — after the Huntsman had had a word with the signalman beforehand. I went on to the Cotswold Foxhounds, at Naunton Downs farm and then the Heythrop Foxhounds at Wyck Rissington, Gloucs.

October 16th: Heythrop Foxhounds, Hook Norton, Oxon. Master and Huntsman Captain Ronnie Wallace lost his temper with us.

October 23rd: Old Berkshire Foxhounds, Watchfield Common.

October 30th: South Herefordshire Foxhounds, *New Harp*, Hoarwithy. This was their Opening Meet.

November 6th: Oxfordshire Coursing Club at Combe at 9.30a.m. We had 60 hunt saboteurs out. We walked in beat lines across the fields from 7.00a.m. to 9.00a.m. to drive the hares away. Had some run-ons onto the fields. I took plenty of photographs. The coursers claimed to have killed one hare before we arrived out of 26 coursed.

November 7th: Protest at Sporting Art exhibition at Blenheim Palace. Seven of us were thrown out for not having tickets.

November 13th: Dummer Beagles at Roundhill farm, Brailes. We managed to save one hare that was being hunted.

November 27th: Heythrop Foxhounds, Harford Bridge. The son of the Hunt Secretary chose to drive round after us wherever we drove. When we had to stop suddenly to avoid an accident he collided with the back of our vehicle.

December 4th: Tried Old Berkshire Foxhounds, Sparsholt; Chiddingfold Leconfield & Cowdray Foxhounds, Heath End; Garth & South Berks. Foxhounds, Spencers wood; and Hampshire, "H.H." Foxhounds, Crondall but all were cancelled due to snow.

December 11th: Heythrop Foxhounds. SNOWED OFF

December 18th: Cambridgeshire Foxhounds, Everton.

December 27th: Heythrop Foxhounds, *The Fox*, Chipping Norton. I took photographs at the meet.

1977

January 1st: Puckeridge & Thurlow Foxhounds, Meesden Green. Cambridgeshire Foxhounds, Ashwell Bury.

January 3rd: Puckeridge & Thurlow Foxhounds at *The Bell*, Clare, Suffolk.

January 8th: Heythrop Foxhounds, Fifield, Oxon. Hunters used their horses to block us on a road.

January 15th: Enfield Chace Foxhounds, Northaw church. The 'Hunt Protection Association' were supposed to be out but we saw nothing of them.

January 29th: Devon & Somerset Staghounds at Dunkery Hill Gate. I took photographs of this hind hunting day. There was no kill.

February 5th: Whaddon Chase Foxhounds, Swanbourne station, Bucks then over to see the Vale of Aylesbury Foxhounds meeting at Braziers End farm, Cholesbury which was a 'women only' sab.

February 11th: Waterloo Cup Hare Coursing at Altcar, Lancashire. 38 hunt saboteurs were arrested.

February 12th: Christchurch and Farley Hill Beagles at *The Swan*, Islip, Oxon. There was no kill and I took photographs.

February 19th: Heythrop Foxhounds, Sherborne, Gloucs.

March 5th: Cotswold Vale Farmers Foxhounds, *Red Hart*, Blaisdon, Gloucs.

March 12th: North Cotswold Foxhounds, *Farmers Arms*, Guiting Power, Gloucs.

March 20th: Protest against service conducted by the Reverend Eric Wheeler — a hunting vicar — at Steeple Bumpstead church, Essex.

March 26th: Heythrop Foxhounds, Rockliffe. This was Ronnie Wallace's last meet with the Heythrop.

April 23rd: Eastern Counties Otterhounds at North Elmham, Norfolk. Hunt supporters tried to dent our cars. I took photographs of the day.

"Well, them's vermin lad." "What *is* vermin Sir?" "Vermin be rabbits and foxes and weasels and stoats and rats and squirrels and owls and hawks and crows and magpies and jays and cats and rooks and otters and some dogs and hares and some other things and I shoots 'em all for my master."

"What's left in the woods then Sir?" "Pheasants sonny, and the master shoots *them*."

CHAPTER FOUR
Beyond the legal front line

As a counter to the success of saboteurs the hunters began to use low-key vandalism against our vehicles as well as personal violence. It started harmlessly enough with the hunters letting down our tyres. We countered this by making foot-pump and spare tyre valves standard sabbing equipment and whenever possible we left someone to guard our vehicles.

The hunters then went a stage further. They were aware that our use of hired vans made us vulnerable. Firstly we would have to pay for any damage to them secondly if there was damage we might be denied the opportunity to hire them in future. Accordingly we became the victims of a spate of denting, scraped paintwork, smashed windscreens and they even went so far as the dangerous practice of putting sugar in our fuel tanks (few cars in those days had lockable fuel caps).

With the police and the media showing a near total lack of interest in the combination of physical violence and vandalism by hunters the sabs had little option but to reply in kind. Though sugar was occasionally added to the fuel tanks of hunters most responses were more subtle. Road signs were changed to direct people away from hare coursing meetings and bloodsports events such as point-to-points and country fairs. Hunt kennels were visited at night and chains of rook-scarers strung up in their vicinity to keep the hounds and hunt staff awake.

Hunt supporters took to following us and snooping around our homes. The remains of slaughtered foxes would be thrown into sabs' gardens or strung up on their gates. One leading member of the HSA even had his beloved pets pitchforked to death by hunt followers.

Such actions generated a great deal of animosity towards all connected with hunting and inevitably some response, but always without violence. In 1976 the annual BFSS Country Fair at Deene Park near Corby, Northants, was more than a little impaired when adverts were place in many local papers beforehand announcing its cancellation. The bill for these adverts was sent to the BFSS.

The annual hunt balls arranged by fox hunts also became targets as they were perceived to be fundraising events. They were subjected to sudden, very localised, power cuts and the parked vehicles of hunt supporters were immobilised.

The activists encountered two problems during these raids: firstly the blinding flash which followed the cutting of the power cable

50

destroyed night vision; secondly whilst creeping through the grounds of the mansions to find the marquee they had to avoid the many courting couples. During one such mission in Suffolk in mid-Summer one raider almost fell on top of a very welcoming near-naked girl. One of the inebriated revellers, she mistook him for her lover who presumably had gone to the bar to fetch more drinks. The raider mumbled his apologies and beat a hasty retreat.

As the seventies wore on the tit for tat conflict between hunt saboteurs and hunters escalated into small scale rural warfare. Worryingly it became widely accepted that irate hunters could attack hunt saboteurs almost with impunity. One hunt Master explained this to the media thus: "*Horse-whipping a hunt saboteur is rather like beating a wife. They are both private matters.*" (Comment by Tim Asplin, Joint Master Essex Union Foxhounds [1976-1984] following an incident at his hunt on November 27th 1976, quoted in *HOWL* No.8 Spring 1977)

Hunt saboteurs trying to save lives would often be ambushed and left bloody and badly beaten. In response nuisance raids at night on hunt kennels with rook-scarers were replaced by full scale onslaughts aimed at stopping the hunt even meeting. The target was the equipment necessary for fox hunting, tack would be destroyed and vehicles wrecked. Assault groups typically consisted of five or six people in two cars, well equipped and carrying walkie-talkies.

There was never any intent to look for physical violence against people, the target was the property vital for fox hunting, but if hunt thugs attempted to interfere they would be dealing with people who could and would defend themselves and their colleagues.

Such an assault could stop a hunt. Unaware of what was taking place elsewhere I was engaged in undercover observation at a dawn cub hunting meet of the Essex Foxhounds in August 1976. At the scheduled 7.00a.m. start on August 14th I drove up and joined the riders and followers gathered at the appointed meet but the hounds were conspicuous by their absence.

Eventually a hunt supporter drove up to explain that all the vehicles at the kennels had been immobilised overnight. He explained that the hunters had repaired one lorry and set off with their hounds but, a few hundred yards on, the water added to the diesel had taken effect.

The kennel staff had then phoned the Master and another stalwart supporter living nearby for help only to find that their vehicles had been treated similarly. The Essex Foxhounds did not hunt at all that day. It was game set and match to the allies of the fox and with no physical violence whatsoever.

As well as help in the fields foxes began to receive increasing intellectual support to correct the unjust negative image of the species.

Hunt saboteurs opposed the killing of animals because it was cruel and unnecessary. Their opponents claimed that hunting animals was the most humane way to control their numbers and challenged conservationists to find a better way.

In the mid-1970s wildlife experts led by John Bryant, a member of the RSPCA Council, exposed the fallacy at the heart of this challenge by pointing out that the fox population was self-regulating and that the species could be easily accommodated in our countryside if sensible precautions were taken to protect vulnerable livestock such as poultry and if efforts by hunters to encourage foxes were ended. Hunters should be stopped from building artificial earths for foxes to live and breed in and hunters should be stopped from putting out food for foxes.

In addition the very real benefits of foxes in our countryside were highlighted. Foxes play a vital role in our ecosystems and are the most humane and natural way of controlling the numbers of genuine agricultural pests.

Contact with other animal welfare groups made me think about other animal abuses; about vivisection, factory farming, the fur trade and whaling. I became vegetarian. For the first time groups began to talk about extending the tactics used in hunt sabotage against all animal exploiters. Banner waving protests had been mildly effective at generating publicity for the cause but many felt that carefully targeted direct action was also needed if lives were to be saved.

So in the early 1970s a new militant more active animal welfare movement emerged, pledged to fight for the cause of animals and relieve their suffering — whatever the personal cost to the activists.

The first activists to strike at vivisection called themselves the 'Band of Mercy'. This copied the name of a militant and radical youth group of the RSPCA who operated during the nineteenth century.

The basic ethos of this modern Band of Mercy was to attack and destroy property used to abuse animals, but to harm no living creature in the process, either animal or human. Prime targets were therefore animal exploitation centres that were still being built and before they housed any animals.

Hoechst Pharmaceuticals built a laboratory in Milton Keynes where, despite strident local opposition, they planned to undertake experiments on animals involving radiation. Whilst still under construction the building was subjected to arson attacks in November 1973. As a result the radiation experiments were abandoned though other tests continue.

At other finished premises vans used to transport the helpless animals were the target. The night intruders exposed themselves to great risk of capture by pushing them well away from any buildings that might house animals before igniting them.

Boats used in the slaughter of the grey seals in the Wash were also attacked and some sunk.

These operations went on regularly throughout the early part of the decade but once arson was used the police took the matter very seriously. Vulnerable establishments tightened their security greatly.

In August 1974 at the Oxford Laboratory Animals Colonies (OLAC) complex at Blackthorn near Bicester — a registered breeding place for laboratory animals — two Band of Mercy operatives, Cliff Goodman and Ronnie Lee, were caught.

The police charged them for that incident and a whole string of earlier offences. A young man was also arrested and charged as an accomplice in the burning of a seal cull boat. At the subsequent trial he admitted the charge and his lawyer pleaded for mercy claiming that he had been led astray. He received a suspended sentence and was fined.

On March 24th 1975 at Oxford Crown Court the other two pleaded guilty to fourteen different charges including setting fire to vivisection laboratories still under construction, damaging vehicles used to transport animals for experimentation and seal hunters' boats in the Wash.

Cliff Goodman was defended by a solicitor who told the court: "*Cliff Goodman is not a crank. He is basically an honest young man of integrity. There is a substantial body of opinion that takes the same view as he does.*"

Ronnie Lee, a trainee solicitor, chose to defend himself. His statement to the court included the following: "*My intentions were to prevent suffering. I did not do it out of hatred and I am not sorry for trying to save weak and helpless animals from death and torture. I have not come to beg for mercy for myself. I ask for justice for those animals, creatures who are so brutally treated by the human kind.*" [quoted in *New Musical Express* November 12th 1977.]

Judge Kenneth Mynett sentenced them both to three years in jail. Supporters staged a march through Oxford and a banner demonstration afterwards around the Martyrs' Memorial. They carried placards with a variety of slogans including: "*Can Compassion Be Condemned When Cruelty Is Condoned*?"

*****

With the jailing of Cliff Goodman and Ronnie Lee for what at the time were lengthy sentences other activists hesitated to face similar consequences and illegal activities largely came to an end. Hunt sabotage and banner demonstrations continued, but the night activists had temporarily had their wings clipped.

Partly as a result of the actions of the Band of Mercy newspapers had taken a renewed interest in animal exploitation. In the spring of 1975, following months of determined undercover work by reporter the late Mary Beith (1938-2012), the *Sunday People* published the scandal of the smoking beagles experiments at the research premises of the Imperial Chemical Industries (ICI) at Alderley Park in Cheshire.

Fearing that proven links between smoking and cancer would cause the collapse of their valuable cigarette markets, the large tobacco companies were involved in a frantic race to produce a safe tobacco substitute. ICI called their product, "New Smoking Material" (NSM).

To test it for safety they used beagles. Mary Beith worked undercover at the laboratory and used a small camera to photograph what happened. The beagles were clamped into stocks and forced to inhale the smoke from up to thirty cigarettes a day. After three years, they were killed and post mortems carried out to gauge any ill-effects.

The nation was horrified by the callous and cruel nature of these experiments. Man chooses whether or not he smokes knowing full well that if he does so he faces a risk of cancer. Why should animals pay for his follies? Particularly as the experiments were of dubious value anyway.

Dr. Kit Pedlar, Chairman of the RSPCA's Animal Welfare Advisory Committee declared: "*It is well known that if smoke of any sort is repeatedly inhaled into the lungs, it will cause irritation. The tests cannot but prove anything else*".

"*It will take twenty to thirty years of close study on the effects on human beings before any true picture emerges. To subject dogs to such experiments, is unnecessary.*"

Evidence as to the cruel treatment of the dogs came from a variety of sources. Here is a statement made by a former employee, a Mrs P. of Macclesfield, Cheshire to R.D. Marriott, Northern Counties

Organiser, National Anti-Vivisection Society Ltd. on Thursday March 6th 1975:-

"*I worked for eighteen months at the ICI Toxicity Testing Laboratories at Alderley Park, Cheshire, as an attendant looking after the Beagle dogs which were being used in the smoking experiments to test a new smoking material (NSM). These dogs have to smoke thirty cigarettes a day in two four hour sessions.*

The dogs have to be put into a canvas coat which has holes through which the animals' legs go, and it is then fastened over their backs. Their heads are then clamped into a thing like a stocks and a mask fitted over the muzzle. They are made from plastic bottles, with a rubber mould inside and a rubber band to make it air-tight. A cigarette is fitted into the other end so that as the dog has to breathe it inhales the smoke.

The dogs hate them and often try to shake them off. Just imagine having your face fastened in something for hours on end. A lot of them chew the inside of the mask, even though they can't move their mouths much, as the mask fits tightly. Condensation from the dogs breathing and the smoke eventually stains the muzzle and teeth. Their tongues used to be a horrible colour, the smoke irritates their eyes, they get cramp from standing, and they suffer from stress, boredom and frustration.

I'll defy anybody to tell me that those dogs look forward to being trussed up like they are, forced to have a mask on their face and smoke. One dog (Wilfred) used to protest all day long. He used to get out of the mask more than he was in it, and he got smacked something awful. Another dog (Bertha) just hated the experiment altogether, and used to drag the box about all the time. It was terrible. One dog had a very sensitive mouth, he was a nervous dog and very distressed at being used in the experiment and he made his mouth bleed by trying to get the mask off. Sometimes, to stop the dogs throwing the masks off, they are fastened too tightly.

Just imagine, having to stand for hours on end with your head in the stocks. If a fly settles on them, or their ear itches, they can't get to it at all.

These dogs get no regular exercise. Only what they get in the pens. It's up to the discretion of the attendants; there is no regular provision for exercise. They don't even walk from the pens to the smoking machines. The canvas coats are put on in the pen; they are fastened onto a trolley and wheeled to the smoking benches. They never walk. We did once suggest that they made a long run at the side of the dog house for exercise but it was never done.

One dog (Wellington) gave trouble right from the beginning and had to be put on a tranquilising drug. This did calm him down but he used to get so lank and miserable while he was on the tablets. Then his stomach started to swell. First they blamed that on him having too much water; then they decided it wasn't that at all, and in the end they had to take him off the experiment because he became so distressed that he couldn't smoke anyway even if he managed to keep the mask on. He was panting so much that he could not smoke. The second day I was there his mouth was bleeding. On another occasion, one of the attendants hit him and when I remonstrated with him, he put his fists up to me...

Most of the attendants were very good and did their best for the dogs, but a minority were not. Some of them seemed to think that because the dogs were there for experiments, they hadn't any feelings. We were told once that all the natural instincts had been bred out of them. I have seen these dogs get thumped and kicked, and I've fallen out about it many a time. They were often hit with plastic rulers. The supervisor started that by banging his ruler on the bench at the side of the dog to try and frighten it into being quiet and behaving. Then gradually it progressed to hitting the dog with the ruler. He gave the dogs plenty of clouts and I have seen him knuckle them on the heads and pull their ears. Quite apart from the rulers, I have seen many a dog get such a crack from several of the attendants. Some of them seemed to think that just because the animals were going to die anyway it did not matter if they suffered in the meantime.

One attendant, who used to work in a circus, was one day trying to get one of the dogs onto the smoking machine by sitting astride it as though she was riding a horse. (At first the dogs used to go frantic, jump up and down and pull the boxes over. It must have been a terrifying experience for them). Anyway, she was determined that she was going to be the boss; it was her idea of training, so all she did was to terrify it into submission. That was the sort of thing we had to put up with. If we complained we were told that we were too soft. It's when they lose their temper that they start to hit the dogs. If a dog gets out of its mask, they give them a good smack and force them back in. I have seen them fastened up so tight, it's a wonder they haven't screwed their head off. They just want to keep them on smoking, and it is a nuisance to them if they keep coming out of the masks and making them more work..............."

There was a massive public outcry against these experiments and petitions demanded that they should be banned. Along with other animal welfare radicals, I wondered if the Band of Mercy would have reacted more militantly, if their leaders had not been behind bars.

For me, the situation altered dramatically when I learned on Friday June 13th 1975 from an article in my local paper the *Kent Messenger* that the smoking beagles were to be killed at the end of the following week.

The time for petitions and protests was over. If these beagles were to live — to enjoy any of their birth-right — it was time for swift, decisive action.

I had just finished my university finals and consequently I was free to act. I made contact with some of our most trusted and experienced saboteurs who lived near to our target — the large ICI complex in Cheshire.

On Monday, June 16th, I left my London home and rode north on my trusty motorbike. My destination was ICI's Dog Toxicity Unit at Alderley Park, Cheshire. My plan was simple: to get some, or all of the beagles out.

The next day was spent doing ground surveillance in the fields and woods around the perimeter of Alderley Park. The whole complex was set in quiet secluded countryside and despite the intimidating security of the main front entrance I found that there was an easy approach through the woods at the rear.

Making sure I was not seen, I climbed the perimeter fence and settled down in the undergrowth. My task was to locate the dogs and take note of security posts, fencing and any alarms.

When I found the beagles it was in broad daylight in the middle of the hot summer's afternoon. I had spent long, sweltering hours watching the comings and goings of personnel and observing the buildings through binoculars. In the end the dogs made their presence known to me by their barking. They were housed in a low, brick unit, some distance from the main buildings.

That day the back door of the kennel block, a fire door, had been left open because of the heat. When I was confident that no-one was looking I left my hiding place and ran across a few yards of open space to the building.

I entered cautiously. Peering around the door to make sure no one was inside I found row upon row of metal kennels with a dog in each. There was a front concrete run and a back compartment to each kennel. The doors had locks, but when I tried one, it opened. Despite the available security, the staff were so over confident that they had become lax. This was perhaps the first time that activists anywhere had contemplated rescuing dogs from such a laboratory. In later years security at such places would be greatly increased.

All too soon I heard voices approaching along the corridor. Shutting the kennel door gently, I made a rapid retreat and slipped back into the safety of the woods.

I decided to take immediate action that night. Operating in conjunction with a trusted colleague, who had a car, we planned our mission. We would take the back route to Alderley Park, switching off all but the car's side lights as we approached and drive some way into the woods for cover.

The only other person who knew of the operation was our back up contact in the south of England. If we did not report back to him on time he would know the plan had misfired and could alert the Press.

At 3a.m. we were safely in the woods parked about three hundred yards from the dog unit. Between 3a.m. and 4a.m. is a great time for such actions as any security is usually at its lowest state of awareness then.

We approached stealthily and cautiously. Using a screwdriver I levered the fire door open. It opened easily. We then held our breath anticipating security alarms going off. Nothing happened.

We waited another ten minutes to see if any silent alarms had been activated that might bring security staff running to our location. When no one came to investigate I entered the building.

My torch beam illuminated the first beagle in the row, Major, who cowered away from me in fright.

I opened his door and entered his kennel talking softly to reassure him. Gently I picked him up and carried him to my colleague waiting outside. There was a moment's panic when, like the amateur I was, I let the fire door close shut behind me. I fumbled with the screwdriver, forcing it open again.

Going back to the adjacent kennel I found another terrified beagle who dashed into the back and forced himself, shaking, into the tightest corner.

Dogs are always likely to bite in this situation but there was no time for a formal introduction. Anyway, one reason why scientists choose beagles for such experiments is that the breed is so docile. When I had hold of this cowering dog he calmed down. I took this second dog, Noddy, outside. It was then that the two dogs decided to take their own part in our canine version of the Great Escape. As soon as they met they started to fight. This was neither expected nor planned for. It was as if they had spent ages threatening each other

58

through the mesh and now the blissful moment for combat had arrived. Nothing could have been so badly timed.

We had taken lots of leads, planning to build up a collection of dogs outside the unit and then walk them back to our car. But the aggression between these first two dogs made that plan impossible. Their only thought was to fight. I should never have selected dogs from adjacent kennels but how could I walk by and leave him behind? Major simply would not cooperate when we were walking and Noddy fought to escape the lead.

We ended up passing the dogs to each other over the fence and then carrying both dogs all the way back to the car which consumed a considerable amount of time. I wanted to go back for another couple, but we had problems. We could not leave them alone in the car as they would fight, my partner would have to stay with them.

This meant I was on my own to traverse the wire, get a dog and ferry it back to the car. We had planned to get many out, now we would be lucky to get even another one.

Every other dog rescued would take time and jeopardise the safety of the two we had. It only needed one security man to pass by on a routine check to ruin the whole operation.

The faces of the other beagles left behind haunted me as we made the reluctant decision to pull out there and then. To this day I bitterly regret the fate of the dogs we couldn't take to freedom. When I had chosen the two dogs from the 48 in the unit I was in effect playing God — deciding who could live and who would be left to die.

We left Alderley Park at speed heading south. Once on the motorway we slowed. It was the early hours of the morning and we had to be careful not to attract any police attention by exceeding the speed limit.

We made one stop to make two telephone calls. One to our base to say we were on our way, mission accomplished. The other to the Press Association, who would make sure all newspapers told the British public of the beagles' escape.

Then we drove on uneventfully to our destination where the beagles were passed over into safe hands. They had further adventures but eventually both Major and Noddy enjoyed long and happy lives in great homes; Major at the home of Richard Course and his family and Noddy with the family of hunt saboteur colleagues.

Haunted by the beagles I was forced to leave behind I returned alone on my motorbike two nights later to try and remove another dog. I was successful but I was caught with the poor dog, Snap, in the outskirts of nearby Manchester. On the last day of my University career I was in police custody and Snap was returned to ICI. I was thoroughly miserable over my failure. Sympathisers made offers to buy Snap and the other beagles but ICI would not sell them.

I was charged with theft of the beagles and going equipped to steal. A colleague, John Bryant, was charged with receiving, handling and disposing of stolen goods. The case was resolved at Knutsford Crown Court on December 17th 1975 when the prosecution dropped the charges against us if I agreed not to take any more dogs (by agreeing to be bound over). Here is the relevant press report:-

"*Smoking Beagles' Pair Are Cleared*
Two men in the 'smoking beagles' storm were freed by a court yesterday.

No evidence was offered against them.

Zoologist Michael Huskisson, aged 21, pleaded not guilty at Knutsford, Cheshire, to stealing three beagles.

John Bryant, 33, an animal-centre manager, denied receiving two dogs.

The beagles were in an ICI laboratory at Alderley Edge, Cheshire, where they were used in tests on the effects of smoking.

The two men are animal-lovers who objected to the experiments.

Huskisson admitted taking the dogs but shouted in court: "I didn't steal them."

Judge David Morgan-Hughes said the only matter at issue was whether there was dishonesty.

Mr Alex Carlile, prosecuting, said that in offering no evidence the men's "genuine motivation" had been borne in mind.

Huskisson, of Abbotsley, Huntingdon, Cambridgeshire, and Bryant of Ferne, Wiltshire, were bound over to keep the peace." (*The Sun*, Thursday December 18th 1975) [Ferne animal sanctuary was at that time in Wiltshire but has now moved to Somerset]

Subsequently on occasion I was able to see both dogs enjoying running about in open countryside with fellow canines.

We get but one go at life on this planet and to spend the entirety of it locked up in some miserable research unit is a crime the magnitude of which will one day be recognised.

*****

Ronnie Lee and Cliff Goodman were discharged from prison in March 1976. The early raids by the Band of Mercy and mine on ICI had opened the eyes of animal welfare supporters. No longer need they stand back helplessly while animals suffered.

In the absence of any co-ordinated political drive a new militant body emerged — the Animal Liberation Front (ALF). Their aim was the protection of wildlife, relief from suffering for the laboratory animal and liberation for the captive animal. A whole host of raids were carried out on various exploitation centres.

Word filtered back to the radical animal welfare organisers that as a result the police were taking a particularly serious view of animal welfare orientated crimes. It was rumoured that even the famed police Special Branch were involved in tracking the culprits.

However, one of the biggest problems facing the police was the attitude of their own officers, who are like anyone else when it comes to compassion towards animals. Called out to investigate ALF raids at animal exploitation centres many realised, perhaps for the first time, the full extent to which animals are forced to suffer in modern society.

They found battery houses with hens living in near perpetual darkness, in tiny cages, upon piles of their own excreta. They entered laboratories to find blind rabbits, cats and dogs with their skulls split open to implant electrodes and living monkeys literally crucified in the name of science. I know that many felt more sympathy with the raiders than with the raided.

There can be only one real explanation for the dismal conviction record for ALF crimes in those early days — that many of the police detectives simply did not want to know. When they investigated 'crimes' at hunt kennels, doubtless they found the hunt staff, as always, arrogant and ignorant and I personally am convinced that many officers simply turned a blind eye to what they saw.

It was perhaps this aspect that terrified the authorities. When the police themselves give tacit support to law breaking the possibility does exist to subvert society. To counter this police were sometimes themselves put under great pressure to come up with 'a result'.

In January 1977 the grave of legendary huntsman John Peel (1776-1854) was desecrated by a small group of anti-bloodsports activists that included me. His headstone, decorated with hunting memorabilia, was toppled and a corner broken off. Regarded as the patron saint of hunting his grave and headstone in the small Cumbrian village of Caldbeck were viewed by hunters as a shrine at which to pay homage.

The year before, on the bi-centenary of his birth, the hunting press made much of his key role as the father figure of hunting. Images of his decorative headstone were widely publicised but I and others had seen just too many animals tormented and butchered by hunters following his lead. Being young and headstrong I rose to the bait and joined a team seeking to decry this glorification of killing animals for fun.

During the early hours of Sunday January 23rd 1977 we dug a hole over the grave allowing his headstone to be pushed over and a small corner broken off. A fox's head (a hunting trophy bought from an antique shop) was left in the hole along with this note:

"John Peel John Peel come blow on your horn,
Come blow till your cruel heart turns blue,
No rest for the thousands of foxes you've torn,
But at least this one's got the last laugh on you".

The toppling and breaking of the sacred headstone, the entombment of the remains of a hunted fox above him in his grave, the taunting doggerel were all calculated to incense the hunting fraternity — the self-styled 'pillars of society'. It certainly did that.

It is hard with the murky view of many years hindsight to see why people should feel driven to commit such a crime. Perhaps it is easier if you picture yourself back in that time. All manner of animal abuse was not only legal, it was glorified. The courageous young hunt saboteurs who tried to save the lives of hunted animals were all too often ignored or persecuted by the rural police and attacked by hunters. If you were trying to save the life of an animal and a hunt thug seeking to stop you punched you, some police seemed more interested in charging you for provoking him than in charging him for his assault on you. The media, in awe of the royal hunting connections offered by Prince Charles and his sister usually sided with the hunters.

Initially, to hype a story that the press showed little interest in, there was an inaccurate claim made that the remains of John Peel had been exhumed and thrown in a cesspit. This caught the attention of the media, made headlines and caused outrage — but it never happened.

The storm of publicity put intense pressure on the local police. As an officer later told me, Cumbria only had two heroes, Donald Campbell and John Peel, and here was the latter apparently despatched to the sewage works!

During routine early morning checks at Forton Services many miles south of Caldbeck on the M6, an alert police officer had noted a particular car as belonging to an anti-bloodsport person. He was simply checking car number plates with the police computer to see if they were stolen. With the intense ALF and HSA activity at the time it was and still is the practice to enter all cars seen at demonstrations on the computer. The actual entry for this car was: Member animal liberation anti bloodsport supporter CR0 TX 47 11.1.77. Refers.

This revealed for the first time that the police were using their new National Computer to gather and retain intelligence about UK citizens.

The officer thought nothing of this at first, but when he learnt of the raid he informed his superiors. Following up this lead the police quickly pounced on the registered owner and her friends, me included. Routine monitoring of police radio transmissions by a colleague alerted us to the fact that the police were searching for our car. Police officers raided my Gloucester bedsit, searched everywhere tipping drawers out onto the bed and they found my precious camera.

On the day of the raid I had taken some totally innocent pictures of ourselves in Workington some 25 miles from Caldbeck. I had taken no pictures in Caldbeck but I should still have destroyed my film when I knew the police were coming as, whilst there was nothing directly incriminating on my film, Workington was still a very long way from my home. Seizing my camera the Detective Sergeant realised that it was valuable and had the courtesy to offer it back to me for me to take the film out. I faked a blunder and opened the camera back hoping my film would be ruined by the light. Seeing my action another officer lunged forward and grabbed it from my hand.

I was almost successful. Only half of one frame remained intact, but it was enough. That half photograph showed two colleagues standing in a car park in front of a wall daubed with graffiti. There was also a green Fiat in the picture.

The work of the police detectives after that was impressive. By enlarging that half frame and circulating it amongst their officers they identified the location — Workington. The graffiti was unmistakable, perhaps for the first time the police were grateful for such vandalism.

Next, they concentrated on the number plate of the car in the picture. Although only partly visible, by meticulous analysis they came up with 12 possible combinations of numbers and letters. Only one of these belonged to a green Fiat.

When they contacted the owner it turned out to be a lady who had been in Workington that day to book a holiday which subsequently, due to tragic circumstances, she had to cancel. Because of the nature of her visit she was sure of the date.

Not destroying my own film was a major blunder on my part. The police had other evidence of course but my error contributed significantly to our downfall. The police now had a case against me, it was entirely circumstantial, but they felt it was enough to charge me and my two companions.

From the start the police and authorities were keen to dispel any thoughts that any remains had been disturbed. The first local press report in the *Cumberland News* Friday January 28th 1977 quoted a police spokesman saying that there was no evidence that any of the bodies in the grave had been disturbed.

This statement of fact was emphasised at our very first court appearance by the prosecution. Here is the press report quoting the Crown prosecutor at our committal proceedings at Wigton Magistrates court in October 1977: "*Mr John Kay, prosecuting, said the headstone outside St Kentigern's Church at Caldbeck, in the Lake District, was found uprooted on January 23.*

Mr Kay said it was not true that the body had been disturbed." (*The Sun* October 4th 1977)

The judicial establishment had no sympathy for us and we can be certain that if there was any suggestion that the body of John Peel had in any way been disturbed the evidence would have been photographed and deployed against us in court.

Cutting through all the media hyperbole, whilst this was certainly a novel and shocking crime, it was small in legal terms. It was outrageous for hunters certainly, distasteful for the general public, but as a crime minor. Yes, a large hole was dug to push over the headstone but there was never any intention to disturb remains. Had that really been the aim a January night in Cumbria with the ground likely to be frozen would not have been chosen.

Initially we were charged merely with criminal damage to the headstone but after the prosecution learned that we planned to defend ourselves — and perhaps because of that — a second Common Law offence worded as follows was added: "*Unlawfully and indecently opened a grave and subjected the remains therein to indignities.*" [Lawyers later told me that this was a charge unknown to British law and should have been contested].

At Carlisle Crown Court in November 1977 we faced charges of criminal damage to the headstone and desecration of the grave.

Given my involvement I should have pleaded guilty, but a lot of the evidence against me was 'doctored' (sadly not unusual at the time) so I chose to fight it out, defending myself. My two colleagues chose to do the same.

Following a trial of eight days the jury retired and subsequently brought in a verdict of guilty.

The judge ordered us to be held in custody pending sentence. Although we had recognised the possibility of imprisonment, the

Bucks and Courtenay Tracy Otterhounds. King's Mill, Marnhull, Dorset. April 28th 1973.

Left: the hunt sets off.

Right: hunt saboteurs Robin Howard and Dave Wetton spray ahead of the hunt to mask the scent of any otters.

Left: at the end of the day the hunters and their hounds wait by an unusual hound van.

Rorke Garfield (with arm in plaster) North Bucks Beagles. October 6th 1973.

Ronnie Lee sprays to mask scent of hare. North Bucks Beagles. October 6th 1973

Hunt saboteurs care for hounds. New Forest Beagles. October 13th 1973

Peaceful protest. South Down Foxhounds. November 13th 1973

Hunt saboteurs at Oxfordshire Coursing Club February 2nd 1974

Political campaigning Sunday October 6th 1974. Supporters of the HSA and the LACS combine to leaflet in the Gainsborough constituency of keen hunt supporter, Marcus Kimball, who was standing for re-election as Conservative MP.

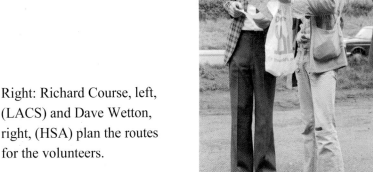

Right: Richard Course, left, (LACS) and Dave Wetton, right, (HSA) plan the routes for the volunteers.

Hunt saboteurs draw media interest. Chiddingfold, Leconfield &
Cowdray Foxhounds, February 8th 1975. Above: Dave Wetton
gives a quote to a reporter. Other hunt saboteurs carry placards.

Right: television
cameraman films hunt
saboteurs at the meet.

Smoking Beagles at ICI laboratory (Picture by courtesy of *Sunday People*).

Above: The author and Sue Smith with two beagles liberated from ICI (Picture by courtesy of *Sunday People*). Below left: Former Smoking Beagle enjoying a run on a beach. Below right: Safe in caring hands. Freed Smoking Beagle with Richard Course.

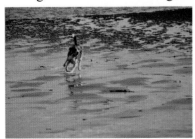

Waterloo Cup hare coursing protest
February 13th 1976. Above: the
slipper looks a bit angry at the
incursion by myself and others onto
the field to save hares. Right: my
arresting officer.
Below: my view from inside the
police van.

South of England show, Ardingley, June 12th 1976. Hunt saboteurs run into the arena to protest against a parade of hounds. Top left: Dave and Cee Wetton with banner. Above: a hunt supporter tears at a banner.

Below: Oxfordshire Coursing Club, November 6th 1976. Below left: Richard Course from the League Against Cruel Sports complains to Sandy Mackenzie, founder of the Coursing Supporters' Club. Below right and bottom right: hunt saboteurs try to save hares. Bottom left: hare coursers look on.

Essex Foxhounds August 25th 1976.

Top: a young fox cub (arrowed) bolts from a covert. Hunt rider and foot-follower try to head him back.
Above: the remains of a cub killed by the hounds.

Duke of Beaufort's Foxhounds cub hunting, October 2nd 1976.
Above: riders and foot followers surround the covert.

Left: hunt terrierman
with the remains of
dead cubs.

Hunt saboteurs save lives.

Top: Enfield Chace Foxhounds, January 15th 1977. Hunt saboteur Sue Roberts takes control of a foxhound found straying onto a busy road. This kept the hound and passing motorists safe.

Bottom: hunt saboteurs sit in a fox earth to stop hunt terriermen digging out an exhausted fox. Eridge Foxhounds, November 1st 1980. Left to right: Liz Varney, Bob August, Robin Howard.

Hunt saboteurs protesting against the slaughter of hares at the Waterloo Cup, February 11th 1977

Above: police escort the column of hunt saboteurs towards the hare coursing field.

Right: Ian Pedler and Cee Wetton negotiate with a mounted police officer.

Waterloo Cup hare coursing protest, February 11th 1977.

Left: Alan Knight explains the cruelty of hare coursing to a police officer.

Above and left: hunt saboteurs run onto the coursing field to save hares.

Right: hunt saboteurs create a smokescreen to conceal the hares.

Eastern Counties Otterhounds hunting from their meet at North Elmham, Norfolk, April 23rd 1977.

Below: hunt saboteurs in the background run to catch up.

Hunting vicars.

Hunt saboteurs condemn men of God for their delight in killing God's creatures.

Right and below: protest against otter hunter Rev. Robin Ray September 26th 1976 at Boscombe Church.

Left and above: protest against fox hunter Rev. Eric Wheeler, March 20th 1977 at Steeple Bumpstead Church.

Croome and West Warwickshire Foxhounds, November 24th 1979.

Above: thin line of hunt saboteurs attempt to get between hounds and their quarry. Hunt riders mass on the high ground behind.

Below: lone hunt supporter holds up vans packed with hunt saboteurs.

Hunt saboteurs lead the line in a mass rally against the seal cull, London, March 8th 1980.

Above: my very popular 1979 t-shirt design. This slogan was also sold on badges and car stickers.

Left: protest against whaling outside International Whaling Commission meeting. Brighton July 19th 1980.

reality came as a shock. It hit us even harder as we had walked about as free men until that cold winter's day.

It was December 7th, the build up to Christmas. Hand-cuffed and sitting in the prison transport we could look out onto the streets milling with Christmas shoppers. We felt as if we had stepped out of the real world.

Our destination was Durham Jail. At the time this was one of Britain's top security prisons, normally reserved for dangerous criminals and IRA terrorists.

As we clambered out of the van hand-cuffed together, on a dark night illuminated by security lighting, four burly prison officers with Alsatian dogs stood guard. The dogs hurled themselves the length of their leashes, their teeth snapping only inches from our arms. It was an effective display and deterrent.

Next came the indignity of the medical after which we were split up and scattered amongst new inmates and short sentence prisoners on A-wing.

My mind was in turmoil. I certainly did not appreciate that my prison cell high up on the right side of the wing was one of the most coveted in the prison. It overlooked the maximum security E-wing, which held some notorious women criminals.

Regularly these women provided one of the most provocative strip shows outside of Soho — in exchange for the men doing their own display.

The first night was a depressing experience. The cell light was controlled from the outside. Once it was turned off we were plunged into darkness until morning. There was no toilet in our cell, only the pot and when one small bowl is shared between three men it pays to get in first. One learned to hold the pot with your thumb over the rim so that you could tell if it was getting full.

It was also difficult to get used to all the night sounds of prison: cell-mates snoring, or talking in their sleep; distressed and unstable people shouting in their sleep.

After the first night the prison authorities in a welcome gesture of compassion, put the three of us 'animal loonies' in a cell together. We were vegetarians and the prison went to extraordinary lengths to accommodate our diet.

In fact, prison has one of the largest proportions of vegetarians (and today vegans) in our society. This is not because vegetarians/vegans are more prone to criminal actions, nor because animal welfare raiders are always getting caught, but simply because in prison vegetarians/vegans get better food.

I saw not only diet conversions, but also religious ones. That there are a lot of practising Christians in prisons reflects the fact that sitting in Chapel for an hour on Sunday is infinitely preferable to sitting in the cell.

For those first two weeks on remand pending sentence we were in a strange kind of limbo. We were convicted, but not sentenced. The judge had remanded us for reports and told us to seek legal help, so we had a whole series of briefings with solicitors and chats with probation officers.

My solicitor warned me to expect anything from a community service order to nine months imprisonment. The cell lawyers, or fellow prisoners, could not believe that we were there in the first place, on a first conviction for criminal damage amounting to just £71.75. They and the prison officers were convinced we would be released with a suspended sentence or community service order.

On December 22nd we appeared before Judge A. A. Edmondson and stood in the dock awaiting his verdict — nine months imprisonment. I was tempted to wish him a Merry Christmas too, but recalled the warning of a fellow prisoner that for a similar contempt he had had his sentence doubled.

We were returned to Durham jail and appeared before the Governor the following morning. We were told our earliest day of release — June 7th 1978.

From only two days before Christmas the balmy days of the following summer seemed a long way off. I consoled myself with the thought that in the grand scale of things my problems were small. I could look forward to the certainty of freedom whereas for millions of animals held prisoners in far worse conditions death is their only form of release.

Also, for me personally prison as an adult was easy compared to coping with boarding school as a youngster. With my Dad in the army and facing a posting abroad in 1965 I was sent to a boarding school at the age of 11, a decision that my parents saw as best for my future. But it was a cheerless place, a Methodist school in a Cathedral town where bullying was rife. Some thrived, I merely survived, but many endured a miserable existence. A lad in the year above me hung himself. I never joined in with the bullying, I just sought to avoid it and was happy if I was not the victim. To my shame I was too cowardly to oppose it — a failing on my part that I have worked during the rest of my life to rectify. Boarding schools pride themselves on preparing pupils for life in the higher echelons of society. Mine prepared me well for prison.

CHAPTER FIVE
Prison life

After sentencing we settled down to accept our lot as best we could. I changed from being a name to a letter/number — E13171. We were split up from the cosy like-minded threesome and scattered about D-Wing. I was put in a cell with a young lad who had a long track record of stealing cars.

The other mainly Geordie prisoners found us hard to understand, and not only because of our strange southern accents. Their previous lives had often been a training ground for prison. Many had numerous convictions and had progressed through the various legal stages: warnings, approved school orders, detention centres, borstals, probation and community service orders and suspended sentences before graduating to Durham prison.

Yet, there we were, plucked straight off the streets, not even held in custody before the trial, and plunged immediately into prison. All for £71.75 worth of damage. No wonder our fellow inmates could not believe it.

Before the court case, we had expected that in the unlikely event of conviction we might face a rough time in any of the northern jails, where John Peel was supposedly such a hero. Our fears were completely unfounded.

Other prisoners were very friendly to us, as if they welcomed someone different to talk to. During our whole time in Durham only two prisoners were against us. One shouted that we should have got nine years instead of nine months.

Similarly only a few prison officers were hostile and then only in a joking manner. One, in charge of the wash house, would shout out: "*Look out, lads, here come the body snatchers!*"

Other officers made a point of coming to our cells to chat about animals, their protection, vegetarianism and our beliefs. They told us about their pets and their sympathy for hunted animals. To a man they felt that it was futile our being locked away as we could achieve no useful purpose in prison. They were right.

Exercise periods were the highlight of the day. That Christmas at Durham it was bright and sunny and the exercise yard had a great aspect, overlooked as it is by the Cathedral. It was laid to grass, but with concrete oval paths. The prison itself formed one wall, and the others, exceedingly high, were topped with razor wire — thin razor blades embedded in wire — which had the fearsome reputation of being able to slice a man to ribbons.

At the four corners were concreted squares where prison officers with dogs stood on guard.

For exercise, prisoners were unlocked in strict rotation and there was no worse fate than to be forgotten. Great long lines would be formed up on landings and on the shouted command, "*D-Wing for exercise!*" we would wind our way down the stairs to the outside.

Exercise never took place in the rain, presumably because the officers did not like getting wet. For us it was not too bad, as we were short termers, but for people in for many years it must have had a strange effect to never feel the rain. We were not allowed to stop and by tradition some of the paths were walked in a clockwise direction, others anti-clockwise.

At one side of the rectangle was a brick toilet block. These toilets were a haven because there one actually had time to perform the necessary function although officers made sure you did not take too long.

Doctors were another prison diversion. Prisoners were always going sick with all kinds of imaginary ailments and the doctors were well versed in the traditional army cure for such malingerers — an injection in the backside.

There was also much sadness and misery in prison. Two fears were ever present: that a loved one would run off with someone else, or that someone dear to you would fall seriously ill or die.

The rules only allowed prisoners out to visit the death bed of a blood relative or spouse or their funeral. While I was inside one man learned that his young child had been gravely injured in a road accident. It was heart-breaking to witness his grief. I was fortunate in that I had neither wife nor special girlfriend on the outside, but I did worry about my family.

One abiding memory of Durham jail is of Paul McCartney's *Mull of Kintyre* Christmas record. That was in the charts all through my stay and seemed to permeate to every cell in the vast building.

A sadder memory concerned a young man whose cell was adjacent to mine on D-Wing. He was married with numerous kids, had a terrific sense of humour and seemed to have spent all his life in conflict with the law. He was very easily led into trouble and hated all kinds of authority.

He first came to Durham remanded in custody on a minor charge. One of the rules that officers were strict in enforcing was getting up in the morning. When this lad failed to rise as ordered, an officer tipped him out of his bed and in the following skirmish the officer was hit.

68

Ironically, when he went to court the lad was acquitted of his original charge, but convicted of assaulting the officer and jailed. To be in Durham jail for assaulting a prison officer is a serious predicament to be in. The other officers made his life a misery. After I left Durham to go to an open prison I learned that he had been transferred to another closed prison and had hanged himself in the punishment block.

In terms of prison work we were lucky. After a boring spell sewing mailbags we were given one of the plum jobs, working in the catering and cleaning division. Prisons only function at all thanks to the work of the prisoners. There are convict cooks, cleaners, barbers, librarians and gardeners all contributing to this subculture.

Working in the catering section we gained considerable freedom, our cells were seldom locked. This was valuable as we had previously been separated.

Most of our day was spent on our hands and knees scrubbing appointed landings or the main floor with a bucket, a green scouring pad and a bar of soap.

At mealtimes we collected the food and served it out. We were always closely supervised to ensure we did not show any favouritism.

Our last daily routine was to take the soup and buns around the cell blocks in the evening. By visiting each cell, we were a vital link in the prison telegraph system. Nearly all prison information was transmitted through the catering division.

In due course I was transferred to Kirkham open prison, near Preston, Lancs. Open prisons are worlds apart from closed ones. Kirkham, a former RAF camp, was a prison farm where inmates were housed in rows of open billets with twenty men in each. Every hut had wash basins, toilets and that almost forgotten luxury — baths.

The routine was to work through the day in one of the many greenhouses or the vegetable packing station. In the evening we watched colour television, played table tennis, or took part in other sporting activities.

The camp had an enthusiastic football team and the officers were able to arrange matches against local teams. Of course, ours always had home advantage and an enthusiastic captive audience. On one occasion they even brought in a local police team. As expected the tackles went in extra-hard on both sides.

I worked in the packing station, cutting the eyes out of potatoes moving by me on a conveyor belt. The work could hardly be described as interesting, but we had the freedom to talk and it was infinitely preferable to working in any mailbag shop.

Time passed surprisingly quickly. The routine was little different to the boarding school life of my youth — but without the malevolence. We had a film show once a week and even had the first telephone installed for use by convicts in the entire prison system.

We were warned that our calls would be regularly monitored. Even so there were massive queues to use it, despite the dent it made in our small allowances.

The ethos of open prison is that you are on trust. The fencing is minimal, designed more to keep people out than inmates in. However, anyone who abused the trust and tried to escape, or was caught outside the wire was immediately returned to a closed prison and lost their remission.

People with a history of escapes or of violence were barred from open prison. Only those with the lowest security rating were allowed to go there.

At one time in my hut people did start to go out at night, slipping out to the local pubs. They came back reeking of booze, boasting of their romantic conquests. Inevitably they talked too much, were caught and did the rest of their sentence behind closed doors.

Perhaps the saddest aspect of prison was the complete absence of any form of counselling to help prisoners not to return. The system seemed only to be geared to holding people, keeping them out of trouble until their release when they were waved goodbye. It seemed to cry out for someone to talk to the men, to try to help them go straight.

Eventually our time for release came. Early on June 7th 1978 I was given back my civilian clothes, a rail warrant to my chosen station and shown to the gate.

On walking out to freedom my first task was to pick up the hand scrawled diary I had thrown over the fence the previous evening. Prison officers were notoriously keen to confiscate diaries. I was determined that one day mine would serve a useful purpose.

CHAPTER SIX
Life after jail

Waiting to board the train for home I realised how cushioned we had been from the rigours of the outside world. Now I was plunged back into the simple responsibilities I had forgotten, like buying food and washing clothes.

Throughout my time inside prison officers continually warned me that I would never get work, that I had ruined my life. It was hard for an ordinary person to get a job; it would be hopeless for an ex-prisoner. They could not have been more wrong.

I was released on a Wednesday morning and I was in regular full time employment the following Monday. This was thanks entirely to a close friend in the HSA, Alan Knight, later to be my best man when Sue and I married in 1985 and who now runs International Animal Rescue (IAR). In 1978 he worked for a T-shirt printing firm in Brighton and when he learned that they were looking for a full-time van driver recommended me for the job. I was still inside at the time, so he had to stall for a few weeks by saying I had to work out my notice!

I knew that I had been given a rare chance to make a new start and threw myself wholeheartedly into this job. I was prepared to work all hours and drive any distance. It was always possible that my employers might find out my previous record and I wanted to get some good record of service under my belt first.

My return to animal welfare work started soon after my release. Whilst working for the firm I paid for the printing of some animal welfare t-shirts including one against the fur trade. I am no artist but I laboriously created an image of a big cat with the slogan: *Fur Coats are worn by Beautiful Animals and by Ugly Women*. Then it was pointed out to me that many men also wore fur coats so the last word was changed to *People*. Printed in gold on a black shirt (t-shirts and sweatshirts) this proved very popular.

I went out on hunt sabotage expeditions but mainly to take photographs. Throughout the 1970s I joined a number of peaceful protests and marches in London against the Canadian seal cull, whaling and the fur trade. These events were supported by tens of thousands and it was clear that concern for animal welfare across the world was growing rapidly.

By the late 1970s the saboteurs had developed a new tactic to save exhausted foxes that had sought sanctuary below ground to escape the hunters. Usually the terriermen would move in to dig out the fox so to

71

thwart them the saboteurs would simply sit in the holes and refuse to budge! It was a risky business for the sabs as it could provoke extreme violence from frustrated hunters but if the sabs were determined and there in number it could very effectively save lives.

With plenty of time to think carefully in prison, it had dawned on me that our long-term goals would not be reached by militant direct action alone. Such actions could save the lives of individual animals and certainly generated public interest and exposed the magnitude of the problems facing animals but real permanent change needed solid groundwork and political action. We had to plan a course of action that would save our children and their children in turn from having to fight the same battles over and over again for the fair treatment of our fellow creatures.

Short of a revolution, animals in the UK will only be helped by Parliament. It requires a groundswell of public opinion, a wave of anger based on sound, proven arguments to bring new legislation. Even changing the law is not enough. Public pressure is then required to ensure that the humane legislation is fully enforced.

Forced into a critical analysis of animal welfare from the outside I perceived the movement as a broad front, embracing all ages and classes in society; encompassing people whose idea of action varied from writing letters to papers and MP's, holding banner demonstrations, marches and hunt sabotages, to more direct approaches.

Forms of direct action such as hunt sabotage and protest marches against the likes of vivisection and seal culling certainly fulfilled the role of attracting young people to our cause. These youngsters felt a real need to achieve something and to do so quickly. For them political action lacks any charisma and its wheels move far too slowly.

With animal suffering ever on the increase there was tremendous pressure on newcomers to enter the realms of illegal activity to try and stem the tide. Before people embark on such roads they should consider all the angles. In the months before I was jailed I can recall many discussions as to alternative methods of attack. Removing animals from laboratories was all very well, it gave the vivisectors bad publicity by exposing what they were doing, but the animals were easily replaced.

Arson and other destructive attacks on premises will certainly delay the infliction of cruelty, but they will not end it. Buildings can be rebuilt and new vans purchased. Moreover in the face of sustained criminal attacks, media and therefore public sympathy had a tendency to favour those who had been attacked — the animal exploiters.

I felt that instead of night raids to cause damage, photographic evidence should be collected and released to the media for the public to see what was done in their name. Directly or indirectly the public paid for the research; they had a right to know what was going on.

Such attacks were later refined in the early 1980s to near perfection by the South East Animal Liberation League, the Northern Animal Liberation League and other associated groups. It was one of their raids which had exposed that pets really are stolen for vivisection. It is so easy to move on into totally illegal realms, becoming a hot-headed, no holds barred militant. The extremist will certainly catch the attention of the media and is of value to the cause, but we must remember the old cliché that today's headlines are tomorrow's fish and chip papers (or chip papers for vegetarians/vegans).

I remember in the mid-seventies a plan being hatched to send a team over to Spain to disrupt a bull-fight by running into the ring with banners during a bull-fight. We knew it would near enough be a suicidal action, with the bull, the matador or the crowd 'accounting for' the team. The plan was advanced to the point of getting passports and making travel plans before wisdom prevailed and it was shelved.

Had it gone through and the group been killed, the incident would have made a few columns in national papers, loved ones would have wept over the coffins, but bull-fighting would still continue. [Some Spanish activists have recently taken to doing protests like this against bull-fighting — I salute their courage!]

On the morning of October 4th 1971, the day of St. Francis, Patron Saint of Animals, Mrs. Olive Parry, housewife and mother knelt down in the churchyard of St. John's, Worcester, doused herself with paraffin and turned herself into a human fireball. It must have hurt. Her last message, with her when she died, read:

"I am Mrs. Parry. This is my last protest against vivisection and other cruelty inflicted on defenceless animals."

This supreme act of sacrifice was intended to draw public attention to the awesome burden of suffering inflicted on animals. It did, but for so short a time. That suffering still continues and Mrs. Parry is now forgotten by all but her closest loved ones.

Publicity is very transient. If an ALF team seized control of our entire media and forced every national paper and news bulletin to concentrate solely on animal welfare issues for a whole week it would still change nothing. People would simply see, read and say, *"That's bad, but where's the TV page?"*

After many years in which the full horrors of war and famine abroad have been brought to our living rooms by the ever efficient media, the nation is in danger of being desensitized. [I wrote that paragraph in 1983 — it is even truer in 2015!]

I became certain that a spiral of increasingly spectacular actions was not the way in the long-term and that within the confines of my own specialist interest — bloodsports — the forces favouring these cruel pastimes could be defeated without recourse to illegal action. All that was needed was clever scheming on our part.

I began to look beyond the realms of hunt sabotage and other militant actions for ways of building the wave of public opinion that would bring about political action and new laws to protect wildlife.

Whilst I was in prison six of my photographs that I had taken as a hunt saboteur, including two that I had taken when working undercover (pretending to be a supporter of hunting) were used to illustrate a two-page article by Ena Kendall "*When hunt is a four-letter word*" that was published in the *Observer* colour magazine on February 26th 1978. That suggested to me a key to unlocking one of the many doors needed for political change — increasing public awareness as to just how badly animals were being treated.

I had lengthy private chats with Richard Course. He was then Chairman of the LACS. Always a close friend particularly after he gave a home to my smoking beagle, Major (renamed Bonzo), we had several meetings and chats about the direction the movement was taking.

I was aware that political campaigners like Richard could be inventive. In the campaigning for the October 1974 election I helped Richard Course, Dave Wetton and others distribute 20,000 leaflets in the Gainsborough constituency of Marcus Kimball, at the time Chairman of the BFSS, outlining the full extent of his bloodsporting interests. We had met at the *Plough* Enfield at 7.30am on Sunday October 6th to catch our private coach north. Compared to the previous election Kimball suffered a 13.6% drop in votes and a 36.1% drop in his majority!

In the 1979 election on May 3rd (that brought Margaret Thatcher to power), the LACS and the HSA combined in support of Bob August, chairperson of the HSA, standing as a Conservative Independent (anti-hunting) candidate against Kimball — he cost Kimball 570 votes. The election leaflet for Bob August, published by James Barrington, included the following:-

"CONSTITUENTS' INTERESTS
I feel that Mr Kimball, in his position as Chairman of the British Field Sports Society, spends too much of his valuable parliamentary time in the defence of the bloodsporting interests of stag hunters, otterhunters and hare coursers when he could be more gainfully employed in furthering the interests of his own constituents."

There was alongside a fox hunting image with the caption: *"Is this the image that Conservatives should be promoting?"*

Aggressive and imaginative political campaigning like this appealed to me and in the same year I joined the League. [The political work carried out by Richard Course and his colleagues at the League, in particular Angela Smith and Chris Williamson (both later to become MPs), set in motion the sequence of events and created the concepts that would ultimately lead to the passing of the Hunting Act 2004 that banned the hunting of wildlife with dogs and hare coursing.]

The League had trundled along quite happily since being founded in 1924. By combining the future HSA tactic of banner demonstrations with some political guile they were to a degree successful. Due notably to the determined opposition of one League stalwart, Gwen Barter, the practice of carted deer hunting in which tame stags were hunted by hounds, caught, then hunted again, was abandoned on the English mainland. The pastime continued for some time afterwards in Northern Ireland.

With the birth of the HSA in 1963 and its growing influence the League inevitably declined. The policy of buying up land to serve as sanctuaries for wildlife, particularly deer, was started; this proved to be very popular with the middle aged, but it could in no way halt the draw of young people to the HSA.

As mentioned earlier during the 1960s the LACS Chairman, Raymond Rowley, had courageously carried out numerous undercover projects within bloodsports covertly photographing and filming fox hunting, stag hunting and hare coursing. His efforts resulted in the conviction of one fox hunter. To expose hare coursing he created his own secret camera equipment that was years ahead of its time.

However by the second half of the 1970s the League was in the control of elderly conservatives who it was felt had too much sympathy for the establishment. After their numerous successes it was the HSA that caught the imagination of youth. But there was political awareness also and a slow drift began so that HSA activists also supported a faction within the League. This was led by the inspiring personality of Richard Course, a man who had the vision to see, even

75

at that time, that the only real future lay in the political drive. In addition Mark Davies, later the Chairman, was doing excellent work in the League office as its Secretary.

By the mid to late seventies matters at the League came to a head and there was a power battle between the new militants and the established old guard. The old guard made the fundamental error of forgetting that a campaigning organisation is judged only by its latest achievements. Those who control it may say whatever they like, but it is their strength of mind, fire and determination to succeed now and in the future that really counts in the eyes of the members. In the end Richard Course won his battle for control with almost embarrassing ease.

Accordingly it was a re-born League that I had joined — a League that had regained its sense of direction.

In the autumn of 1979 I switched jobs. I had loved my time as a delivery driver calling at many locations along the south coast and elsewhere but it was time to move on. I had a spell of stacking produce shelves in a supermarket in Tonbridge then after a few months of that I went on a three week blinder.

*****

I had always fancied my chances as a professional photographer. Not so much for any technical expertise but rather for my genuine concern for my subjects and the need to accurately record their situation. With the years passing I realised that if I did not make the opportunity for myself no-one else would. Over Christmas 1979 Russia invaded Afghanistan. Their paratroopers landed in the capital, Kabul. Soon afterwards western photographers and journalists were streaming over the border from Pakistan into Afghanistan to record this conflict. I was determined to try my hand as a caring photojournalist so I collected the little money I had, bought an air ticket and on May 9th 1980 flew out to Pakistan.

Normally photographers are commissioned for such trips. I had nothing other than a vague promise from the *Daily Express* that they would look at my work when I returned. I had no contacts and knew no-one when I arrived in Peshawar, but I quickly made friends with other journalists and photographers making the same trek. Through them I made contact with the local guerrilla groups, the Mujahideen (later to evolve into the Taliban).

After two weeks, I linked up with a Mujahideen group that was due to cross into Afghanistan many miles to the north, near Chitral.

Also in our group was Colin Smith, the highly regarded Middle Eastern correspondent for the *Observer* newspaper, and a Swiss journalist. After many changes of plans that included the daunting prospect of climbing over snow-covered peaks at an altitude where oxygen should be carried, we ended up crossing in at night along steep narrow slippery paths to link up with a small supply group.

We were all disguised as Pathans and were even taught a few choice phrases to use should we be unfortunate enough to encounter a Pakistani border patrol. My trip into Afghanistan lasted only five days, though we covered a considerable mileage on foot.

The fighters we were with proudly showed us their weaponry. Some looked very ancient but there were also many near new AK-47 assault rifles. I found it fascinating to handle these weapons of choice for so many guerrilla groups the world over, and over so many decades. The AK-47 may look primitive compared to Western weaponry but it can be dragged through all manner of hostile conditions and still fire, when high-tech Western arms all too often jam.

We had the dubious pleasure of being witnesses to one night battle that gave every indication of having been stage-managed for the benefit of ourselves, the Western press. The tracer fire being exchanged with the Russian forces was certainly startling to watch and the sounds of battle were awesome but when in response mortar/artillery shells started landing around us I felt distinctly fearful. Hiding behind a large rock is all but useless when the ordnance is falling near vertically from the dark sky. I nearly broke my leg on one occasion diving for cover. In the pitch dark what use were my cameras of that era anyway? I could hardly illuminate the scene with a flash.

I found it somewhat grotesque that men were willing to kill and be killed to produce a few pictures and column inches in papers read by a society that cared little either for their cause or their fate anyway.

The most sickening story I heard concerned the shooting of prisoners by the Mujahideen. A group of Afghans sympathetic to the Russians had been captured. To prove how merciless the Mujahideen were and what a hard war they were fighting, the prisoners were lined up and machine-gunned for the benefit of a photographer, whose pictures of the event were subsequently published throughout most of Europe — earning him a lot of money. When I asked the photographer if the men would have been shot had he not been present, he said, "*Of course not.*" The horror showed on my face. "*You're too sentimental,*" he said.

77

The other disconcerting feature of life with the Mujahideen is their fervent belief that they can only attain their Islamic version of heaven if they die in a religious war. This certainly explained their occasional use of kamikaze-style tactics, but it did nothing to ease the qualms of Westerners travelling with them.

I came home from Afghanistan more than a little disillusioned with my fellow man. If there was any pleasant memory it was of the fact that despite the decadence and destructive nature of Western civilisation man can tread lightly on the earth.

In the beautiful scenic mountains of the Hindu Kush the people live a life that, though undeniably hard, given the freedom to farm as they wish, can be perfectly adequate. They seemed to exist on a diet of the equivalent of two slices of bread a day and a glass of milk, and a piece of fish or meat every other day with the occasional fruit, yet they were tough and superbly fit. When we complained of the rigours of the heat, the march and the weight of our rucksacks, one young lad picked up all three rucksacks and ran up the mountain side. No wonder our armies never conquered that nation.

Their animals were treated with compassion and consideration, they had to be, their well-being was their owners' well-being too. Like us, the rural Afghan enters the world with nothing and leaves with nothing, but unlike us he destroys very little in between — no pollution, no environmental destruction, complete harmony with the countryside. The young children that we found on one occasion playing by a stream had the brightness of eye and the innate will to play the simple, human, games that Western man, submerged beneath his technology, has long forgotten. In reality they had nothing, but in that they had everything.

On my return in June I attempted to sell my pictures, but only succeeded in gaining minimal payment from the *Daily Express* for my black and white portfolio. It was a paltry contribution to my £1,000 expenditure. Near penniless in August 1980 I went to work for my close friend, former HSA Chairman and later League colleague and founder of International Animal Rescue, the late John Hicks who, with his wife, Jo, managed Foal Farm Animal Sanctuary near Biggin Hill, Kent.

Foal Farm is an animal rescue centre, taking in all manner of unwanted or injured animals and re-homing them wherever possible. When I joined the farm existed in the middle of an uneasy truce between the new enthusiastic workers and the old conservative committee. There were tensions that revolved mainly around the evolving concept at the time of rights for all species of animals.

When it came to caring for the resident animals there was agreement between the factions where the cats, dogs and horses were concerned, but sadly conflict over the other creatures. The differences were fundamental and I mention them because they are the essence of so many of the arguments that have continued within animal welfare.

To the committee at the time, sheep, pigs and hens were food animals and it was dangerous to care for and love them, while their fellows were offered for sale in sandwiches and pies in the canteen. Instead of getting rid of the sandwiches and pies, they wanted to get rid of the animals. John Hicks named one large rescued pig 'Rasher' to highlight the point. Wild animals such as foxes were wrongly damned as vermin and were unwelcome. The farm had a policy of re-homing as many animals as possible. Wisely the homes were checked before and after the animals were placed. Though countless numbers of animals were helped it was obvious to us that we were only scratching the surface.

The problem of finding homes for stray and unwanted cats and dogs remains massive. There is a desperate need for free or at least heavily subsidised spaying and neutering that could be paid for by a Government tax on the profits of the pet food industry. It is disgraceful that it is left to voluntary animal welfare groups to do the best they can.

Work at Foal Farm was often heart-rending, caring for the living cast-offs from an affluent society. There was Bud, a beautiful 'Lassie' Collie with a badly set front leg. He was dumped at the end of the drive, tied to the barbed wire fence with a scrawled note attached to the boot-lace round his neck: "*Bud 3 years old, please help.*"

There were the people who achieved the amazing feat of making a six month old golden retriever puppy vicious. This adorable looking puppy was in fact a near killer that would bite on sight. It took a great deal of patient care to teach that dog that not all humans were cruel.

There were also amusing incidents like the all too frequent ritual of hosing out the ducks. There were a considerable number of chickens, ducks and geese roaming free-range about the farm. To protect them from predators they had to be rounded up and locked away at night. The chickens were easily conned into their hutches by the lure of food. The cockerels made a run for it across the fields and it usually required several rugby tackles to stop them, but the mallard ducks were the worst. They would take up residence under one of the wooden sheds, well out of our reach and simply refuse to move. To shift them we had to bring up the hoses. A soft gentle spray and they simply preened their feathers. It took a good hefty jet before they tumbled out with much indignant quacking. They never really appreciated that it was all done for their own good.

Sadly when Foal Farm was back on its feet and thriving the internal rows returned. When the final power battle came, the radicals rallied round John and Jo. For a time, there even appeared to be a possibility that they might win, but the Foal committee held the trump card. According to their constitution they could expel anyone who disagreed with them, which is exactly what they did. John and Jo left Foal and in time set up their own rescue centre. Initially this was here in the UK and then later in Goa, India. Foal Farm continued and remains a thriving rescue centre.

Some months before the final conflict at Foal Farm I left to take up my new position with the League. The possibility of this undercover operation had first been raised in November 1980 and after months of meetings and lengthy discussions I commenced work at the end of April 1981, operating at first against stag hunting in the West Country.

CHAPTER SEVEN
Deer hunting

"To be moved by the terror in the eyes of a hunted stag might be sentimental: to live its fear as it faces the hounds, anthropomorphic; but to imagine that one day people will not look back on stag-hunting with the abhorrence they now feel for bullbaiting or cockfighting is the sheerest delusion."
Ena Kendall *Observer* Colour Magazine. January 24th 1982

[This and the following chapters on hunting/hare coursing are written in the present tense because at the time of the original *Outfoxed* all this was legal. With the protection for wildlife given by the Hunting Act 2004 this is not the case at the time of writing (2015). All the hunts — and the hunters who are still hunting — mentioned in these chapters now claim to fully abide by the Hunting Act.]

It was April 28th 1981. From a grassy hedgerow I looked across the grey, misty Devon fields, my binoculars trained on the pink coats of the huntsmen and tri-colour patches of the staghounds. Ahead of them, heading for cover in a wood, was a small stag.

It was my first day out with the Devon and Somerset Staghounds in my guise as a full supporter. To mingle with the regulars I had adopted their way of dress and their way of talking. My car was covered in hunting stickers including the most important sticker of all, the BFSS roundel.

I wore the traditional tweed cap and waxed ¾ length shooting jacket that is the prime indicator of the genuine hunt supporter. This 'uniform' alone was one of the main reasons why so many hunting people accepted me.

My earlier hunting experience as a saboteur now came into its own. I knew the jargon and knew other hunts well enough to pass muster as a genuine hunt supporter.

The one thing I lacked was stag hunt supporter stickers, which could only be obtained by attending the hunt and paying the 'cap'. This is collected before the meet by supporters with armbands, standing on all access roads. In return for a donation a coloured day sticker is put on the windscreen of your car. Anyone who does not pay is severely hassled and their car is blocked. I collected my first stag hunt sticker that day.

The stag hunters and their supporters had gathered an hour before the meet. I arrived some twenty minutes before the off. I was friendly but avoided too much discussion as to my identity.

Lengthy conversations could have been dangerous, as I had not at the time decided on a false name, a false address and background. I was simply an observer. From past experience I knew that this gossiping time before any meet was a chance to hover and learn from other people's conversations.

That day, as in those that followed, I listened to horrific tales of deer threshing about entangled in barbed wire, of stags swimming reservoirs only to be attacked by hounds as they emerged exhausted. I learned to hide my feelings and join in the uproarious laughter that followed.

When the hunt moved off I joined the long crocodile of motorised traffic that trailed after them. Cars, Land Rovers and motor bikes roared around narrow country lanes, for an occasional glimpse of the hunt and the stags.

It went on and on from morning until five in the afternoon when I found myself with four cars and their occupants gazing over flat empty fields. Other supporters began to filter past us. I stopped one and asked where the hunt was. Pointing into the distance he said: "*They killed about 20 minutes ago, in the brook over there.*"

I jumped into my car and headed in that direction, but found my way blocked with double parked cars. I pulled hard into the left hand side and got out. I pondered about my camera. I had made a point of taking plenty of pictures at the meet and during the hunt saying I was a budding Jim Meads, a well-known hunt photographer of the time. Could I risk taking my camera in to photograph the aftermath of a kill on my very first stag hunt in the undercover role?

I recalled the old ALF maxim: "*Once decided, it is as good as done*". This was no time to hesitate so I ran ahead, camera at the ready. I must admit though that seeing the alarming bunch of burly thugs gathered around the carcass, my heart did miss a beat.

I was a late arrival; they had already sliced up and shared out the liver to the following throng. Children were running everywhere clutching pieces of steaming liver, often in their bare hands, sometimes in handkerchiefs, or carefully wrapped in empty crisp bags.

As I arrived the hunters tipped out the stomach and entrails and were helping the dead stag to his feet to shake out the last remaining drops of gore and blood. People looked menacingly at me when I aimed my camera and reeled off some photographs, but no-one said a word.

With the stomach removed, the carcass was dragged aside and the hounds called to it, as their reward. Before they were allowed near the steaming intestines a strange, almost primitive ritual took place. Huntsman, Dennis Boyles, shouting and waving his whip over the remains, goaded the hounds into a frenzy of excitement, holding them back all the time. When they were judged to be sufficiently excited he stepped aside and allowed the hounds to surge forwards tearing at the stomach, ripping it to shreds in seconds.

In close-up to get pictures, like the rest of the supporters, I was showered with blood and the foul smelling, part-digested grass, the recent contents of the stag's stomach — his last meal. My discomfiture clearly showed and the rest of the supporters laughed at me being caught in such a fashion.

Dennis then turned his attention to the main carcass. The skin on each leg was cut just above the knee and peeled back to the ankle. The ankle was then broken, twisted off and the resultant slot, or hoof, with a glove of skin was offered as a souvenir to anyone prepared to pay a small donation to the Huntsman.

After all four slots were taken the carcass was left to the inquisitive supporters. The hunt staff moved away to joke and chat with the Masters, accepting coffee, soup and sandwiches from other supporters. Those around the stag poked and prodded it, examined its teeth to try and gauge its age and pulled tufts of hair from it to tuck under the flaps of their caps. Some favoured hounds were allowed to move in on the carcass, to lick the blood off its legs, or stick their heads inside the torn belly and lap the blood within.

After about 30 minutes the riders began to drift away, the foot followers shuffling behind them. The carcass was left on the ground. I was told that someone would come to collect it and take it away to be shared as venison. I lingered to take a photograph of the dead stag with the supporters walking away in the background. When they saw me most turned round and smiled, pleased at their success.

I followed the subsequent and last hunt at the end of April, but there was no kill.

Though it is called stag hunting the quarry hunted varies according to the time of year. From August till the end of October the big old males with the full spread of antlers (Autumn stags) are hunted. Then from November to the end of February the females (hinds) are the quarry. The hinds often run with their young calves. During March and April the Spring stags with their very short, newly formed antlers, are hunted.

This separation of sex and age range is in no way designed to help the deer. Red deer rut in early Autumn, during October.

AUTUMN STAG HUNTING

"It is astonishing how deer will often loiter about in front of hounds, often to their own ultimate undoing, presenting a very different picture from that of the terrified creature fleeing in dread for its life conjured up by the sentimentalist. That there is a bad ten minutes at the last is undeniable, but we all have to face that sooner or later."
(The Fairest Hunting. *Hunting and Watching Exmoor Deer*. H.P. Hewett. Pub. J.A. Allen & Co., 1963. Page 45)

Autumn stag hunting starts for the Devon and Somerset and Quantock packs early in August. The Tiverton, whose hunting country covers the lowlands south of Exmoor, have far more problems with crops so they start considerably later, usually well into September.

The autumn stags are creatures of habit and accordingly are harboured. The harbourer employed by the hunt checks their location the previous night and reports on their whereabouts to the Masters at the meet. All the hounds are paraded at the meet and are then returned to a horsebox. Only five or six couple (10 or 12) of the most experienced hounds, known as tufters, are selected.

The tufters are also the steadiest and the most responsive to commands. Once they are started on the selected stag they can be expected to stick to it and not riot after any other deer. Their job is to find the deer and hunt him for some time. Once the deer has been running for a while he begins to emit a distinctive scent (caused by fear) which can easily be tracked by the remaining inexperienced hounds that form the bulk of the pack.

In August 1981 I returned to the West Country in my undercover role and started the new season at the meet of the Quantock Staghounds at Volis Cross on August 19th. This time I was driving a hired Ford Escort, which avoided the problem of my having to use my own extremely recognisable car. Little happened that day of any interest other than I enjoyed a marvellous view of a beautiful stag running at speed through high corn. All that was visible was his head of antlers. Of course the tufters piled in behind him and together they cut a great swathe through the corn, which seemed ironic considering that the chief reason given for hunting deer in the first place is that they damage crops!

The day was hot, scenting conditions bad and even though the main pack was released, the hounds were never able to get on terms with the stag and fortunately he escaped.

Next day I was with the Devon and Somerset Staghounds, meeting at Potters Cross. I soon learnt that one of the biggest problems with stag hunting was to find the meets. The country for the Devon and Somerset covers a massive area and it is possible to spend hours scouring Ordnance Survey maps looking for obscure 'Cross's' and 'Gates'. Unlike fox and hare hunts, stag hunts more often than not meet on the open moorland. The easiest solution was to phone the kennels and ask them for directions. Though these were usually readily given, one was vulnerable to being asked for name and phone number, so I was reluctant to do so. The best way to find meets was to ask the experienced supporters at the end of the previous one.

Again there was no kill, but the hounds stuck very close to the stag and pushed him extremely hard. He saved his neck by running through sheep foil to lose his scent just north of the main A361 and then crossing this busy main road. The most interesting incident occurred when the trailing hounds entered the field of sheep. The sheep flocked together and charged the hounds putting them to flight, looking almost as if they were on the side of the stag. It caused astonishment to the stag hunters; almost invariably when hounds meet sheep it is the hounds chasing the sheep.

On August 22nd the Devon and Somerset Staghounds met at Mounsey Hill Gate, right in the centre of Exmoor. With the morning misty and wet I knew the scent would be good and when one of the Joint Masters, seeing that it was the turn of the dog hounds, commented, "*These are a right bunch of killers,*" it was clear that the deer were in for a hard time. The stag was quickly away. Riders were directed to try and prevent him reaching the safety of any League sanctuaries and the main pack was laid on. The hunt progressed into the afternoon with the tiring stag twisting and turning. When he tried to run in amongst thick gorse and lie down for safety the hounds checked, but the riders moved in cracking their whips to evict him.

Eventually in late afternoon the stag arrived near Marsh Bridge, west of the B3223. The tiny, winding, downhill road to this landmark was soon completely blocked with riders and traffic as the hunt supporters competed for a closer look.

I parked and ran down the line of cars, hearing whistles and shouts from hunters in the river below. The stag was only just in front of the hounds. Then the traffic moved on and downwards towards Marsh Bridge. This isolated, quaint looking, bridge appears totally insignificant to tourists stopping to stare at the waters below, or to eat their lunches in the shade of the nearby trees, but for many deer it represents the end of the hunt and the end of their lives.

That summer's afternoon the whole area was packed solid with Land Rovers, cars, motorbikes, horses and milling followers. The hounds were heard baying frantically nearby. The horn was being blown triumphantly. It was all mayhem and confusion. No-one really knew where the deer was; only that he was approaching the bridge, along one of the small tributaries.

Supporters lined the bridge and others peered over the hedgerows. I followed a group into a grass field adjacent to the tiny stream that formed the tributary.

The baying from the pack rose to a crescendo to herald the coming of the stag. I removed the lens cap on my camera, checked the aperture and shutter speed and noted with alarm that I had only a few frames left on my film. Those closest to the trees lining the brook were holloaing, and screaming that the stag had passed them. The hounds were following through the undergrowth and on the grass alongside. The bridge ahead was too low for the stag to pass under, and with so much shouting and screaming on either side he was headed back.

He saw the hounds ahead and jumped left handed into the grass field where I was standing. I raised my camera, but he had jumped back into the undergrowth before I could even focus my lens. The supporters around me, many of them young kids, screamed "*We've got him now!*" Hurriedly I changed my film.

I ran down the sloping grass, climbed through a barbed wire fence and fought my way through the undergrowth surrounding the brook. The terrified stag crashed just past me, his antlers missing me by barely a few feet. I knew the end for him was near. The area of marshland was full of supporters and hounds; there could be no escape. I circled right-handed towards the bridge thinking that the kill would be there. Then the commotion shifted to an area behind me.

The hounds were now baying their blood-curdling cry of death. All hunting hounds will speak to a scent and they will bay even more excitedly when they close on their quarry and can see it. Fox and hare hounds will go straight in and attack their quarry and for them the baying is soon replaced by ripping and tearing. Staghounds are different, fearing reprisal from the stag's antlers they hang back, baying. The sound at such a time is chilling. The baying rises to a whole new pitch of excitement and the sound of some 40 hounds growling in this fashion is truly menacing. Once heard it is never forgotten.

Hearing this sound for the first time I fought my way towards it. Other supporters were struggling along narrow footpaths, but I knew that I had to be first. I went straight through the marshes and ended up wading up to my waist, camera held high to keep it dry. As I closed on the dreadful cries, my only fear was that it would all be over before I arrived. I knew that I could not help this stag but if I could record what happened it would help others. I forced my way over and through some flimsy barbed wire, pulled aside some bushes and encountered a scene that haunts me to this day.

There was a small pool no more than 20 yards in diameter, surrounded by encroaching foliage. In the centre the stag was swimming frantically, with his head twisting from side to side, looking up and staring with fear. In the pool with him and swimming after him were the bulk of the pack, while other hounds stood on the margins of the pool baying viciously.

I knew that seconds counted. I swung my camera to my eye, focused on the staring eye of the stag and captured the frame that I will never forget. One hound was on the stag's back and 16 others almost on him. There was shouting and commotion behind me as other supporters arrived. Moving round the right hand side of the pool ahead of the stag they caught his antlers when he reached them. The hounds closed in, tearing at his flanks and back. The supporters tried to fend the hounds off, kicking out and beating them back with their caps.

I quickly took some photographs, but unfortunately the head of the stag was concealed by the dense vegetation on the pool margins. The hunt servants arrived and I knew that it was time to make myself scarce with my camera. My experience with the Border Counties Otterhounds had taught me that hunting people will readily seize valuable pictures and both they and I knew how valuable that photograph was.

I moved back as crowds of supporters swept in. It was difficult to make out what was happening, but eventually after minutes that seemed to drag on interminably I heard the crack of the pistol that indicated for that proud stag at least suffering was over. The stag had been dragged out onto the bank and the pistol pressed to his head.

After the kill, I felt safe returning to the scene because hunting people are slightly less wary of dead animals being photographed. I adopted the attitude that I had only just arrived and they gleefully told me how they had caught him in the pool.

The ritual I then witnessed was unlike anything I had ever seen previously in all my hunting experience. The Whipper-in had hold of the stag's antlers and was feverishly banging the head on the ground and screaming to the hounds like a dervish. The hounds responded by baying, barking and snapping. Warm blood, oozing from the stag's gaping head wound, was spraying everywhere.

It was gruesome and darkly satanic, a blood ritual designed to whip hounds and supporters up to a passionate intensity. When it had subsided a path was cleared through the undergrowth and the body of the stag dragged out into the open. There was a pause whilst a supporter in a Land Rover was summoned to collect the body. In the delay curious children crowded round the carcass and some of the adults peeled off small pieces of tattered velvet from the antlers and gave it to them.

The stag was loaded into the back of the Land Rover and taken to a clearing at the top of a nearby hill. Dubious about following and not wanting to risk losing the pictures I had, I eventually trailed along behind them. There was the usual crowded huddle of supporters round the body whilst the liver was shared out.

I was surprised when the Huntsman wrenched the stag's mouth open and started fiddling with his victim's teeth. I had seen supporters do this to the spring stag in April, I presumed to try and age it, but what was Dennis Boyles up to this time? The answer was not long in coming. Taking out a pair of pliers he began pulling the teeth out. These 'tushes' are revered trophies sold to supporters to wear on neck pendants.

My last stag hunt meet of that particular trip was of the Devon and Somerset Staghounds at Wheddon Cross on August 25th. The League have a sanctuary right in the middle of their woodland draw at this meet and with increased patrols by John Hicks, the League Warden, the hunt have to be particularly careful. On that day they were also concerned to prevent the deer heading too far south, because of further League sanctuaries in that direction.

It was a scorching hot day and with the scent poor it seemed unlikely that the hounds would kill, particularly as the stag was content to run round and round in the first draw, reluctant to leave. But eventually, late in the afternoon, the stag made the mistake of coming away from the protection of the woodland, crossed the main A396 at Sully Corner and was soon in dire trouble.

Again I was caught up in streams of hunt followers in single file traffic on the narrow lanes. When all the cars stopped and the occupants ran on ahead, I did likewise. The action moved further downstream and three other supporters ran back to bring up their cars, I left mine where it was and ran ahead on foot. Vehicles could just squeeze by me, but it would certainly hold them up. I may have been posing as a supporter but there was nothing like a bit of inadvertent sabotage!

I was moments too late to witness the kill. Running alongside the woodland I heard a shot. The stag had come out of the brook and stood at bay in some slight cover — then it was all over. I returned to my car to find some mighty irate hunt supporters held up behind it but the usual profuse apologies were enough to convince them of my innocence. The carcass was taken right back to the original meet. I was there in good time to see and photograph all that happened. I had by that time made some good friends in the hunt and they were kind enough to hold back the swelling throng to enable me to photograph Dennis Boyles cutting up the liver.

After the hounds had been given their reward and the slots taken, Dennis went to work to remove the teeth. These were sold to a group of keen young children from the Pony Club whom I also photographed. A middle-aged man then proudly shepherded forward his two young daughters and asked Dennis to blood them.

The practice of blooding children is a barbaric ritual — a rite of passage for some new hunters. Its aim is to form some kind of satanic bond between the new aspiring hunter and his or her chosen sport. People are usually only blooded once in their entire lifetimes. It is an initiation ceremony that is still regarded as essential by the old school of hunter.

In fox hunting it is traditional for the blood and faeces stained stump of the fox's severed brush to be daubed across the child's forehead and possibly down each cheek as well. The recipient is then given strict instructions not to wash the blood off.

In stag hunting there is obviously no bloody brush to hand but after reaching inside the stomach to tip the contents out, coupled with cutting up the liver, the Huntsman's arms are running in blood from the fingertips to the elbows.

Knowing that there was a valuable picture in the offing I watched Dennis and prepared to act. I had anticipated some kind of formal ceremony. Consequently when Dennis simply reached across, smiling and quickly dabbed each child on the cheek, I was too slow. However, when I asked one of the kids to pose for my camera she was happy to do so. The looks on the supporters' faces in the background made it quite clear that they were aware of the potential danger of a blooded child being photographed; but I smiled disarmingly at them.

When I reported back to the League, Richard Course and the Executive Committee were well pleased with my photographs and findings. I was instructed to continue my work and to try and take some movie film as well.

I was back in the West Country on October 3rd in time for the meet of the Devon and Somerset Staghounds at Cuzzicombe. It was a day of torrential rain and though the hunt were persistent, carrying on until 6.30p.m., it was clear that the stag had the better of the hounds. October 6th found me with the Devon and Somerset at West Buckland with Ena Kendall a journalist from the *Observer*. Ena had glimpses of deer running hither and thither, but saw nothing of any consequence. There was no kill.

The next morning I followed the Quantock Staghounds from their meet at Seven Milestone, on the fringe of the Quantock hills. For this I was equipped with both movie and still cameras and I was able to get some excellent film of the hounds rioting after young stags, known as prickets. The stag they wanted was most reluctant to leave the thick woodland of the first draw, but when he did he went away at speed towards Holford. The usual hectic chase ensued, with the stag at one point crossing the road a mere 50 yards behind my car, forcing other supporters to swerve to a halt.

The tufters were sticking tight on their quarry and the scent was evidently good. The stag was viewed crossing a grass field heading towards Holford and he was clearly tiring. The full pack was then brought up in their trailer and released. Sensing that the end was near I sped round to the League's sanctuary at Alfoxton, just outside Holford. The stag never made it there though; instead he was headed in the village by a large group of followers and turned back in the direction from whence he had come. The supporters were muttering and cursing about the attitude of the villagers. Some of whom, they complained, had even had the audacity to order hunters out of their gardens!

The near exhausted stag returned through the Quantock Forest, but even that Forestry Commission conglomerate of thick undergrowth could offer no sanctuary. The scent was excellent and the hounds were screaming in close pursuit. On and on the chase went, columns of cars tearing through the forest, stop, look, race forward, stop, look, race forward, clouds of dust ahead and behind like the frantic forward rush of the allied armies after their victory at the battle of El Alamein in World War Two.

Out of the forest and on towards the village of Aisholt I found a small group of supporters who told me that the stag was in the valley

90

below. The hounds were baying frantically. I leapt into my car and drove at speed down towards the reservoir. I was now well to the fore of the hunt. I stopped just past the bridge and ran back with other supporters running in every direction around me.

Then there was that sound: the dreaded menacing baying of hounds that can strike at their quarry. I looked upstream from the bridge and saw the stag struggling pitifully in the deep clinging mud. I whipped my movie camera to my eye and through the viewfinder saw the last desperate struggles of this once proud beast.

The hounds were all around him, snapping, barking and biting at his flanks. With every struggle he sank ever deeper into the strength-sapping mud. Vainly he twisted his great head to present his formidable antlers to the hounds, but to no avail. With the approach of a man from the left hand bank the pack cleared and the merciful shot rang out. The stag keeled over.

At that instant there was a jarring thud in my back and I was barged down towards the river. My immediate thought was that they knew who I was. My anger was replaced by fear, but it was only other supporters sliding down the bank who had bumped into me accidentally.

I regained my composure and ran upstream to photograph the stag being dragged away. It was hard enough to get the stag out of the mud, but then the supporters faced the awesome task of dragging him up a steep, heavily wooded bank, through brambles. Ropes were tied to either branch of his antlers and tug-of-war style teams formed to heave on them. With the stag dead I saw nothing wrong in helping. It made me look like a willing supporter.

Sweating and swearing we dragged the carcass to the top to a grass clearing that turned out to be someone's back lawn. Having helped with the work I felt that I had gained sufficient cover to enable me to move in and take some really close up shots of the cutting up. The heart when ripped out was so warm that I almost expected it to beat. It was given to the wife of the landowner, standing nearby holding a young child on her hips. The liver, slots and tushes were shared amongst other supporters.

The following morning, October 8th, in pouring rain, I joined the Devon and Somerset Staghounds for their meet at Webber's Post. During the morning the stag managed to evade the hounds, but in the end they locked onto his scent and after brief circling, the stag ended up running to water at Luccombe, just south of Porlock.

I had lost contact with the hunt and was roaming ahead. Even at that early time in my undercover career I had learned from supporters that in such circumstances it is best to head for the nearest water. Some hunters refer to this practice derisively as 'bridge waiting'. Seeing a group of supporters crowding the river bank I parked then ran to join them. The stag was standing at bay in midstream surrounded by half a dozen hounds. They moved in at every opportunity snapping at his flanks. The bewildered deer was shifting his position. He looked left and right, fearful of the baying hounds and the supporters who were laughing, pointing, and jeering.

One of the few supporters with a conscience began to scream for a hunter with a gun: "*Where's the gun, get the gun. For God's sake get the gun and put him out of his misery*". There was no-one with a gun nearby. Most of the riders were far away up on the moorland. Normally four or five guns are out — some carried by riders and some carried in appointed vehicles — but on this occasion there was none at the scene.

Shutting my mind off from the horror of it all, I shot some movie film and took some stills. After about five minutes, having gained a second wind, the stag climbed out of the water and ran upstream on the far bank. By now more hounds had arrived and their baying forced him back into the water. He ran upstream for several hundred yards, only to see approaching riders.

There was no escape. I had dashed frantically up and down the bank to try and keep up, but I was some 50 yards short of the final act when a group of supporters waded in and wrestled and manhandled the deer over in midstream. I heard no shot.

The carcass was taken to a nearby field for the ritual breaking up. This was notable for two incidents. Firstly, a vicious fight developed between some of the hounds and secondly, the curiosity shown by a very young child towards the body of the stag. When children are indoctrinated at that early age to delight in such killing is it any wonder that stag hunting continues?

No-one has ever been able to explain with certainty why exhausted deer run to water, but two theories spring to mind.

When deer are first found by the hounds, they go away with mighty leaps at tremendous speed, clearing 6ft fences with ease and making light work of steep hillsides. Chased by hounds that are not bred for speed, but for stamina, the deer are worn down remorselessly and when exhaustion begins to tell they inevitably run downhill. In the rolling valleys of Devon and Somerset there they will find rivers and streams.

Secondly it is reasonable to assume that the deer are intuitively aware that they lose their scent in water. Certainly, they would find the water soothing and cooling to their bodies, cut and torn from the rigours of a long hunt. Perhaps they even find a degree of security standing in mid-stream, up to their flanks in water, where they can use their antlers to ward off hounds that are out of their depth and have to swim?

The following Saturday, October 10th was a memorable day in the annals of cruelty. The Devon and Somerset had met at Morebath and their first draw was in nearby Skilgate Wood. The selected stag was away quickly heading east and there was a mad chase by hunt followers to keep up. Catching a brief glimpse of the beast I took some movie film of him running some 200 yards ahead of the hounds. At that time, still fresh, he was able to clear the hedges and fences with ease. The chase went on and on, winding its way to the north and east. The stag ran in amongst other deer to try and lose his scent amongst theirs, but the hounds were not fooled. The ensemble of car supporters moved ever onwards. No-one wanted to be stuck at the back of the traffic crocodiles.

The hunt headed towards Roadwater and Luxborough and it was expected that the stag would go to water at picturesque Kingsbridge Gorge.

I was with supporters crowding around a stream when a hunt servant galloped up excitedly and told us that the stag had been twisting and turning upstream, now he was coming towards us and we should try to grab his antlers. It seemed foolhardy advice to me as those antlers are fearsome weapons, but the supporters were not dismayed.

Next, I heard some holloaing behind us indicating that the stag had crossed out of the river and circled round. I walked back to my car, knowing that I was then well behind the hunt. A supporter came up and enquired who I was taking pictures for. I said for my own interest and he said: "*Oh I knew you weren't anti — because you've got a BFSS badge, I thought you might be working for the Horse and Hound!*" I breathed a sigh of relief.

I drove towards Dunster and stopped to ask supporters where the hunt was. I learned that the stag had just gone downstream with the hounds in close pursuit. My sense of urgency was rekindled and I dashed on. Finding supporters at a bridge within sight of Dunster Castle I stopped. They told me that the deer had just been headed back upstream. By now it was 4.15p.m. and the weather was dull and overcast. Too little light for the cine camera so grabbing my still camera I ran over the field beside the river seeking to witness the final act.

In the distance ahead I saw an old stone bridge with supporters crowding round, pointing underneath. Getting closer I could see what caught their interest. The exhausted deer was standing under the bridge, with his back to the curved arch. There were just 2½ couple (5 hounds) baying him from either side. Again he had the wide-eyed look of fear and complete bewilderment. Here was a wild animal trapped, terrified and exhausted and all my fellow humans could do was laugh and gloat.

There was no sign of the hunt staff, nor anyone with a gun, nor any other hounds. After a few minutes the stag moved upstream pursued by his five canine tormentors. He then turned downstream and came back again to lie in the water under the bridge. The hounds moved in snapping at his flanks while supporters tried to beat them off. The deer ran off again upstream for the last time, a car follower armed with a gun arrived and there was the crack of a single shot. Much struggling ensued to get hold of the carcass in midstream. The time was 4.35p.m.

The distance from Morebath to Dunster is over 16 miles. As deer and hounds ran it must have been well over 20 miles. That hunt had lasted some five hours. The stag's carcass was broken up in the usual manner in a riding stable at Timberscombe.

I was back in the West Country at the end of October for the last meets of Autumn stag hunting. In August and September the stags are fit and healthy after a summer of feeding, but by October the situation has changed dramatically. This is the time of the rut and stags are preoccupied — fighting for hinds and defending their harems day and night. It is not surprising therefore that, when the hounds find them in late morning, they are already tired.

I was told by supporters that the end of October was the time to see kills and that if I was lucky I might see one of those rare celebrities, the stag that just won't run! Sometimes the stags are so determined to defend their hinds that they simply put their antlers down in defensive posture and stand their ground. The riders having paid for a good gallop do not pay tribute to such a brave stag. Instead they pull the hounds back and send the hunt staff in cracking their whips, to make the stag run. I was told of one such incident with the Tiverton Staghounds some three seasons before. The stag simply would not run. Apparently the hunt was stopped three times and he was given three chances of being whipped on. He went another field and stopped. The hunters gave him up as a bad job, shot him and went to look for another.

It was to witness an incident like that that I arrived at the meet of the Tiverton Staghounds on Wednesday October 21st. A lengthy hunt ensued with the stag twisting and turning in a vain attempt to hide amongst other deer, but in the end he was killed at about 4.30p.m. I had some excellent film of him running out of woodland some 20 minutes before he died, but even at that late stage I was unable to keep up on foot.

The next day was memorable. It was a meet of the Devon and Somerset at Pitcombe Head, near scenic Porlock. Attempting to follow on foot I was left behind so I returned to my car and headed towards Exford. Descending the hill towards the river Exe I knew that something was happening. There was an air of excitement and urgency. I drove on until I heard the hounds. They were running and baying along the far hillside. In the maelstrom of horses and cars it was difficult to pull in. Bumping up on the verge I grabbed my movie camera and ran for the river.

The stag had clearly just passed upstream because the hounds were baying their cry of death. As I splashed and scrambled forwards the stag burst from cover on the far bank heading towards me, with the hounds in close attendance. I whipped up the movie camera to film. The exhausted stag ran past me barely 30 yards away on the far bank. To the left he was headed by riders and he crossed into the stream with the hounds all around. He then ran back towards me on my side of the bank. I should have been fearful of being gored by his antlers, but at the time I was too concerned with keeping him in focus. As he went by I saw that I was low on film and I opted to do a lightning fast change and reload. He was headed again by hunters on the right so ran back past me to my left. Headed once more he returned and the hounds were then all around him snapping at his heels and biting at his flanks. Hunters always swear that their hounds never touch the deer but my film proves the truth.

As I was filming I was aware of hunt servants to my right, ahead of the stag, one of whom was bellowing loudly in my direction: "*He's a photographer from the Daily Star, he's a photographer from the Daily Star, stop him!*" and gesturing towards me. I carried on, knowing that aggressive supporters responding to these claims were approaching me.

The stag had passed me for the last time. As he crossed the river the hounds, supporters and riders closed in; he stumbled and fell, alone. He was wrestled and manhandled in the water, a shotgun brought up and the crack that signalled the end echoed the length and breadth of the valley.

Hunters were then around me and I thought that my best defence was to become really angry: "*What kind of Fleet Street photographer would use a f..... movie camera to take still pictures?*" I assured them that I was not working for any newspaper and that my film was purely for my own interest. They seemed persuaded and left me alone. I filmed the carcass being carried back to a nearby field to be cut up. Women carrying very young infants followed in the cortege.

Afterwards the hunt Joint Masters all tackled me, asking who I was and why I was filming. I used the same story, flashing my BFSS badge and they seemed convinced, but I knew that from then on I needed a proper cover story.

I did make one stupid mistake. A supporter had been chatting to me about my camera and lens and was so impressed that he wanted to take down details of the lens combinations. He asked to borrow a pen and I reached in my top pocket and offered him my biro and only remembered at the last instant that it had *League Against Cruel Sports — Help Write Off Bloodsports* written along its length.

I stopped with it in my hand and hurriedly put it back, saying: "*That one doesn't work; I'll get you one from the car.*" It was a close shave.

There was another time when I pulled a film carton from my pocket, whilst standing amongst a crowd of supporters and a bill fell to the ground. Fortunately I picked it up first. It was for vegetarian pizzas — not exactly the expected diet for the brutish, macho stag hunting image.

To guard against similar incidents happening again I developed the habit of completely checking my car and my clothing — inspecting every pocket and my wallet before every hunt. To improve my credentials as a genuine supporter I could easily offer a hunt supporter a lift, as I did on several occasions and I did not want any hard to explain items slipping into view. On one such pre-check I found a carrier bag blazoned with the name of a well-known health food shop under the seat and a League leaflet. There was a lot at stake and I had to be careful.

For my cover story I decided to stick as close to the truth as possible. My Christian name would remain the same. No matter how proficient one becomes in the art of subterfuge, it is hard to shake the habit of a lifetime and ignore one's own name, or respond to someone calling to you across a crowded bar by a different name.

For my surname I chose Wright (appropriate because I was on the side of right). My cover was simple and not uncommon in the world of hunting. My father was an ex-army officer, with pots of money and

Devon and Somerset Staghounds, April 28th 1981. For this stag the suffering is over. Above: child (right) clutches a piece of liver.

Right: the hounds are whipped up to a frenzy then get their reward which is to rip apart and eat the warm stomach and its contents.

Devon and Somerset Staghounds, April 28th 1981. Laughing supporters leave their victim. The body of the stag is later collected and taken away for meat. The slots (hooves) have been cut off and taken as trophies.

The end of a stag hunt. Devon and Somerset Staghounds, August 22nd 1981.

Above: exhausted stag is cornered in a small pool by the hounds. Below: hunt supporters catch hold of the stag's antlers and drag him to the bank. They try to ward off the hounds that are trying to bite the flank of the stag. The stag was dragged out onto the bank and held for some minutes until a hunter with a pistol reached the scene and shot him.

Devon and Somerset Staghounds, August 22nd 1981.
The Huntsman is collecting trophies from the stag. He is cutting the
slots (hooves) off. The stomach has been tipped out and will be
given to the hounds.

Above: Devon and Somerset Staghounds, August 22nd 1981.

Left: child supporters are given pieces of velvet from the dead stag.

Right: a collection of slots for sale to supporters.

Below: Tiverton Staghounds, October 31st 1981.

Dead stag with a hound that he gored in the final battle. The injured hound is given a ride back to the hunt kennels.

Devon and Somerset Staghounds, August 25th 1981.
After the gralloch (that bloodied his hands) Huntsman, Dennis
Boyles, sells the stag's teeth as souvenirs to young hunt supporters.

Quantock Staghounds, October 7th 1981.

Above: image from 8mm cine film shows stag (arrowed) stuck in mud just before he is killed. Above right: a young child is taken by the hand to witness the butchery. Right: the liver is shared out amongst supporters. Bottom left: the heart is given to the landowner where the deer was killed.

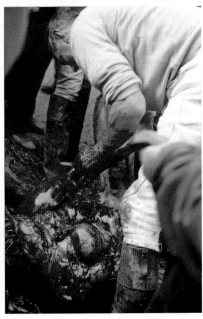

Devon and Somerset Staghounds, October 8th 1981.

Above: stag at bay in a stream at Luccombe, south of Porlock.

Below: after the kill, a curious child supporter looks into the eye of the dead stag. The hounds lap the blood from the sliced open stomach of the deer.

Devon and Somerset Staghounds, October 10th 1981.

Exhausted stag draws an audience of hunt supporters as he stands at bay to five hounds under a small stone bridge at Dunster. This hunt had lasted for around five hours and extended from Morebath to Dunster, probably well over 20 miles as the deer and hounds ran.

Devon and Somerset Staghounds, October 22nd 1981. These four images are poor quality because they are single frames from cine film.

Left: this stag has no escape

Right: hounds snap at the exhausted stag.

Left: after the kill hunt supporters take an interest in who is filming.

Right: the dead stag is carried away to be cut up. Note the babes in arms being carried along behind.

Devon and Somerset Staghounds, October 29th 1981.
Above: Huntsman, Dennis Boyles poses in triumph (young female
supporter obscured because she later changed her views).
Bottom left: young girl contemplates the blood on her hands.

Devon and Somerset Staghounds,
November 17th 1981.
The hunting of hinds when they are
pregnant.

Above left: the hind is tiring. Above right: a hunt supporter clutches
the warm heart of the hind.
Below: together in death. A hind and her yearling calf lie dead when
the hunt is over. The hind gave her life to protect her calf but it was
a futile sacrifice as the hunters killed her calf soon after killing her.
Note how the slots of the calf were not taken, they were too small to
be wanted as trophies.

Devon and Somerset
Staghounds, March 18th 1982.
Top: hunted stag swimming
across Wimbleball reservoir.

Centre: the stag (arrowed)
runs on.

Right: a hound licks the blood
from the stag's carcass.

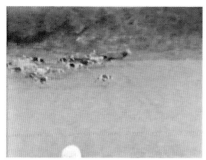

Quantock Staghounds, March 19th 1982. These are images from 8mm cine film. With hounds snapping at his legs the tired stag tried to jump a hedge, caught his front hooves, and flipped onto the road breaking his neck. His body is dragged away (left).

Below: Devon and Somerset Staghounds, August 26th 1982.

Below left: young hunt follower clutches a piece of liver to take home for his tea.

Tiverton Staghounds October 30th 1982.

Top: Huntsman pulls teeth from the dead stag.

Right and below: the body of the stag is dragged away.

Tiverton Staghounds, February 26th 1983. Top: tired stag flees.
Bottom: with hounds tearing at his hindquarters the stag is shot.

in consequence I was a wealthy young gent living in London, dabbling in stocks and shares, with plenty of free time and a passion for huntin', shootin' and fishin'!

I secured two accommodation addresses in London. The first I gave to anyone who wanted to post letters or hunt literature to me. From there, the mail was posted on to the second, from where it was forwarded to me. Once I had fabricated this plausible background I felt more confident to deal with any inquisitive hunt members.

On October 27th, the Devon and Somerset met at Culbone Stables, near Porlock. I did not see the kill, but two supporters who were returning from it told me the stag had been shot at bay on a road in woodland just outside Porlock. They were quite upset and said: "*It was terrible, I don't think we'll be coming again.*"

I could not question them without risking arousing their suspicions, but I found that a lot of car followers in ignorance, genuinely believe it is a clean kill. When they actually see the grim reality they are often deeply shocked.

Many car supporters rarely see a kill. Only the experienced followers, steeped in knowledge of the ways of the hunted deer, anticipate their movements and make sure they are there when it happens. For them the kill and the following ritual is all important.

Stag hunting is not all action — often it is long, drawn out and boring: a procession of slow-moving traffic crawling along narrow country lanes with the occupants not seeing a thing of the hunt. The following day, October 28th, with the Tiverton Staghounds was an example. In torrential rain the tufters were only able to hunt spasmodically and the day ended early with the hunt giving up without even getting the main pack out of their box.

The next day, the 29th, from the Devon and Somerset meet at Bratton Fleming, there was a short, sharp and bloody encounter. It was right at the end of the rut, a time when the stags are at their weakest. I had a brief view of the magnificent stag as he made a short excursion from one wood, before he turned back into it and headed back for Loxhore. By 1.30p.m. the hounds had closed right up on the tiring quarry. He battled through some woodland heading towards National Trust land at Arlington, from which the hunt was banned. There are also League sanctuaries in the area. Not to be outwitted and desperate to score again before the switch to hind hunting, the hunters decided to shoot him.

As the stag emerged from the woodland, on to the road, a man jumped out of a van and fired. The shotgun pellets smashed into the right side of the stag's skull knocking flesh and fur off, bursting his right eye and bowling him over. Rising shakily to his feet, the stag stumbled over the road through a hedgerow and ran in to the grass field below. The gunman leaned over the hedge and fired again. Once more the stag went down, but again his wounds were not fatal. He staggered up, carried on through a water meadow and trickling stream and up into the cover of a small copse, followed by baying and barking hounds. Torn, battered, bleeding and half-blinded the tormented beast turned to face the pack. A third shot rang out, the pellets striking the deer full in the chest and ripping through to the massive heart. The beast tottered and fell dying into the pack. Even in death the stag inspired fear and the hounds backed away cowering. The small stream now trickled red with blood and the supporters, who had gathered in force, rejoiced.

The carcass was taken back to Bratton Fleming and subjected to the usual indignities in the scramble for souvenirs. I watched the supporters laughing and joking as they poked and prodded the carcass. Knowing the suffering that stag had endured it did nothing to enhance my faith in humanity.

For the one and only time during all my time observing stag hunting, Huntsman Dennis Boyles posed for photographs by the head of the stag with an attractive 17-year-old female supporter.

[After the widespread publicity given to my undercover work this girl — Miss 'L' — wrote to me including the following: "*Dear Mike Huskisson, I am writing in response to your article in the* **News of the World** *titled* **'Savages'** *16/10/83. The 'attractive young supporter' you refer to is myself and I am writing to inform you of my reformation since the taking of that picture two years ago. Although I do not belong to the L.A.C.S. I have since joined B.U.A.V.* [British Union for the Abolition of Vivisection] *(Nov, 82) and C.I.W.F.* [Compassion in World Farming] *(Jan. 83) and I am deeply concerned with cruelty to animals, especially in laboratories and factory farms. I take an active part by going on marches and demonstrations, delivering leaflets and helping to raise money for the funds.*" She adds that she was raised from the age of six to enjoy hunting but now believes that stag hunting should be replaced by some other form of culling — but only when necessary. Because of that letter I now obscure her face whenever this picture is printed. (Personal communication dated November 13th 1983)]

The last day of Autumn stag hunting that year was on Saturday 31st October when the Tiverton Staghounds met at Chulmleigh Beacon. At the meet two police officers had words with the Master and we were subsequently warned to keep off certain farms. In that part of their country the Tiverton are hated by the farmers and are banned from many areas. The hunt pay token heed to this by asking their followers to try and prevent deer heading for banned land, but in the final analysis they happily carry on — a point borne out by the fact that many farmers now have to mount shotgun patrols to protect their land from hunt trespass.

That day the hunt quickly found a stag and pushed him around on land down by the river Little Dart. I was running up and down the river bank trying to see what was happening and had the infuriating misfortune to continually meet riders who had just seen the stag, without catching a glimpse myself. Close to the river it can be very difficult to distinguish the baying of the hounds, a sound easily confused with that of fast flowing river water tumbling over rocks.

A supporter told me that the stag was dead-beat and would not last long, so I opted to stay by the river, but that was a mistake. The stag somehow summoned the strength to run up out of the valley, clear the hill and head north. He did not get far and fought his last battle in dense, matted undergrowth around a small stream just south of Brookland Farm. Just before he was shot he managed to deeply gore one of the hounds. I learnt this when I saw a tractor trundling down the road with both victor (gored bitch) and vanquished (gutted stag) in the back.

The following year, 1982, I was out with the Devon and Somerset Staghounds from their meet at the *Froude Arms*, Anstey on Thursday August 26th. The hounds latched onto a very big stag that was clearly too heavy to go far and he was duly killed near Chain Bridge in Tiverton country at 2.30p.m. The notable thing about the cutting up was the presence of a large team of French stag hunters, who gleefully rejoiced in the kill. Seeing me taking pictures, they and a number of other tourists asked to pose by the body and for me to send on their pictures.

Wednesday October 6th, found me with the Tiverton Staghounds for their meet at Witheridge Moor. A stag was soon away and, with the scent good, he was tightly hunted by the hounds. At several points he was only just ahead as he ran near to and crossed the main road just west of Bampton. He circled back and when he was seen to swim the Exe, in a reportedly dead-beat state, it seemed that the end was very near.

However, where were the hounds? From being hot on the trail at the top of the hill they were suddenly way, way behind. Waiting supporters grew ever more frustrated as the chances of a kill dwindled. A few straggling hounds appeared and I heard a sickening thud as one hound was hit by a vehicle on the road. Eventually, after a delay of some 60 minutes, other supporters arrived and we learned that the pack had fallen into a quarry. Many hounds had been injured, some with broken legs. Even so, the hunt tried to continue. The surviving healthy hounds were brought forward, but the stag had gained too much of a start. Despite a prodigious effort the hunt eventually gave up at 6.45p.m. in the approaching darkness.

The Tiverton Staghounds met at Chittlehamholt on October 9th and spent a day that proved boring for supporters. For three full hours the hounds repeatedly drew a covert in which two good stags had been sighted but they found nothing. Supporters looked over hedgerows and gazed intently through binoculars at nothing but flora. I sat in my car but any boredom I felt was alleviated by the knowledge that no deer would suffer that day. The hounds were taken on to draw the nearby woodland at Great Odam Moor, but that too was blank and at 4p.m. 'home' was blown, with no action at all.

Hunting people are always keen to criticise a drag hunt — damning it as too predictable — but one thing is certain, in that humane sport there are no blank days.

My last day of Autumn stag hunting in 1982 was with the Tiverton Staghounds from their meet at the romantically named Kissing Gate, Stoodleigh on Saturday, October 30th. The stag was quickly away from the first draw, heading towards the River Exe. I encountered some hunting colleagues from the Three Counties Minkhounds and was grateful that I had the foresight to use the same name and cover at both hunts, as they immediately recognised me.

The stag criss-crossed in woodland around the river, but he was plainly tired. The gun shot rang out at 3.00p.m. The river was wide and deep at that point and the carcass floated on down, to the consternation of the followers. By slipping and sliding on the far bank the young lads managed to guide the body round obstacles and it was eventually pulled out when it stopped at a weir.

This stag was dismembered in the usual way on the river bank and his prized teeth pulled out with pliers. One interesting feature of this episode was that a supporter asked for and was given the tail. He said he wanted to use it for fishing and the followers joked: "*What are you going to catch — a shark?*"

So ended my two years long observation of Autumn stag hunting, the type of stag hunting that attracts the most support because of the spectacular spread of the stag's antlers, the near certainty of a hunt, and the high likelihood of a kill.

The season is short, but with one or more of the three hunts out on four days of each week there is plenty to see.

During those two seasons I saw the hounds tearing at the flanks of stags and climbing on their backs; I saw stags surrounded by hounds with the hunt staff miles away, messy kills necessitating more than one shot, children being bloodied and deer being whipped to make them run. However, the only unlawful aspect was the willingness of hunt supporters to brazenly trespass on private property.

HIND HUNTING

"It is almost unnecessary to say a word with reference to the proverbial agility of the deer. 'Nimrod' thus adverts to a remarkable leap taken by a hind under difficulties, at the time when the late Lord Fortescue was the Master of the old stag-hounds. "I was shown," he says, "a leap which a hind had taken last season, before the pack, when close at her haunches, after a long run, and not more than ten minutes before she sank before them. What makes it more extraordinary is, that on being paunched, a calf was taken from her almost able to stand."" (*Notes on the Chase of the Wild Red Deer.* Charles Palk Collyns. 1862, Pub. Alston Rivers Ltd., 1907. Page 155 quoting article in "*Sporting Magazine*" Oct. 1824. Page 42)

By November 1981 I was an accepted hunt follower, no-one bothered at my stepping in to take pictures or asking questions. To put them even more at ease I made a point of giving some of the innocuous pictures I had taken at various meets to eager hunt followers who featured prominently in them. I used this increased cover to great advantage during the hind hunting season from November to the end of February, when female deer take over as the stag hunters' prey.

Hind hunting is particularly upsetting as it nears its close. This is the time when hinds, heavily in calf and unable to run far, fall easy victims to the hounds. Furthermore, they often run with last year's calf at their heels as they both try to escape. Refusing to abandon her offspring the hind seals her own fate. The mother, her unborn and the calf carefully nurtured during the last few months are slaughtered. It is a pathetic and sickening sight, a grave indictment of the callousness of hunters.

Less distinguishable from each other than stags (with identifiable antlers), it is hard for the hunters to select one hind and pursue her — and only her — all day. If one hind runs into a wood and four come out the other side it is difficult to pick out the real quarry. Some hunt supporters jokingly suggested that the hind should first be caught and painted red to make her easily spotted!

My first experience of hind hunting was with the Devon and Somerset from their meet at Twitchen on Saturday 14th November 1981. The first two creatures to emerge from the undergrowth were two beautiful stags. Hinds then broke out in all directions and the hunt was on. Hinds will usually run as a group and often with their young from previous years. The first task for the hunt is therefore to split a hind away from this family group and get her running alone.

On this particular hunt the pack screamed on ahead and after a frantic dash I ended up in that notorious killing zone — Marsh Bridge — with the hunt swiftly approaching. A group of five hinds and a pricket (young stag) came by. Three went on to the river and three circled away left-handed. Not surprisingly when the pack arrived they split. There was some confusion collecting the hounds together but, when they had, they were cast on again. This time they put up a stag and a hind running together. Both were hunted back towards Hawkridge and Tarr Steps, the famous tourist attraction.

Here the two split and the motorcycle followers were at fault. In error they directed the hounds onto the line of the stag. The hounds roared away at great speed and by the time the hunters realised their mistake, checked and returned to search for the hunted hind darkness was approaching. Would it arrive in time to save this tiring hind? The scent must have been good because they quickly picked up her scent, pushed her on towards Shircombe and were close to her when, exhausted, she swung for Willingford Bridge. Mercifully the light failed and reluctantly the hunt had to give up soon after 5p.m.

When I commented to a keen supporter that, given the readiness of the pack to split, it was surprising that they ever caught any hinds, he explained some facts to me. With the rut for red deer occurring in October, the hinds in November although pregnant, are still very light and not in any way incapacitated by the burden of new life. They remain difficult to catch until around Christmas; from then on matters change. By the end of February the kills are more or less certain. In the old days, hind hunting used to continue until the end of March. But, when reports started to appear in the media of the most gruesome grallochs, (disembowellings) in which fully formed calves were cut from their mother's wombs, public outrage grew to such an extent that even the insensitive hunting people thought it wise to change their ways. Nevertheless, I encountered many hunt supporters who would like to see hind hunting continue for another month.

On November 17th, I was out with the Devon and Somerset from their meet at Nutscale Drive, high on Exmoor, south of Porlock. The area swarmed with deer. I counted one herd comprising an old stag and no less than 20 hinds. The hounds got in amongst the hinds, splitting them up in all directions and at one point I saw them pressing one particular hind very closely.

Against hounds the hinds are particularly defenceless because of their lack of antlers. When baying exhausted stags the hounds hold back out of sheer fear of the sharp and hard antlers but even then if they can attack, they will. I saw it happen. They will dart in to snap at his flanks and if hunt supporters are holding his antlers, as in the pool at Marsh Bridge, the hounds will even climb on his back.

Against such determined aggressors one can feel nothing but pity for the defenceless hinds. I have seen hounds lunge at hinds and although the hunters are usually very quick to put the hind out of her misery, if they do not, or cannot because of location (they may not even be there) the hounds will do the job for them. I have spoken to an eyewitness who described in graphic detail seeing a hind badly torn by hounds and, even worse, an incident when an exhausted hind made her way into dense undergrowth, closely followed by the entire pack. By the time hunt staff fought their way to the scene all that was left was her head and feet.

One feature of hind hunting that makes it certain that all manner of cruel assaults on deer will occur is its sheer fragmented nature. There are many hinds up on the moor and when they split in all directions the hounds often do likewise following individual groups. In place of one hunt there may be many hunts. Frequently at the end of the day I heard supporters drifting back from all directions reporting to the Masters that they had seen 2½ couple baying a hind here, or a couple baying a hind there. No-one has any idea, let alone any control over, what happens to the deer at such times.

That November 17th deer were chased all over the countryside. Eventually a pregnant hind running with her calf at foot was singled out by the hounds. The hind's progress was impeded by her concern for her calf that was only just bigger than the hounds and struggled to keep up with his mother.

Distressed, the hind stayed with her calf as long as she could, risking her own life. The calf broke away and I then saw the hind standing pathetically in a stream surrounded by hounds. She tried to run downstream, disappeared from my view followed by the baying pack and was killed seconds later.

103

Soon afterwards I encountered a hunter driving a pick-up truck containing the carcasses of both calf and mother. The victims were driven to a nearby grassy field for dismemberment. A supporter told me that the calf had been caught and killed soon after his mother. Both were cut up in the usual way, with the exception that the calf was so small that his slots were not regarded as worthwhile trophies and were left.

When the hounds started to worry (bite at) the body of the calf, supporters nudged it over to the hind with their feet and thus produced the embrace in death, which I managed to photograph. I found it hard to believe that grown adults — men and women — could regard such a pastime as fun, let alone sport.

Hunting on the 18th and 19th of November was inconclusive, but there was an interesting day with the Devon and Somerset from their meet at Wheddon Cross on Thursday 26th November. For nearly two hours we watched hounds chasing various hinds in all directions, but all the time supporters had been aware of one particular hind hiding in the gorse on the far hillside. When it seemed unlikely that hounds would settle on any other individual they indicated her presence to the Huntsman.

The full pack was taken up to find her. She sat tight in the safety of the gorse until the last moment. However, when she did move she went like a bullet with awesome power and grace. In the first 200 yards, she must have gained 50 yards on the pack. Hedges, fences and even narrow roads were cleared with ease. Unleashing such power is often the undoing of hunted animals; they expend too much energy too soon. The hounds are happy to trail along in the wake of their quarry, speaking deliriously to the scent.

Like all pack hounds these are not bred to be fast. Lurchers would have brought the hind to bay, or more likely pulled her down within 500 yards, but that would have provided no prolonged hunt, no fun for the followers.

This hind ran off in a massive circle about a mile in diameter, the supporters tracking her progress across the moor with their binoculars.

She then came right back to the very spot from whence she had started. Instead of laying down in the gorse however, she repeated her very first movements carrying on round the circle. After about 50 yards she stopped, carefully retracing her steps, then broke off the circle at a right angle and disappeared at full speed over the hill. Had I not seen the manoeuvre I would have found it hard to believe.

Sure enough the hounds were fooled. They came thundering round the circle, back past the gorse refuge and on for their second circuit.

Sadly the supporters near me betrayed this clever hind. They holloaed, shouted and gesticulated and one ran to a nearby rider, who galloped on to tell the Huntsman that the hounds were at fault. The pack was stopped, brought back to the indicated spot. They soon hit the right line and sped off following the hind over the hill.

That spoilt an excellent escape manoeuvre and highlighted the fact that car and foot followers are by no means mere observers to any hunt. Many a hunted animal that has successfully eluded the pack has had his or her whereabouts betrayed by an alert follower, another example of how the odds are stacked against the hunted.

Some inconclusive hunting then ensued around the League sanctuary at Pitleigh with hounds running in all directions. The tiring hind ran to water at Sully Corner, where only a few months previous the Autumn stag had been killed. I had run on ahead and was waiting down by the river, when she came tip-toeing daintily downstream towards me. She was not exhausted, but careful. She picked her way along the river bed for some hundred yards, then came out at right angles on the far bank and tried to go on up the hill but was headed back by the car followers. Initially there were no hounds in sight, but a few did appear after she disappeared downstream. They appeared to be gaining on her, so I followed by car. I came to a steep narrow lane, but halfway up encountered all the hunt vehicles coming down towards me.

The lane was too narrow for us to pass. I could not go on, had to go back, but knew that I had to do so quickly. The hounds were likely to be on the hind soon and if I ended up at the back of the crocodile of hunt traffic I would see nothing. Accordingly, I reversed at some speed. The road was wet and covered in leaves and when I touched my brakes to swing into a gateway I merely succeeded in skidding across the lane putting the rear offside into one bank and the front nearside into the other. The road was completely blocked and I had all the hunters streaming down towards me!

What a predicament for an undercover operator to find himself in. It became worse when I climbed out shaken and found that the impact had burst the boot open. I had ignored the boot when checking the car and a whole load of copies of *Cruel Sports*, the League's newspaper were revealed. Hunt supporters were running to help move my car out of the way so that they could rush on for the kill while I was there staring at a whole batch of exposed LACS magazines. If my boot lid did not close, I was done for. Had the impact warped it? I banged it shut but it opened again. I banged it again desperately but again to no avail. The hunters were nearly on me. I cleared some mud from the rim and slammed the boot lid again. Mercifully it shut.

The hunt followers were all about my car. They were keen to help me get out of their way. With six willing, burly men to help, it was soon moved to the side. I was temporarily out of action whilst I levered the front wing off the tyre. Angry over my driving error and my foolishness in carrying such incriminating material in my boot, I cheered up greatly when I rejoined the hunt later to learn that they had lost the hind anyway. She was one smart lady.

Monday 30th November produced an interesting day with the Quantock Staghounds from their meet at Dead Woman's Ditch, an obscure landmark high on the Quantock Hills. Hounds were put into the Quantock Forest and were quickly away. A hind was separated from the safety of the herd. The scent was excellent and all seemed well for the hunt. I drove rapidly round to the League sanctuary at Alfoxton, expecting to find the action there but there were no sounds of baying, nor of the horn, nothing. I found some bedraggled looking riders and asked them what was wrong. They explained that the Master had had a tiff with the riders and had taken his hounds home. The time was just 12.30p.m.

Conversation with the kennel staff back at the meet confirmed that the hounds had been running well but some riders, in their enthusiasm to lead, had galloped ahead thereby foiling the line. When this cardinal sin for hunt riders was pointed out to them, instead of apologising, they were abusive and hence the Master called it a day. Doubtless the deer were more than grateful for the presence of ill-mannered hunt followers.

For the meet of the Devon and Somerset at Scob Hill Gate on December 1st I had a new weapon in my armoury — an all-terrain motorbike. Years before, as a young hunt saboteur, I had ridden a motorbike to my first stag hunt. Now I was back again on two wheels, but this time in full undercover mode. After too many experiences of being stuck in queues of hunt traffic in my car I saw a motorbike as a great asset. It was possible not only to by-pass the jams but also to turn about in an instant when the hunt changed direction and, furthermore, to go straight over the moors, right behind the pack.

Riding my motorbike I joined a most select band of stag hunt followers — the bike brigade. Because of their manoeuvrability they were always at the front of any hunt, usually saw the deer killed and were always on hand to help the hunters.

My first day on the bike was inauspicious. I got lost on the moor, stuck in a bog and only with great difficulty did I rejoin the hunt in the late afternoon. They had changed deer by then and there was no kill.

The Tiverton Staghounds killed from their meet at Chain Bridge on December 2nd, but out of my sight. I made an error of judgement and was waiting at the wrong bridge.

The following day with the Devon and Somerset at Morebath was a better day for observation. Three hinds and a stag were quickly away from the first draw at Morebath Manor and went like rockets towards Shillingford. It looked as if the chase was on, but the hounds checked, then reversed course, hunting a young calf. They were stopped and taken on to draw near Skilgate Wood.

A hind was reported by followers crossing the road towards Haddon Hill and Wimbleball Reservoir and the hounds were laid on. I saw the hunted hind running in company with another. When they both jumped into woodland and separated, only the lead hounds took the correct line, the rest of the pack switched to the fresh hind. The hunt switched to this fresh hind and pushed her south towards Bury. Hounds were closing on her as she went to water. When she came out and went up over Bury Hill she was only yards in front. She was now in the vicinity of the League sanctuaries at Barlynch and Baronsdown and I was praying that she would make the right turn and reach safety but it was not to be.

She crossed the River Exe somewhere near Bury Castle and some desperate hunting ensued in the vicinity of Dulverton. Any hunted animal has a repertoire of tricks to elude hounds, but this one was running out of hers fast.

Determined to keep up, the hunt followers, myself included, raced in circles into Dulverton and back again. On 50 yards, stop and listen, back 200 yards, stop and listen: from one bridge to another and back. Then, from a bridge near Dulverton, I saw the hounds stream across the grass bank, plunge straight into the river and swim across baying. Camera at the ready, I rushed down in hot pursuit. When I heard the menacing growls of the death bay I knew they must be looking at the hind. But there was no sign of her. She must have been there moments before and in her exhaustion stopped to rest. Now she was gone. A bitter argument as to tactics ensued between the Huntsman Dennis Boyles and his Whipper-in David. Dennis took the hounds away towards Exebridge and I had just reached the village when I heard the shot ring out. The hind had been killed in the river well away from the road.

That was Thursday. On Saturday December 5th after the meet of the Devon and Somerset at Aldermans Barrow I ended up in a particularly good observation position ahead of the hunt. I was in cover by a river with the hounds coming baying downstream towards me. I expected at any minute to see the hind break cover with the hounds around her. Nervously I prepared my camera. At almost the last instant the hounds suddenly switched direction, turning off at right angles after a fresh hind.

It later transpired that this hind was hunted to Porlock, coursed down into the village and trapped in a small children's playground. She was killed with a pistol when unable to jump the wire to escape. Her body was brought back to the Whitstones, a landmark high up on the cliff's overlooking Porlock Bay, to be sliced up. In the summer a popular tourist spot, in the winter the hunters lay claim to it. The carve up was just as usual, the only feature of note being that by way of a joke Dennis blooded one of the elderly, if not positively geriatric, male riders.

Back in the area in the New Year, the first hunt I attended was the Tiverton Staghounds on Wednesday, 20th January. It was a triumph for the deer: the hounds rioted and split into groups, with the majority going off after a young stag.

The next day, Thursday 21st, with the Devon and Somerset at Horner near Porlock was entirely different. The hounds drew first around Webber's Post and then hunted a deer towards Cloutsham. I followed and she soon went to water but instead of standing she doubled back attempting to lose her scent in the snow on the banks. The hounds appeared disorganised and, even though obviously heavy with calf, that hind escaped. Deer were running everywhere and the pack split completely, so that a whole variety of different hunts were taking place.

One group of hounds latched on to one hind and she was killed far to the south, at Larcombe near Exford. Another group pursued a lame hind and she was killed in Horner Water.

The hunt always make a point of saying that the deer they kill are wounded, crippled or ailing in some way and that they are doing the herd 'a service' by putting such casualties out of their misery.

Like other hunt claims this is simply not true. Aside from this kill, the Autumn stag that was killed at Dunster which had a clean bullet hole in one ear and a hind killed by the Tiverton Staghounds in January 1983 which had a deformed hoof, were the only infirm victims I saw.

I no sooner learned of the killing of this lame hind than the hounds were in full cry again around Horner. In near darkness, at 4.45p.m., a hind came downstream at Horner Water, with the hounds some 100 yards behind. Tragically it was too dark for me to record any of this on film. The hind paused at the weir, looked towards me, and struggled out onto the bank. The pack streamed by me, their baying rising to a crescendo, echoing the length and breadth of the cold valley of leafless trees. The hind, stumbling on, cleared the first fence she came to, but at the second, burdened by the weight of the life within her, she collapsed exhausted into the barbed wire. The pack was on her. I heard no shot. The 'sporting conservationists' who dragged her body back were splattered with her blood.

Three deer died that day. As they so rightly said — hinds are easier to kill after Christmas.

The meet of the Devon and Somerset from Mounsey Hill Gate on January 23rd 1982, was a demonstration in hunt perseverance. Deer were quickly found and the hounds settled on to three hinds that were separated away from the herd. The hounds were checked and riders moved in cracking whips to separate one from the others. A protracted hunt then ensued on either side of the River Barle with supporters able to see very little. In the afternoon the hounds latched on to another hind with a yearling calf by her side. They separated the yearling off and killed him, then were taken back to draw for his mother, but without success.

As darkness approached I headed for the nearby favourite killing site, Marsh Bridge, and met up with an experienced supporter. An exhausted hind came down the river bank towards us but, seeing us, veered away and ran up over the hill into the darkness. That manoeuvre probably saved her life. The hounds were just a few minutes behind, but they lost precious time picking up her change of direction.

With a gloomy murk engulfing us I thought that it would all be over for the day and the hunt would give up, but the supporter assured me that it was still worth us following. He had often heard of the Tiverton killing by the light of torches.

The Tiverton Staghounds were known to be in the area having crossed the road north from their meet at Knowstone; in fact it was quite possibly 'their' hind and hounds that we had seen.

In total darkness we drove on around the bridges near Dulverton looking for the tell-tale signs of torches down by the water but we found nothing. The whole scenario appeared to me to be totally ridiculous. I wondered what we would find next — a Huntsman wearing a miner's hat — with light blazing?!

*****

In the 1982/83 season I spent most of the time fox hunting and beagling, but I did manage the occasional trip to see the staghounds. On 1st January 1983, I was with the Tiverton Staghounds for hind hunting, meeting at *The Fortescue Arms* at Kings Nympton Station.

At the meet the Master, John Lucas, asked supporters not to repeat any of the 'silly' behaviour of the previous time they had met in the area, as it had caused him a lot of work and gained a lot of bad publicity for the hunt. This was a reference to the much publicised incident near Chittlehamholt, in which hunt supporters had wrestled an exhausted hind to the ground and stabbed her to death with a penknife.

Hounds were taken to draw Snydles Wood and a hind was quickly away westwards. Headed back by supporters, she joined up with another group of five deer. One from this group was split off by the supporters and the hunt continued. When the hind was seen to run onto a railway line only minutes in front of hounds it was thought that she would soon be caught, but thankfully she reached and found sanctuary in a large wood from which the hunt was banned.

Hounds were then taken back to draw again near to their starting point. There was a long wait but eventually fresh deer were found. I circled round in the traffic jams, through Kings Nympton and on the way back heard a shot from deep inside Kings Nympton Park. I was later told by hunt staff that the hind had been caught tangled up in barbed wire.

The carcass was brought out of the park to be dismembered by the bridge over the river Mole. I was cautious about taking pictures. One of the senior staff of the *Shooting Times* was present and I felt sure that by this late stage someone must be getting suspicious. However, suddenly a car and a motorbike pulled up on the bridge, people piled out of the car and hurled not only abuse at the hunt, but also rotten eggs and plastic bags full of mud!

The local HSA had arrived. Though too late to save the hind they were in time to give me the perfect cover. Muttering about the 'bloody antis' I moved in close taking pictures freely. The supporters were totally distracted from me by the more obvious saboteurs. If they were annoyed at me for anything, it was for photographing the dead hind and not the hunt saboteurs.

110

On January 15th, possibly as a result of the sabotage attempt on January 1st, the Tiverton did not advertise their meet at Spurway Moor Gate and it took me some time to find them. Groups of hounds were running in all directions chasing numerous hinds and it became so disorganised that everything had to be stopped to get the pack back together. From the restart a deer herd was quickly found and a very small hind was soon killed. This was the hind that had one of her back feet deformed.

January 20th found me at a meet of the Quantock Staghounds at a place called Warm Corner in the Quantock Forest. Hunting was inconclusive on and around Robin Uprights Hill and Holford and is only worthy of mention because of a comment from one of the supporters. Late in the afternoon the hounds were baying, particularly excitedly and the supporter said that she thought they were 'hocking' the hind. The use of this term in these circumstances plainly indicates that some supporters know that their hounds will attack the deer.

The hind hunting meets from mid-February 1983 to the end of the month were disrupted by a hard frost. I had hoped to take *News of the World* reporter Maureen Lawless to them but they were all cancelled, or replaced by deer drives — barbaric practices that the hunt are always secretive about.

SPRING STAG HUNTING

With a summer and winter of stag hunting behind me, the start of the 1982 season of Spring stag hunting found me experienced in hunt tactics.

These younger male deer are hunted during March and April, and because they are not hampered by the rigours of the rut or by carrying huge spreads of antlers that make passage through dense undergrowth difficult, the chase usually lasts all day.

The Devon and Somerset, from their meet at Wheddon Cross on March 16th 1982, had protracted hunting in the snow on Dunkery Hill, eventually losing their stag, as did the Tiverton the following day from their meet at Swineham Hill. The next day, the 18th, the Devon and Somerset were more successful from their meet high on Haddon Hill.

The stag went away quickly, out through Bury, on towards Dulverton, then circled back over to Upton and swung round heading towards the massive Wimbleball reservoir, which is banned to the hunt. I was with supporters on a hill beside the reservoir as they watched through binoculars and described the action below as the hounds closed on the tiring beast. *"He's at the water's edge, the hounds are going through the wire, he's in, he's in!*" With that I ran for my car, did a 'Le Mans' type start to the accompaniment of a shower of dust and raced for the reservoir.

Seconds were precious. The hounds could be on the stag at that very moment. Foot to the floor, change gear, foot to the floor, change gear, foot to the floor, change gear, all anchors on, slide to a halt, grab my camera and run. I ran and ran along a finger of land into the reservoir hearing the hounds baying like mad on the other side of the slight ridge. I ran up to climb over the wire and go over the ridge but paused to look round to see if any hunters had followed. The stag was behind me swimming strongly, near the middle of the reservoir some 200 yards away. I swung my camera up and photographed.

It is quite a feat for any cloven-hoofed beast to swim a reservoir, particularly when it has run several arduous miles beforehand. Anyone who has tried to swim a couple of lengths of their swimming baths with their fists clenched will know just how useful the open hand is. I looked at the stag and felt immense sorrow. The great creature was striking out bravely in a determined effort to live. His supreme efforts were fruitless though; the hounds were simply taken around the reservoir by road and were waiting for him to emerge from the water.

An audience of supporters formed up ahead of the stag and when he eventually landed and shook himself down they jeered him on his way as he was forced to run for his life again. The hounds were unleashed immediately so I knew the hunt would not last long. I turned back to the car and drove towards Luxborough, but I was well behind and it was all over before I arrived. I was told by an eyewitness that the stag was shot when he stumbled into a hedgerow and was unable to get through it. He was killed about 3.30p.m. Just a few hours previously that stag had cleared all such hedgerows with ease. His carcass suffered the usual indignities.

The meet of the Quantock Staghounds on March 19th was by invitation in Devon and Somerset country at *The Ship Inn*, Porlock. At the meet I sensed a great deal of suspicion towards me. I was in the discomforting position of being pointed out to other hunt followers by the senior hunt staff, but nothing was said to me directly.

The selected stag tried every trick he knew to elude the hounds. From the Parks he went out at speed up onto the moor towards Lucott Cross then over to Holnicote and back to Porlock, before going out towards the *Culbone Stables* pub. Then he headed towards the coast and back to Porlock. Knowing that he would by then be exhausted and looking to go to water, I waited by a likely stream in Porlock.

Some hounds arrived but there was no sign of the stag. Then I heard the remainder of the pack baying as they ran the high ridge behind me. I drove out from Porlock towards the sea at West Porlock. It was a common feature of stag hunting that exhausted deer would, if they reached Porlock, swim out to sea to escape the hounds. They were either left to carry on swimming until they drowned, or were chased by hunters in boats, brought back to the shore and killed.

Nowadays, perhaps because of the bad publicity that such incidents attract, the hunt takes measures to avoid it happening.

Nevertheless with the deer running strongly for the sea it looked likely to occur that day. I joined a long line of hunt cars parked just west of Porlock with the supporters all gazing intently up a grass slope towards a small covert. The hunt could be heard nearby. Suddenly the stag broke out of the covert and ran down the slope towards us. Reaching the hedgerow separating him from the road, he began to look for a gap to pass through, but supporters running down the road shouted, heading him back.

He ran back up the slope and encountered the pack piling out of the covert towards him. Turning about, he ran towards us but now there was no longer a spring in his step. He headed for the corner in the hedgerow some 100 yards in front of me, beside the road.

The hounds were right behind snapping at his heels. Motorcyclists ran forward over the grass to try and grab him. He reached the hedgerow and tried to clear it with one mighty, desperate leap. Earlier in the day, he would certainly have done so, but by this stage after some five hours of hard running, exhaustion had taken its toll. His front feet pecked at the hedge top, his whole body swung over on to the road and he never moved. His neck was broken in an instant. The keen hunters felt cheated.

Following that incident I spent two days with the Quantock Staghounds in April. The first from *The Blue Ball*, Triscombe on April 26th there was no kill, despite the fact that the hunt continued until 6.45p.m. The second day started from *The Carew Arms*, Crowcombe on Friday 30th April and was more successful.

The stag was quickly away over Robin Upright's Hill. He then ran over the moorland towards the League sanctuary at Alfoxton. Instead of staying in the safety of the sanctuary he ran on to the peaceful village of Kilve that had made the headlines earlier in the year after the bloody killing of a hind in the garden of a tea shop. Circling away from Kilve, I saw the young stag running on the edge of the moor in company with three hinds. Entering a tiny copse the three hinds ran on, while the stag doubled back. This manoeuvre split the pack, half

113

going with the hinds and half returning with the stag. I predicted that the stag would swing north towards a holiday camp and the sea and I headed in that direction. When he failed to do so I lost him.

When contact is lost at such a late stage in the hunt, as the hounds are closing in, it is best to go round to the known killing points. I visited Weacombe, Kilve, and Holford, three such killing sites where small streams come off the moor, but I found no sign. Later I was told by riders that the stag was killed on the side of Longstone Hill, high on the moor at about 2.30p.m.

Spring stag hunting in the 1982/83 season was limited for me by my concentration on fox and hare hunting. The meet of the Tiverton Staghounds at Benley Cross on February 26th, by the date, should still have been hind hunting, but mercifully for the females it was changed to Spring stag hunting. The reason was because the hounds had been inactive for about two weeks due to the frost. There are always slight problems entailed in switching the pack from hunting one sex to the other because of the difference in scent, so, after the long lay-off, the hunt opted for the immediate change to Spring stag hunting.

There was extra interest in this hunt because I was guiding in a reporter — Maureen Lawless of the *News of the World* — to see the truth about this pastime. We had calculated that it might immediately blow either of our covers if she was seen in my car. So the League's Promotions Manager, Jim Barrington, a man with extensive knowledge of hunting, was brought in to help.

We would stay completely separate and never talk. But they would stick close to me as I knew the back routes and the likely places for the kill to occur. At the meet another League employee, the Sanctuaries Manager John Hicks, turned up to warn the Hunt Masters to keep off the League's sanctuaries in the area.

Hounds were taken to draw woodland north of Affeton Moor and a magnificent young stag was soon away running down towards Chawleigh and the A379 near Eggesford Station. The hounds were well behind at this point, so far in fact that the supporters took over the hunting — like Indian trackers they were on their hands and knees trying to slot the stag (follow his hoof-prints). Other followers sighted the stag and the hunt veered away south of Chawleigh towards the bridge at Stone Mill. In the water the stag paused to gain a second wind then headed out eastwards again.

Following in the wake of what was rapidly turning into a frantic dash, I encountered a menacing looking farmer on a tractor with a high powered rifle. He made clear his dislike for hunt followers — such as he took me to be. This is one of the many areas in which the

114

hunters are distinctly unwelcome and the farmers will go to great lengths to protect their land. I would have dearly liked to have told the farmer exactly who I was and what I was doing, but to do so would blow my cover.

We wound our way back towards the meet at Benley Cross and it seemed for a time that the hunt had lost the stag. Such an event might actually have pleased some of the followers, several commented on what a magnificent creature he was and that he should be left to breed to produce strong stock.

Sadly though there is no room for such sentiment in stag hunting. The quarry was observed slipping away by an alert follower and betrayed by the white handkerchief raised to attract the hunt. The hounds closed in as the tiring stag headed for the wood from whence he had originally started. Knowing that the end was near I indicated to Jim and Maureen to stick particularly tight to me as I raced for the front of the hunt column.

We arrived at one corner of the wood just in time. The stag crossed the road in front and jumped the fence into the grass field with the hounds baying, barely 30 yards behind. I swerved to a halt, cranked off some photographs and saw Jim and Maureen just behind me. Before allowing our cars to be boxed in by the supporters that were flooding in I had to predict whether the stag would run on further or, exhausted, die there and then. When he veered right-handed into the woods I knew.

Gesturing to Jim and Maureen to follow me I ran up the roadside. The blood-curdling baying started, and I knew that the hounds were on the stag. Hunt supporters were whooping with glee. I ran up the road and into the wood through the first gate. There was a deep muddy marsh that I had to wade through and my left wellington became hopelessly stuck. The baying was now reaching a crescendo. There was no time to attend to such minor problems, so I simply ran out of it, carrying on in my sock. One boot on and one boot off I ran and ran and stumbled into a partial clearing. The stag was standing there alone, bewildered and terrified. The hounds were all around him baying frantically and those to his rear attacking his flanks. To the right, one of the riders, now on foot, was snapping home the cartridge in the shotgun. I whipped my camera up, snap focussed and pressed the trigger at the instant I heard the bang.

The beautiful creature shuddered under the impact of the heavy pellets and fell dying into the hounds who soon engulfed him. Careful to be inconspicuous (I did not want to lose that valuable picture) I slipped out of the wood back to the road where I found a group of yokels staring amusedly at my half submerged wellington boot protruding from the muddy pond.

I looked for Jim and Maureen but they had entered the wood from another direction. Maureen had been fortunate enough to witness the kill and Jim was also there taking photographs. Their eyewitness account of stag hunting appeared in the *News of the World* the following Sunday week.

Earlier in February, when the hunting was impaired by frost, Jim, Maureen and I went to rearranged meets of the Devon and Somerset Staghounds.

The first, on February 15th, was at *Culbone Stables*, a well-known hunting pub on the coast, west of Porlock. We travelled in convoy to the vicinity of the meet but then, knowing that by that time I was under suspicion, we separated, allowing the slow hound-van to trundle in between our cars.

I swung into the car park opposite the pub, to the glare of watching hunters. Joint Master Norah Harding approached me: "*There's no hunting today,*" she said. "*But I checked with the kennels and they directed me here.*" I replied. She was emphatic: "*This is a private meet, we do not want visitors, will you please leave!*" With that I apologised and drove off.

Norah then went over and welcomed Jim and Maureen. When they asked if they should leave also, she said: "*Oh no, you're welcome. We just don't like him about as he takes too many pictures.*"

My colleagues soon realised that far from being a normal hunt this was in fact a Deer Drive. They then understood why the hunters were so secretive. Such shoots to cull deer are always denied in hunting circles.

At such events hounds are used to locate the deer herds which are then driven forward towards lines of hunters waiting with shotguns. The shooting is hit and miss. Many deer limp away wounded to die in agony. That the hunters deem these drives necessary amply demonstrates their own inability to control deer numbers by hunting.

The following week, February 22nd, I went with my colleagues to another such drive organised by the Devon and Somerset Staghounds, starting from Court Place, Porlock, but again it was so secretive that I was made distinctly unwelcome.

I later learned from Jim and Maureen that in the course of these two drives the hunters had gaily blasted away with shotguns at many deer, killing several.

CHAPTER EIGHT
Fox hunting

"Ethically it is wrong to inflict unnecessary suffering for the gratification of a mere thrill, and for that reason fox-hunting is a disgrace to the civilization of a country that permits it, and a reflection on the mentality of the people who take part in it. To contend that it provides employment is to put it on a level with crime and lunacy, for which the same thing could be said. The work and trade associated with the sport could be put to more productive and creative use." (*The Farming Ladder*. George Henderson. Pub. Faber and Faber Ltd. 1944. Page 20)

Whilst in the West Country following the stag hunts I also took every opportunity to follow the local packs of foxhounds.

My extensive experience as a hunt saboteur prepared me well for my undercover work amongst fox hunters. It also taught me that fox hunting exists on three distinct levels. There is the glamorous image, the one that is portrayed in the books and articles that the hunters are so keen to distribute.

Then there is the side that is usually seen by hunt saboteurs and anyone else who is prepared to follow and closely observe. Though such observers will see hounds work and maybe even foxes killed the hunters will always behave in guarded fashion.

The third level is the true fox hunting — the inner sanctum to which only the most trusted supporters have access. This is the cruel, brutal, private conflict between huntsmen, terriermen and fox that takes place away from prying eyes and out of sight of the mounted field.

I knew this savage reality lurked behind the glossy facade and I was determined to infiltrate, to expose it.

To first gain access to the trusted minority I ran the gauntlet of searching questions. I had to draw on all my experience of hunting with various packs to produce an impeccable hunting pedigree to match the inner core of the hunting set who are born and bred to their sport.

Strangers are seldom welcomed at hunts with, *"Who are you?"* but rather, *"Who do you hunt with?"* Such diehards never move from place to place — they move from hunt to hunt.

Choosing at random a hunt as reference was no use as for any named hunt there was nearly always either a member of the hunt staff or a follower who knew something about your chosen hunt and could ask testing questions.

To start with I found that my credentials as being a known follower of the local stag hunts stood me in good stead. Acceptance to the inner circle was not a matter of being given a special pass that allowed me through where others were blocked. Rather, when I arrived the hunt staff and terriermen would exchange nods and winks and carry on as usual despite my presence.

The best guide as to whether I was accepted was the attitude not of the riders but of the terriermen. The hunt riders expect their fun as much as anyone and if that fun depends on the fox being thrown live to hounds or released from sacks then so be it, but if the presence of a strange face means that none of this can happen they will happily put up with it, hide their feelings and keep on smiling. Most riders are of course unaware of such goings on anyway.

For the terriermen it is different. They know full well what is required and make quite clear their displeasure if the presence of strangers constrains their behaviour.

I was able to gain the full trust of three West Country fox hunts — the Dulverton West, the Tetcott and the South Tetcott. At these hunts I was totally accepted. Their terriermen behaved as normal whereas at the other fox hunts I visited, the terriermen were far more guarded.

Safe in the inner sanctum I was not only allowed to watch but also to photograph. I was able to record some of the most callous, calculated, cruelty to wildlife imaginable.

Just as the stag hunting calendar is divided up across a hunting season so is the fox hunting one. There is a difference in that in fox hunting it is according to the age not sex of the quarry. Fox hunting starts with the training process, the hunting of young cubs in the summer.

CUB HUNTING

The process by which foxhounds are trained to hunt as a pack and to kill — cub hunting — is vital for fox hunting. It is however usually overlooked by those followers whose only interest is in riding and is always ignored by hunt apologists in debates about the cruelty of fox hunting.

The public are generally unaware of the tremendous turnover of hounds that occurs every year. Foxhounds are lucky if they last five hunting seasons in the pack. Each year the hunts kill many hundreds of hounds all of whom have to be replaced by a new intake.

Recruits for the pack are given preliminary training when walked as puppies by keen hunt followers. They are entered to their hunting

118

life in cub hunting so as to be settled in before hunting proper starts early in November.

To give the longest time for training cub hunting starts as early as possible in the summer, typically as soon as the corn is cut. Techniques vary according to the hunt country.

In some areas the coverts are 'held-up' — a practice whereby a wood or copse known to provide a home for a vixen and cubs is completely surrounded by riders and foot followers. The pack, a mixture of inexperienced puppies and older hounds draws through the covert and any foxes that try to escape are chased back in.

Thus trapped, the young cubs are easily caught. The hunters hope that the new puppies will be involved in the fury of the kill and the worrying of the carcass and will learn the art of hunting.

Cub hunting curiously is also a means of training foxes. Those that are so petrified that they run in headlong terror are often allowed to go. The hunters judge that having learned to fear the horn and the baying of the pack those foxes will provide good 'sport' when the hunt returns later in the season.

No less a hunting expert than the Duke of Beaufort confirmed the nature of cub hunting in his book as follows:-

"The object of cub-hunting is to educate both young hounds and fox-cubs. As was said earlier, it is not until he has been hunted that the fox draws fully on his resources of sagacity and cunning so that he is able to provide a really good run....I try to be out cub-hunting as often as possible myself, and the ideal thing is for the Master to be out every day....Never lose sight of the fact that one really well-beaten cub killed fair and square is worth half a dozen fresh ones killed the moment they are found without hounds having to exert themselves in their task. It is essential that hounds should have their blood up and learn to be savage with their fox before he is killed." (Fox-Hunting. The Duke of Beaufort. Pub. David & Charles. 1980. Pages 68-69)

In many areas the terrain renders it impracticable to 'hold-up' the coverts. Instead the hounds are simply cast forward, hunting in the usual manner, the only difference being that steps are taken to avoid prolonged hunts after old foxes.

Whatever the method, cub hunting takes place when the scent is best. This is in the early morning or late in the afternoon before or after the heat of the summer sun.

I attended my first cub hunting in full undercover role at the meet of the Dulverton West Foxhounds at Mockham Down Gate, near to their kennels on Monday August 24th 1981. The start was at 7.00 a.m.

119

The meet was certainly a picturesque sight with the rising sun gradually gnawing away the mist that clung to the tall summer grass. After a brief display at the meet the hounds were away. There was no question of 'holding-up' the coverts here; the hounds were simply cast forward as normal.

Foxes old and young were soon running in all directions and it was not long before the pack locked on to hunt one cub. As the hunt progressed I found it difficult to keep up on foot over the hilly terrain. I learned later that the youngster was quickly forced to ground, dug out and killed.

When I was next with this pack at Burcombe Hill near South Molton on October 5th the passing of summer had enabled the meet to start at 10.00 a.m. Hounds drew some woodland first and I had a good view of two cubs escaping before the hounds settled on a third and pursued him south across the river.

When they returned I observed an old fox, way ahead of the pack, making his way through a flock of sheep on the opposite hillside. The fox took no interest in the sheep nor did they in him. The owner of the land standing near to me remarked to other supporters: "*It's amazing you know, we have plenty of foxes here, the sheep are in the open, yet we have never lost a single lamb to a fox.*"

This tiring fox took refuge in a badger sett that the landowner confirmed was unoccupied and was left.

Two weeks later these same hounds met at West Buckland near Barnstaple. I knew the area having spent some time following staghounds there. The day was foggy and exceedingly wet.

I spent much of the morning in a wood being drenched whilst the hounds chased foxes in every direction and readily changed from one to another. Changing quarry is a common fault of hounds; it greatly reduces their chances of catching anything as of course they tire.

To prevent it happening in fox hunting efforts are made to recognise the chosen victim. Some foxes are particularly dark, others light, some are large, some small and some have particularly white brushes, others not so.

On well-supported hunts conducted in open country where the fox can be viewed many times, if the hounds are at fault for changing they can soon be put right. However there are many small hunts such as the Dulverton West that operate in hilly, wooded country. On a good day such hunts may only attract 15-20 riders and about 20 car followers so there are few about to correct the hounds. In the classic case of changing, the foxes run in relays. One fox flees in a great wide circle then returns to where he started from and goes to ground. A second fresh fox then pops up, repeats the circle and returns for either a third fox to take over or the first one to do a second circuit.

Thus pursuing hounds are run to exhaustion and catch nothing. Hunting pundits anthropomorphise on this, putting such behaviour down to superior vulpine cunning, but the more likely explanation is the obvious one — exhausted foxes return to their homes and seek sanctuary underground, whilst fresh foxes readily run if disturbed by the pack.

It takes a good hound indeed to lock onto the scent of one fox and mark him to ground when another fox is running in front of him — as with all dogs, hounds prefer the excitement of a chase to merely barking at holes.

All in all it was not surprising that the Dulverton West were changing foxes frequently that morning. Eventually a rider approached me searching for the terriermen as the fox had been marked to ground.

The exhausted fox had sought sanctuary in an earth and the hounds were baying at the entrances to mark the spot. A fox running to ground is most unwelcome in hunting as the chief attraction of the sport is a high speed pursuit with the followers at full gallop.

Many hunts, particularly the more fashionable ones, will take precautions to prevent foxes hiding in this way. Before the meet the terriermen and others block all the known earths and drains in the area, often with fertiliser bags filled with rubble.

This practice has long been criticised by conservationists and naturalists as it disturbs other wildlife, particularly badgers. All too often whilst the holes can be blocked with enthusiasm there is far less enthusiasm shown for unblocking those same earths after the hunt has finished.

With their fox to ground hunters are faced with three choices. They can give it best and search for another. They can bolt it by leaving the holes open, putting terriers in to chase the fox out and resume their hunt, or they can dig it out and kill it.

Knowing that the Dulverton West have a reputation for killing foxes below ground I clutched my camera to my chest and battled through the densely matted bracken to reach the scene. The hounds were scrabbling furiously at the steep hillside with only the Master, Bertie Hill and the Huntsman, Terry Beeney, armed with a small calibre pistol, in attendance.

The earth was soft and it appeared that the hounds might catch hold of the fox themselves before the terriermen arrived, but the latter reached the scene, sliding down the bank armed with two Jack Russell terriers and a whole battery of tools.

One terrier was entered to the earth and from the frantic tone of his barking I knew he had located and trapped the fox. The top of the earth was dug away forcing the fox further and further back until his retreat was cut off by a well-positioned spade. Terry then reached inside, gun in hand. The shot was muffled by the damp earth.

Bertie had been restraining the hounds but he released them and they surged forwards. The muddied, bloodied and dead fox was dragged out by the scruff of his neck, blood streaming from the wound to his head and thrown down the slope. He soon disappeared beneath the melee of hounds. Terry took hold of his hunting horn and blew the kill.

That was Monday October 19th. At the end of the week on Friday the 23rd the same pack met in the heart of Exmoor at the *Royal Oak*, Withypool. Mingling with supporters I savoured typical West Country hospitality in the form of a particularly large stirrup cup. This was one of those days when the foxes had the beating of the pack by running in relays. The hounds were heartily confused.

The following week, Friday October 30th, from another meet at Burcombe Hill it was a different story. Hounds drew first in woodland south of Holridge, but this time they were unsuccessful.

They were taken further on and eventually found. With the scent excellent they pressed this fox hard and he only just made it to the sanctuary of the badger sett but, unlike at the previous meet here, this fox was not left. The terriermen arrived at the scene and every hole was blocked bar one. With the prospect of a lengthy dig the hunt moved on.

As nearly always happens the riders lacked either the patience or the stomach to linger and witness their adversary despatched, preferring instead to gallop off in search of other prey. Only the elderly Master, Fred Smythe, remained to supervise proceedings. A terrier was entered to the open hole and the fox quickly located.

Part of the standard hunt digging equipment is a long steel bar that is pushed into the soil at various points searching for tunnels. When a tunnel is pierced the diggers listen at the hole, straining to catch any sounds of the terrier and fox fighting below — that is the old-fashioned way of locating the adversaries. The modern method is to use electronic devices attached to the terriers' collars in conjunction with small loudspeaker boxes that bleep or click when held above the collar — a sort of underground sonar. The Dulverton West use both methods.

This exhausted fox was gauged to be trapped in a narrow passage that ran for some 10 yards. However, the terriermen were puzzled as, when a dog was put in at either end, it bayed.

When baying, terriers hang back from the fox and exchange barks and other threats and only attack when the opportunity arises. If a terrier is put to earth and encounters the backside of a fox that cannot turn round however it will certainly attack, grabbing the fox's brush and trying to drag it out. The ensuing grunting and growling is totally different to baying.

If the terrier bays no matter which end of the tunnel it is put in it usually indicates that the fox can turn round but in this case the tunnel was too narrow to allow such manoeuvring. The hunters chose one end, entered one terrier and progressively dug the roof of the tunnel back and back, advancing towards the baying. The terrier was fighting, returning to the mouth of the tunnel to show the bloody proof of combat, deep wounds to its nose and mouth.

When first exposed the fox had locked jaws with the terrier and was wedged to one side. A long spade was jammed in the tunnel behind him blocking his retreat. The brush was hooked with the iron bar and grabbed, pulling the fox forward on his back. The terrier was then pulled off and away and the live and panting fox pinned to one side with the spade.

The pistol was loaded and its long barrel pointed at the fox's head. As expected, the fox bit it. The terrierman then thrust the muzzle forward into the fox's mouth cutting it badly.

By then the fox was helpless. He was held by his brush and both back feet. A second spade was thrust into his chest to prevent him biting at the hands that restrained him. He was then goaded with the gun muzzle.

The terrierman kept saying: "*Want some food? Want some food? Get a mouthful of this!*" as he thrust the muzzle into the fox's jaws.

Eventually, he was careless and the fox nearly bit him. Retaliation was a single shot between the eyes that ended the vulpine suffering. The carcass was pulled out and dumped on the grass bank in front of the Master who had observed the whole proceedings.

Thinking that the complex of earths might hold other foxes a terrier was put in again to search the tunnels and immediately bayed. This explained the mystery. All along there had been two foxes fighting back to back — hence the terriers baying at either end of the tunnel.

Only twenty minutes were required to deal with this second fox. He too was goaded before being shot, the iron bar and gun being jabbed into the terrified creature's face. The elderly Master had challenged me for taking photographs of these events asking who I was and my hunting credentials but several of the terriermen recognised me from stag hunting days and vouched for me. I had entered the inner sanctum. With no hounds in the vicinity to break up the foxes their carcasses were taken away in sacks.

That was 1981 cub hunting. The following year I again took an interest following whenever the staghounds were not meeting. On Friday August 27th 1982, I was out with the Dulverton West for evening cub hunting at 4.00p.m. at Worth Farm, Withypool. The late Ronnie Wallace (1919-2002), formerly of the Heythrop Foxhounds, later Master of the Exmoor Foxhounds and his former colleague Tony Collins, at the time Kennel Huntsman to the Heythrop, were both there.

Immediately recognising them from days of sabotaging the Heythrop Foxhounds some six years earlier I knew that I had to be careful. But whereas I was on maximum alert they thought they were amongst people who were all hunting friends. Even though they looked straight at me they cannot have recognised me as they ignored me.

The hounds drew first in the immediate vicinity of the farm and were soon away after an old fox. Surprisingly, considering it was cub hunting, he was hunted. He dodged in and around some marshland before being marked to ground in a flooded hole beneath a hedgerow. The foot followers, terriermen and Huntsman Terry Beeney all gathered around. The riders and hounds went to look for another victim. When the terriers were first entered there were immediate sounds of fighting, then silence. We could smell the fox ourselves but despite extensive excavations no further trace could be found. They reluctantly had to give that fox best, presuming that it had either slipped away in the tunnel system, or possibly even crept away unnoticed through the dense foliage of the late summer hedge line.

The day ended at about 7.30p.m. with no kill recorded — but the terriermen were confident that their dogs had gained sufficient hold on that one fox to injure it severely.

Early in October I switched hunts to follow the Tiverton Foxhounds from their meet at Queen Dart Cross on Monday the 4th. Connoisseurs of hunting regarded this as being one of the sharpest fox hunting packs in the country.

Huntsman Bob Street was on foot with his hounds when they drew through crops beside the Little Dart River. The pack stumbled upon one cub and after a short chase he was killed. In my eagerness to gain a closer look I waded across the river, but only succeeded in filling both my wellingtons with water which retarded my progress significantly and gave watching hunt followers much amusement.

The hunt had 30 couple out (60 hounds) and they certainly were an impressive sight in full flight. It seemed a particularly uneven contest as even an adult fox is less than twice the size of an average tom cat. By contrast I saw only five riders including two hunt staff and about ten foot/car followers. Clearly for all its supposed quality this pack is poorly supported.

Hounds soon found plenty of foxes. One was marked to ground. I went to watch the dig-out but, as it was my first time with this hunt, the terriermen were very suspicious of me. I did not push my luck, did not try to get too close and only learned later that the fox was killed. With the abundance of foxes the pack readily split. Early in the afternoon some of the hounds were even more 'naughty' when they rioted on a hare. Rioting is to be expected in hounds that seldom kill and are in consequence bored but this pack had killed six cubs just the previous Saturday and one that very morning with another marked to ground.

The next morning, the Tuesday, I changed hunts again to follow the Tetcott Foxhounds at Wainhouse Corner near Bude. At the meet I recognised many of the followers as being supporters of the Devon and Cornwall Minkhounds so I benefited from their introduction. I was vouched for and accepted unlike the previous morning.

Almost immediately a cub was put up from amongst a field of kale and after a short chase torn to shreds. Fox hunts usually make a bee-line for kale fields as they are notorious for holding foxes. When drawing them the hounds make an amusing sight with only their tails visible except for when they rear up on their hind feet to see where they are.

After the kill the heavens opened. In the deluge of rain the hunting was extremely slow. I foraged ahead and found a good vantage point from where I could hear the hounds working towards me. They bayed excitedly for a moment but before reaching my position marked their fox to ground. I could tell because the baying was at a crescendo but stationary. As I had seen no terriers in attendance I expected the fox to be left but the Master, Peter Hunkin blew repeatedly on his horn as if to summon the terriermen. I drove round to see what was happening.

I arrived to find the riders disconsolately galloping up and down a grass field. I enquired about the location of the earth and they directed me to a small copse in the valley bottom where the foot followers were gathered.

Activity centred on a large badger sett and excavations were in progress. There were terriers present — one was to ground with Peter tracking his position by the bleeper on his collar. As Peter moved the receiving box over the ground it emitted various clicks according to whether it was above the dog, or not.

For all the keenness in the hounds that were biting and chewing the very soil to get at their quarry the terrier was singularly unwilling; it kept coming out. This dog apparently belonged to a local follower. It did not impress Peter and he eventually sent someone back to the hound van for the two hunt terriers. When these arrived a small white dog was entered and quickly bayed the fox.

The dog was tracked as it forced the fox back in the tunnel. The tunnel roof was dug off and eventually the fox was trapped in one corner. There was no escape, it could retreat no further. I knelt down and looked into the remaining tunnel. The terrier was barking and snapping at the bleeding, terrified fox which was pressed back into the furthermost extremes of its muddy tomb.

Spades were wedged in to secure the live fox and the terrier was pulled off. Peter took the gun, reached into the hole and fired. As the fox still struggled he thought he had missed so the gun was re-loaded but it was not necessary, those were its death-throes.

The torn carcass was pulled out. Peter held it and shook it in front of the hounds, whipping them into a frenzy of expectation. When they seized the body they fought over it and tore it to shreds. The brush, mask and pads of this old dog fox were rescued from the canine maelstrom and kept as trophies. I later found them adorning the landowner's tractor.

That was Tuesday October 5th. Two days later on the 7th the meet of the same hounds at Morwenstow on the coast north of Bude was interesting for a reason other than a kill. Peter had hurt his hand so was relegated to foot following, his place being taken by Claud Harris his Huntsman. Claud spent most of the day at loggerheads with the 2nd Whipper-in — Loveday Miller — and the hunting suffered accordingly. With plenty of foxes about the pack split all over the place and when 2½ couple went missing I accompanied Peter and another supporter to the valley bottom to search for them.

The exertion of running down one slope and up the other had a marked effect on Peter's ability to blow his horn so he offered it to me to try. I was reluctant, fearing that my ability might make them suspicious, but then decided that if questioned I would explain that I had learned from a keen hunting friend. I was helping the hounds, not the hunt as, when the former riot and scatter, there is a very real risk of them being injured on the road.

So it was that with the Master's blessing a hunt saboteur ended up blowing the horn to attract hounds! One couple did eventually turn up, looking distinctly sheepish.

We returned these to Peter's transit van and went to look for the others via a private garden in the valley bottom. The owner stormed out demanding to know what we were doing. Our explanation that we were collecting hounds merely stoked his temper — he was emphatic that he did not welcome the hunt as they had done a lot of damage in the past.

Out of hunting pink Peter was not recognised as the Master and such was the man's temper that he had no inclination to admit his identity. Peter muttered some excuses and we carried on. Our search proved fruitless. We rejoined the hunt to find that the hounds had made their own way back anyway. The day ended at about 2.30p.m. with no kill.

The next morning, Friday October 8th, I was back with the Dulverton West Foxhounds at Willingford Bridge in the heart of Exmoor on a wet and overcast day.

The hounds ran well, pushing one fox out towards Worth Farm, site of their evening cub hunting meet earlier, but then losing his scent when he ran the road. Finding again they quickly locked onto this fresh fox. The scent was clearly good. He twisted and turned desperately trying to shake the pack off. The hunt moved steadily back towards the meet and eventually a very tired fox was marked to ground in an earth near the curiously named Clogg's Down. As always nearly all the followers stayed in the warmth of their cars, sipping coffee, gossiping and waiting for something to happen. I went over to watch the dig.

I saw a huddle of men and found the hounds scrabbling frantically at the earth, located in thick dying heather about 30 yards up a steep slope from a stream. One hunt terrier was battling with and holding the fox. The roof of the tunnel was dug further and further back until the fox could retreat no more.

The victim could be heard coughing and grunting. I wondered whether he would be goaded as I had seen happen previously, but no, the terrier was pulled to one side and the fox shot. The body was hurled down the hillside for the hounds to fight over; a move that showered one terrierman with the still warm blood that spurted from the gaping wounds to the fox's head. His mates joked at his discomfiture.

The fox's brush was rescued from the worry and the remains tossed into the stream. I was careful to observe where as I aimed to return for photographs. I helped with carrying the heavy tools back up to the Land Rover but then declined the offer of a lift to rejoin the hunt, offering the excuse that if I waited in the area they might well return anyway.

As soon as the Land Rover was over the brow of the hill and out of sight I crept back for photographs. The secret of undercover work of whatever form is to always appear to do the expected. It is certainly not expected that a genuine hunt supporter will wade around in a river to recover the torn body of a fox just to take a photograph. In doing so I knew that, if caught, my behaviour would take some explaining.

I was still searching for the remains when a Land Rover appeared on the slopes above me. I cursed, judged that I had been spotted and crossed the river continuing up the opposite hillside as if I was following the hunt as normal. Fortunately the Land Rover went on and I returned and managed to take the required pictures.

I found the hunters again later. They were in hot pursuit of a fox between White Post and Moorhouse Ridge. I headed for Molland Common and late in the afternoon, when it appeared more likely that they would blow for home, I heard the horn sound the three short blasts that indicated that a fox had gone to ground and that the terriers were needed.

Whilst the terriermen set off on a massive circle round by road I hiked straight over the moor and reached the earth before them. It was sited at the base of a hedgerow. The hounds however had beaten us all to the hole and had dragged the fox out themselves. These hounds had always appeared likely to do this as I had previously witnessed them digging feverishly at earths.

They had even succeeded in taking the brush — quite a feat as taking this trophy intact is an art. It usually necessitates the Huntsman ringing the bone with a knife at the base of the tail, forming a tight loop from baling string or the thong of a whip around the base and drawing the brush back and off.

By the behaviour of the hounds Terry suspected that there was a second fox in the earth so the terriers were put back in and confirmed it by immediately baying. I crossed through the hedge and found the hounds sitting like an impatient audience straining and staring at the hole.

The earth was shallow and the mud-caked fox was clearly visible. At one point he tried to escape but was barged back with spades. The terrier named Cricket, a notorious fox killer, was fighting with his

128

adversary, both creatures inflicting and receiving injuries. Periodically Cricket surfaced with deep cuts to his nose and mouth. After a while he gained a firm grip on a paw and the diggers dragged him back hoping that he would in turn pull the fox out. But Cricket lost his grip and ended up with only a mouthful of fur.

Terry summoned a hound and urged him into the hole to grab the fox but he refused to enter. A second hound was called but, although keener, it too was unable to retain a solid grip on the victim. Cricket was entered again and after a further lengthy battle managed to gain a hold on the fox's throat. The sounds of the fox choking and gurgling were dreadful but the supporters merely cheered Cricket on, "*Get him! Get him boy!*"

Terry had earlier boasted to me that Cricket could kill foxes in the tiniest of holes by worming up beside their trapped bodies until he reached the throat, then sinking his teeth in. I suspected that the unequal contest would not last long. Soon all that was audible from the hole were the sounds of Cricket. The supporters judged that the battered and bleeding fox was dead. Cricket was pulled back on to the muddied earth in front of the hounds, still locked onto the fox and the straining pack was unleashed. No effort was made to check that the fox was dead and, more surprisingly, no effort was made to pull Cricket to safety. Many onlookers said that the terrier was lucky not to be bitten by the hounds in the ferocity of the worry.

When the hounds had finished I grabbed the remains. I expected Terry to order the carcass to be thrown into the hedge and I knew that the best way to find it again would be if I threw it, which I did. Terry later blew for home and I left with them but then slipped back to retrieve and photograph the shattered fox body, building up my dossier of vital evidence against the hunting world.

I attended four more cub hunting meets in 1982. On October 27th I was with the Dulverton West at Croyde, a typically sleepy picturesque Devon village — and surfer's paradise — on the coast north of Barnstaple.

Though sunny, the strong wind, so welcome for surfers, made for appalling scenting conditions for the hunt. The hounds were unable to detect the line of a fox even when I watched as they crossed a field immediately after one. Consequently it caused some surprise when after a short, sharp chase they marked a fox to ground beneath some dense brambles.

The terriers were entered to this earth but despite a prodigious effort were unable to make any progress. The pack waited patiently straining to catch every sound. The hounds were a picture of close attention. Eventually the hunters gave up, gave that fox best and went to look for another — but without success.

The following morning, Thursday October 28th, I had an interesting time with the Eggesford Foxhounds meeting at Wixon Farm, Chulmleigh. Foxes were soon found in the woodlands lining the deep valleys adjacent to the farm but the hounds were distracted by deer.

At one point whilst I was with supporters on the slopes of a hill a terrified hind came towards us closely pursued by nine foxhounds. We let the hind pass safely then stopped the rioting hounds with a cacophony of shouting — quite the best I had heard since my days as a hunt saboteur!

I learned that elsewhere a fox was pursued to ground, bolted by terriers, hunted again but lost. My informant said that, considering the number of foxes in the area, that one should have been trapped and killed. However the diggers were suspicious that their terriers might be baying a badger rather than a fox so did not wish to trap anything.

He told me that terriermen have a great respect for the fighting qualities of cornered badgers and that ordinary fox terriers would suffer a severe mauling if pitted against one. He said that though the hunters could certainly assist their dogs with iron bars and spades it would be a poor public relations exercise for them to set about killing badgers in that fashion.

I recalled a stag hunt follower who had gleefully recounted to me in full graphic detail how a fox terrier had been skinned alive by a badger. I felt a trifle sick.

After helping the hind to escape and discussing foxes and badgers with a supporter I had lost touch with the hunt. I drove round and joined up with them as they headed south towards Chulmleigh. I opted to follow a man whom I recognised to be a keen stag hunter.

On the fringe of a large wood named Parsonage we observed a hind and yearling calf running together closely pursued by a group of foxhounds.

We moved in to stop this riot. As the deer passed between us we were able to divert and stop some of the hounds but not all — four couple still charged on in pursuit of the deer across Horridge Moor towards Kings Nympton.

The Huntsman came by labouring in pursuit of his wayward flock and told us that other elements of his pack had marked a fox to ground in a quarry near the wood. I reached the scene but too late, the fox was already dead, its body held in the terrierman's sack.

Later, when the rioting hounds were eventually brought back to the main pack, the dead fox was taken out, his brush cut off and the pack given the remains. The Huntsman then blew for home.

My last day's cub hunting with the Dulverton West Foxhounds was at Cuzzicombe Post on Exmoor on Friday October 29th. Hounds drew first a long combe out towards Molland but it was blank.

They were then taken to draw an area west of the meet. I accepted a lift with the terrierman. We arrived at the new location just in time to see a fox driven out of covert by the pack. He made a frantic dash up the adjacent grass slope and hunt riders galloped desperately to try and head him back. This was the nearest I ever saw to the practice of holding up coverts with the Dulverton West. Their inexperience at such tactics showed when the hunted fox reached the hedgerow and was away to safety.

Scenting conditions must have been appalling. When the hounds were brought up they failed to hit the line even though cast on precisely the same route the fox had taken. Perhaps after being coursed by the riders the fox had lost its scent. The hounds however persevered and were eventually able to pick up the line left by the fox on the plough on the other side.

Hunting was never brilliant though and to cap it all, from the enthusiasts' point of view, the only time hounds were on good terms and speaking well to the fox, Terry stopped them, thinking they were rioting on deer!

My last cub hunting of all was with an obscure little pack, the Mid-Devon Foxhounds meeting on Tuesday November 2nd at Caddiford Cross.

Though the hounds tried hard, this part of their country is full of deer and with plenty of foxes as well, the pack readily split. In the afternoon I found one couple completely lost on the road. The day ended at 2.15p.m., early because of their opening meet the following Saturday.

I had secured some graphic images of cub hunting. Back in the LACS headquarters in London they were locked carefully away in a vault ready for the moment we would present our evidence to the British public.

THE MAIN SEASON

The main fox hunting season starts early in November. By then the new entry of puppies have been entered and settled into the pack. The season lasts until March or April and in some areas even into May.

Inevitably some vixens that are hunted and killed from February onwards are pregnant or even nursing.

In the 1981/82 season I was concentrating mainly on deer hunting so I attended just four meets of the Dulverton West Foxhounds. Nevertheless, because I had been with them during their cub hunting and was a known follower of stag hunting I was completely trusted — even to the point of being driven round in the terrierman's Land Rover.

My first meet was on November 16th 1981 at Stoke Rivers, near to the hunt kennels. In the bright sunshine the hounds and red-coated followers made a most picturesque sight as they picked their way along valleys whose sides were clothed in golden, autumn bracken. It was an excellent day for foxes as none was killed and few were even chased.

It was then that I first realised what an inefficient hunting pack the Dulverton West were. Their hounds ran with all the eagerness in the world but they lacked something in terms of forward drive and speed. They seldom kill foxes above ground. In hunting parlance they are not very sharp.

In fact during two seasons following I only once heard of them catching a fox fairly above ground. When asked to explain this, the supporters said that in their opinion it is because the Kennel Huntsman Terry Beeney is too 'soft' with his dogs.

In most hunts there is a rigorous selection to ensure that the pack remains sharp but not too sharp. The aim is to breed hounds that work in a fashion that gives the fox a slight advantage in speed but no advantage in stamina — the ideal hunt being a brisk 40 minutes to an hour ending with the exhausted fox killed in the open and the riders enjoying a good gallop in pursuit.

If the hounds are too slow through breeding, poor exercise or age, they will be unable to press their foxes hard, will probably change foxes and most likely catch nothing, unless their quarry can easily run to ground.

The converse is equally a fault. If the hounds are bred with too much speed, being crossed with a sight hound such as a greyhound, they will be too fast, killing too quickly ever to be welcome in the hunting field.

It is clear that hound breeding and selection is a delicate balance. The subject is often debated in hunting circles. There are differing approaches. In the most callous, as many puppies as possible are bred but only the best are kept. This new entry sets the standard for the rest of the pack. Any that are not up to it, through age or injury, are killed.

Here from hunting literature are a couple of insights on this topic:-

"When asked the secret of his success, the greatest hound-breeder of all time, Lord Henry Bentinck, replied laconically, "I breed a great many; I put down a great many." His were the highest of standards, and even if he put down many hounds for the slightest fault—hounds that, with patience, might have proved themselves—Lord Henry did prevent what he thought were indifferent hounds from begetting their kind."

(*Come and Hunt*. The Hon. Charles Willoughby. Pub. Museum Press. London. 1952. Page 144)

"And how are you going to start drafting your hunting hounds? It has been said, somewhat humorously, that you should place a man behind a tree with a gun and tell him to shoot the leading two couples and the tail two couples, and there is something to be said for it!.......Before the war, in Leicestershire, a hound was regarded as too old to keep at five seasons." (*Fox and Hare in Leicestershire*. Eric Morrison. (Ex-Master, Westerby Basset Hounds, Joint-Master, The Atherstone Foxhounds). Pub. Eyre & Spottiswoode. 1954. Page 119)

Other more humane hunts such as the Dulverton West Foxhounds keep their hounds as long as possible. Puppies are bred only to fulfil requirements and any surplus hounds are drafted on to other packs, even to the other 'sports' such as mink hunting.

My next day with the Dulverton West was at Tarr Steps Post by the tumbling River Barle on November 27th. This was the day following my minor car crash during hind hunting and I was delayed by the need to arrange repairs.

I arrived to find the hounds thundering through the woods in full cry. They soon ran their fox to ground. The earth was almost inaccessible, located under a dense mat of brambles high on a steep slope that had us all scrambling and sliding to reach it. Sadly for the fox it was very shallow and he was quickly exposed and killed.

Hounds were taken on and, after a period of hunting in the vicinity of Shircombe, the terriermen beckoned me and gave me a lift to another dig-out. After a bumpy ride over farm tracks and through several fields we reached the scene — a badger sett located on a hillside open from trees but shrouded by bracken.

All the entrances were blocked bar one through which the terrier was entered. Normally a badger sett is a difficult dig but this fox must have made an early mistake and backed into a dead-end because he was soon trapped.

I crawled closer hoping to take some film of the kill but though they trusted me there was something significant about this earth for they shielded it from my view. The gun was fired and Terry called the hounds forward to a position down the slope.

As he whipped the dead fox out of the hole and hurled it towards the hounds I commenced filming with the movie camera. I then saw, out of the corner of my eye, Terry moving up the slope holding a struggling object. While the terriermen laughed I turned in time to see him throw a live fox into the bracken. He then holloaed, shouted and blew his horn to attract the hounds. They wheeled about from dismembering the first fox and charged up the hill in hot pursuit of the second.

The terriermen found it hilarious that Terry had been able to hold the struggling fox by the scruff of his neck and brush without being bitten. They told me that the fox had been 'done' in the hole to ensure that he left a better scent but at the time I had no idea what they meant.

As everyone clearly expected the hounds screamed away on an excellent scent. The fox was desperately twisting, turning and jinking but the pack had locked on and they pressed him inexorably. Only the intervention of darkness saved him. Hunting people are always quick to convince the naive that the fox is either killed instantly or escapes unscathed but here was one that, though alive, was far from unscathed at the end. It had been bitten by the terriers and 'done' by the Huntsman.

After those two November meets it was nearly two months later that I attended this hunt again at Newtown Bridge near South Molton on January 22nd 1982. This was a rearranged meet, the planned one, a joint meet with the Eggesford Foxhounds, having been cancelled due to snow. Hounds were taken to draw woodland west of the B3226 and then across into Molland wood. Once again I was offered and accepted a lift from the hunt terriermen.

In time an exhausted fox was run to earth in a shallow hole in a dense forest. During the dig I occasionally saw the terrified creature peering out of the tunnel, perhaps gauging whether to make a break for it. Declining that option he backed further and further into the tunnel. Eventually he could retreat no more and was cornered — backed up to the earth, grappling with terriers and wedged in with spades.

There was no escape. Once again the end was unnecessarily extended. Taking advantage of the privacy of the woodland the diggers jabbed their iron bar repeatedly into the fox's face before he was eventually shot.

The torn body was then tossed to the hounds and, when they had finished mauling it, the remains recovered and buried in the hole. The digging party then clambered back through the undergrowth towards their Land Rover. I was dismayed to see Anthony Adams standing by it.

Anthony, a former whip to the Heythrop Foxhounds was at that time Kennel Huntsman to the Exmoor Foxhounds but he later moved on as Huntsman to the Warwickshire. I recognised him immediately from my days operating as a hunt saboteur against the Heythrop. Would he identify me?

I took a deep breath and hoped for the best. I was fearful that if exposed as an anti I would be given a similar dose of the iron bar treatment. Fortunately he gave no obvious hint of recognition but it strained chance to the maximum when we returned to the main road with Tony and I sat huddled opposite each other in the cramped and cosy back of the Land Rover!

Hounds drew on and soon put up a really big fox that gained some small revenge for his kind. He ran a massive circle about a mile in diameter before returning right to where he had started. He then broke off the ring, ran off straight and left the hounds labouring on round for their second lap of the scent circuit. That fox escaped.

The following month, on February 26th at Hawkridge, not far from Tarr Steps Post, was my last meet with the Dulverton West that season. It was a most interesting and revealing day. Hounds marked their first fox to ground in a complex earth below one of those stone wall and hedgerow combinations that are so common in the West Country.

When the terriers were entered a really bloody battle ensued. Even the much vaunted Cricket came out streaming blood from fresh wounds. The fox may have been exhausted but he was securely lodged, protected by boulders and the hedgerow stumps and he fought like a pocket tiger. The smallest terrier was put in but quickly came out again.

To 'soften up' this valiant fox the terriermen reached for their iron bar. This was thrust into the hole and waggled vigorously but still the fox fought on gamely. Eventually the waiting riders became bored and the hounds were taken away to find another victim, leaving the terriermen to complete the job.

It took a good hour of solid digging, heaving and levering to manoeuvre out sufficient of the large boulders to uncover the fox. By then the hunt must have returned to the vicinity as some hounds showed up; attracted no doubt by the sounds of battle.

The fox was evidently exhausted. Half immersed in mud, wedged in by spades and boulders, he was savagely attacked by the terriers. He was defenceless and helpless. The dogs freely tore at his head and ears. The only mercy he ever received was the burning crack of the close range shot.

It was difficult to extricate the body but after a good deal of tugging the diggers succeeded. It was then revealed that their victim was not a 'he' but a 'she'. One of the terriermen rolled her lifeless body onto her back, pressed her stomach and gleefully remarked that he could feel her cubs.

No wonder she had fought so tenaciously. She was defending both the life inside her and the home she had chosen. It is a common fallacy put about by hunters that they grant foxes a safe close season to breed in. Hunters claim never to hunt pregnant or nursing vixens. This vixen was killed on February 26th just a few weeks before she would be expected to give birth.

In many areas hunting continues well into April and, in some, even into May. Hunting is stopped not out of deference to fox welfare but rather in response to the state of agriculture, the state of the ground and quite possibly to the lack of scent in the summer heat.

In the final act at this macabre scene some of the hounds moved in to worry the carcass of this vixen. When they had finished the torn remains were stuffed back in the hole and buried.

We then heard that the Huntsman was blowing for his terriers again. This fox had sought sanctuary in a very shallow earth on a steep wooded slope leading above a river. We left the Land Rover at the top of the ridge and walked the considerable distance down to the earth. Terry was at the hole and his Whipper-in John Norrish (later with the Devon and Somerset Staghounds) was holding the hounds in check. [In May 2012 68-year-old John Norrish was jailed for 4 years after being convicted of raping a 33-year-old woman after the Tiverton Staghounds hunt ball. (*Daily Mirror* May 22nd 2012)]

A terrier was put in one entrance of the earth and it was soon obvious that any dig would not last long. We could hear the two combatants bumping as they fought and jostled only inches below the surface.

I prepared my 35mm film and 8mm cine cameras. The roof of the earth, soft leaf-mould, was soon dug back exposing the brush and backside of the fox — another vixen.

She huddled ever deeper in the non-existent hole, desperate for protection. Her coat was beautiful; she can hardly have been pressed at all by the hounds. Heavy with cubs she must have gone straight to ground.

Terry grabbed hold of her brush and, taking care to wedge her in with spades to prevent her escaping, asked the watching terriermen for the gun. The word was passed from man to man but no-one had it. In their rush to reach the scene it had mistakenly been left in the Land Rover way back at the top of the hill.

One of the young lads volunteered to run back to fetch it but Terry said not to bother, that he would do it the old fashioned way. He turned to me sternly and said: *"Don't film this, no pictures at all!"* I was in no position to argue.

The hounds were positioned some 20 yards down the slope and the supporters gathered up the hill. The live and clearly pregnant vixen was drawn out from the tunnel by her brush and held struggling upside down. Desperately she kicked and twisted — trying to bite at Terry's legs — but her efforts were blocked by the iron bar.

Terry then whipped her up and, to the cheers of those watching, hurled her towards the hounds. Like a cat she span in the air to land feet first, but there was no access to mother earth as she landed amid the snarling pack. The briefest squeal and it was all over. She was torn limb from limb.

I bit my lip to contain my anger and swore that one day our nation would know the real facts about this pastime. That was two pregnant vixens dead in one day both killed in a singularly brutal manner.

Next season, 1982/83, the opening meet for the Dulverton West was at Yarde Down on the western edge of Exmoor on November 1st. It was a meet held in thick, eerie fog.

From the first draw near Beara Hill the hounds quickly found and flew away on a screaming scent. In the dense fog banks the hunt soon lost their hounds and they, in turn, lost their first hunted fox and split up after several others. Total confusion reigned. After much muttering and cursing the hunters eventually managed to gather a semblance of a pack and succeeded in pressing a fox hard enough to run him to ground.

I accompanied the terriermen in their Land Rover with the terriers Cricket and Mischief. Again after parking up there was a long hike to the earth. I arrived to find the usual digging party at the hole —

Kennel Huntsman Terry Beeney and Joint Master Bertie Hill. Mischief was put in first and immediately bayed. Next Cricket, the killer, was entered to get a hold on the fox.

The usual excavations began and the fox was trapped. When the arena was cleared and the fox exposed, it was seen to be locked in mortal combat with Cricket. Both were bleeding from their wounds. A spade was wedged between the two to separate them and Cricket pulled back to safety.

At that instant the fox made a final desperate bid for freedom surging forward. He was half clear of the earth before Terry stopped him by ramming a spade into his mouth, splintering his teeth.

A voice from the watching crowd enquired how the fox was doing. Terry replied with wry humour, "*He's biting on my shovel!*" The gun was loaded and with the fox hopelessly trapped it was an easy task to clear the mud from the target area. The muzzle was pressed to his skull, the trigger squeezed and further pain extinguished.

The carcass was thrown to the hounds and some supporters lingered until they had finished before moving in to claim the brush and pads as trophies.

After this opening meet I did not return to this hunt until after Christmas when I attended a Pony Club meet at West Molland, near South Molton on December 31st. As cub hunting introduces puppies to fox hunting so does the Pony Club introduce young children to the pastime. Pony Club meets help youngsters overcome their natural inhibitions against killing animals for fun.

Despite the meet taking place during the school holidays only a few attended. Those that did must have ended up feeling that even if they are not attracted by the humanity inherent in drag hunting at least it guarantees fun. It was a cold wet and misty day. The hounds split to hunt all over the place and the riders and staff were embroiled in total chaos.

As had become the norm I accompanied the terriermen. At one point we found the hounds hunting in dense fog, entirely on their own. We stopped them for their own safety, left one of the gallant Exmoor men standing in the pouring rain to guard them, then drove off hunting for the Huntsman. The day ended in mid-afternoon with no kill to my knowledge. However, it was anybody's guess what the hounds achieved when hunting all alone.

That was the Friday meet. The following Monday, January 3rd 1983, again with the Dulverton West Foxhounds, was at Gunn on the Barnstaple side of their country. The meet gave every indication of being a similar washout. In fact it turned out to be one of the most revealing of all.

There was torrential rain at the meet. Terry was suffering from a severe bout of flu, so instead of hunting hounds he accompanied the terrierman — Stan Richards — and me in the Land Rover. I was sad to learn that one of my favourite hounds, Gaylord, had been put down the previous day. This prompted me to ask Terry about the general age of the pack. He pointed out the two oldest, Primrose and Grasper, both 1975 hounds. Seven years is old for a pack hound, most are killed long before that.

From the meet we went for a stirrup cup to a nearby farm with the downpour continuing. Hounds were taken to draw woodland towards Hutcherton whilst we circled round and waited by the woods between Harford and Birch. In time a rider approached down the steep grass slopes and told us that the fox was to ground in the same large complex where, a few days previously, they had killed three. We drove as near as possible but even so had a long climb to the earth taking with us the terriers Cricket and Midge. The riders had blocked some of the many entrances but Terry asked for them to be cleared. Midge was entered. On Terry's instructions, we all kept well back to allow the fox to bolt; but no fox appeared.

The earth was massive and the fox was constantly moving up and down the underground passages as the terriers engaged him in sporadic fights and supporters tried to help by listening at the various entrances. However, no sooner had the sounds of combat been confirmed at one location and digging commenced than it promptly moved to another.

The mounted field again became bored and galloped off to hunt elsewhere. The departing riders told the digging party that if they did reach the fox they should holloa loudly and the riders would return.

Terry went to put Cricket in but, with that dog's fearsome reputation for killing he wanted the bleeper collar used to enable the dog to be tracked and the fox dug out before it was killed.

However, such devices commonly malfunction due to the abundance of mud and moisture at a dig. Despite trying several combinations of different batteries this one simply would neither bleep nor click.

So Cricket went in with no collar. He quickly bayed the fox and Terry rapidly dug down to the sounds of fighting. The fox was uncovered and Terry made a grab for the scruff of his neck but he was too slow, the fox bit his hand. Other diggers rallied to help and tried to prise the fox out of its partial tomb using the iron bar, but to no avail.

139

The fox squealed like mad with pain as the bar was levered against his body.

Cricket was barely visible throughout this. He was further down the tunnel, behind the fox, savagely attacking his brush and hindquarters. Under this combined assault from man and dog the fox flopped over exhausted.

Terry said that with so little life in him they would, sadly, have to kill him (they had the gun to hand). But when, a few moments later, he prodded the fox with the iron bar and he snapped back in response, he gained renewed hope that they might yet enjoy a hunt.

The earth area was further cleared and eventually Terry, jamming the fox's head back with his spade, managed to grab the scruff of his neck. He then pulled the struggling victim out grabbing him also by his brush.

Twisting the fox on to his back he bowed his head towards his backside. Doubtless out of sheer fear the fox urinated, dousing his hind legs and brush. He was then dropped into a waiting sack held open by Stan Richards and the others. "*Call the hunt!*" ordered Terry so everyone holloaed loudly. We waited for five minutes or more but neither hounds nor riders appeared. A young lad was despatched down the hillside to try and find them. Held captive the fox was grunting, kicking and struggling in the sack. Terry warned Stan to keep a tight grip on it.

Terry was in high spirits now and told the diggers to expect to see some real fun. He claimed that he had seen similar bagged foxes used many times by the Cheshire Forest Foxhounds.

The hounds were a long time coming. Stan was having great difficulty restraining the fox. When the pack did eventually appear, coming up the grass slope beside the covert that contained the earth, I feared that, like the previous spring when the pregnant vixen had been thrown live to hounds, Terry would again bar me from taking pictures.

I hung back hoping to escape notice but, when spotted, I judged it would be best to go right in. I did so with my camera prepared with film advanced but concealed. I stood near to Terry, with Stan higher up the slope holding the fox in the sack as the hounds, approaching from below, were urged on by the mounted field.

Terry shouted instructions: "*Release the fox Stan! Release it now!*" Stan fumbled to untie the knot around the sack. I moved towards him, my back to Terry and surreptitiously aimed my camera. The hounds were closing rapidly yet the fox was still confined, so Terry called to his Joint Master Bertie Hill to check the pack. Eventually, after frantic efforts, the sack was opened and Stan shook the fox out.

The fox was alone, exposed, defenceless and completely bewildered. He was muddied, wet, soaked in his own urine and had blood streaming from the wounds to his hindquarters and tail caused by bites from Cricket. He shook himself, saw and heard the baying hounds just 50 yards behind and set off up the hill, still looking confused.

This was the single most important photographic evidence of my whole two years of work. Jeering foot-followers sent the battered fox on his way as the entire mounted field, including both Masters, whooping and screaming, galloped past me. They had all seen exactly what had happened. The fox was released in open view in an open grass field — not out of sight from behind a hedge or in thick woodland.

The fox turned right-handed, desperate to return to the safety of his earth but was headed away by the terriermen. He tried again, running in a wider left-handed circle and managed to reach the wood but as he crept through the undergrowth towards his sanctuary the hunters moved in on foot beating the undergrowth to thwart him.

With every escape avenue blocked the fox swung about and set off towards Birch Farm. Bleeding and soaked in urine he must have emitted a scent that even the worst hounds in the world could track. On and on he went, twisting and turning as best he could but he had suffered crippling injuries. He made one last vain attempt to lose his scent on the road before being caught in a garden. In stark contrast to this fox the following field had a most enjoyable run.

We had lost touch with the hunt and only learnt of the final outcome from Bertie Hill when we found the hounds back in their transport box at about 3.15 p.m. The hunt officials were immensely pleased with the day. They felt sure that catching their fox in the open would encourage their hounds and improve their drive.

Terry had earlier informed me that scared foxes leave no scent so I questioned him as to this incident. "*Surely*," I enquired "*when the fox was in the sack it was terrified so why, when it was tipped out, did it leave such a strong scent?*"

He offered two reasons: firstly that it was 'blooding' i.e. dripping blood from the injuries inflicted by Cricket; secondly that it was soaked in urine.

I learnt that one or both of these factors are essential for the successful release of bagged foxes. Usually the fox will be 'blooding' anyway from the inevitable terrier bites but, if it is not, it is apparently the practice to cut it. As for urinating, the foxes are either squeezed head-to-brush as I had witnessed or have their stomachs gently stood on to provoke this. Connoisseurs of this technique assured me that dog foxes and vixens differ in their willingness to oblige.

When we returned from the earth to the Land Rover I noticed that no-one was carrying the sack. I enquired of Stan as to its whereabouts. He exchanged knowing looks with Terry and told me that it had been dumped in the earth. Presumably it is poor hunting form for a hunt to be found with a sack reeking of fox and full of fox hairs.

Here is the typically sanitised version of that day that was read by keen hunters. It is the meet report for the Dulverton (West) published in *Horse and Hound* on February 4th 1983:-

"On January 3, hounds met at Tree Beech and, in pouring rain, were taken to Gunn where Mr. and Mrs. Fordham gave a real welcome.

Hounds found in Hutcherton and marked to ground at the higher end of the wood.

They then drew on down the valley and it was a little time before a good holloa on Sandick had them running through Hutcherton Farm and down the valley towards Birch.

They swung right to Gunn and crossed the main road to Tree Beech. There, the fox doubled back over the main road and ran through the outskirts of the village. Hounds were running very fast and they caught the fox on Berry; a fast hunt without check, in yet another day of pouring rain and high wind." JACK SPRAGGON

[The *Sunday Independent* on November 27th 1983 printed some of my photographs of this incident and asked the hunters for their version of events. Asked about the image of him stood in the field holding the sack with the fox near his feet Stan Richards claimed that by pure chance the fox was running past him from the earth and he was waving his bag full of tools at it.

Terry Beeney had his say in the *Times* on October 23rd 1983: *"Mr Terence Beeney, huntsman with the West Dulverton pack, which hunts in north Devon, said of the alleged release of a bagged fox: **"We just would not do such a thing. It is his (Mr Huskisson's) version and his word against those of so many. He came out with us all last season and we took him to be a friend".***

Michael Gabbert, the Editor of the *Sunday Independent* was particularly determined to pursue this case. I had recovered the sack that had been used by Stan Richards and the *Sunday Independent* sent the sack to a Public Analysts' Laboratory for scientific analysis. Inside the sack the laboratory found 'short, light-coloured hairs' from a fox. The laboratory chief's report concluded: *"I am drawn to the conclusion that the state of the sack is not inconsistent with it having*

142

held a fox for a matter of a few minutes." (*Sunday Independent* December 4th 1983)]

Following that meet in January 1983 I had just four more days with the Dulverton West, the first was a fortnight later on the 17th at Hunstone Cross. Hounds ran well despite a poor scent and soon marked their fox to ground beneath a hedge bank. The terriers were entered to the tunnels and Terry said that he could hear the grunts and growls as they battled with the fox.

This earth was immense and complex, consisting of both high and low level tunnels. When the terriers lost their hold the fox simply disappeared. True to form the waiting mounted field became bored and galloped off to hunt elsewhere leaving Terry and his eager team to finish the job.

A determined effort was made to reach their quarry. New holes were dug and the bank probed at every likely site but there was no sign of Mr Fox. To facilitate a more aggressive assault the barbed wire fence was cut down but even so, after an hour's hard effort, Terry reluctantly had to give this fox best.

He assumed that the fox had either slipped away unnoticed or else was laid up in some high level underground chamber that had inadvertently been blocked during the dig. Either way although the fox was alive it was certainly not unscathed — both terriers had been bitten and the diggers were confident that they had inflicted similar injuries on their adversary.

We rejoined the hunt to learn that they had found two further foxes but both had escaped when the pack split. I overheard Stan describing to some riders in graphic detail the 'great fun' that had been had with the bagged fox at Gunn. The only regret that they expressed was that they had not been there to savour it.

That was the Monday meet. Two days later on January 19th from the *Fox Hunters Inn* at West Down, north of Barnstaple, the same hunt had a day of extremely fast hunting that was more reminiscent of hunting in Leicestershire. The scent was excellent enabling the pack to press their first fox extremely hard. The hounds were only thwarted when the fox ran onto land where hunting was banned.

Returning to the original draw the hounds were cast again and soon found again. This second fox ran like a rocket towards Muddiford with the hounds screaming in his wake. There ensued the fastest hunt I ever witnessed with the Dulverton West. It was a very private battle fought out between fox and hounds. One against many; wit and speed pitted against brute force and stamina. The battle ranged up and down the hillsides, over roads, through streams and back again; into sheep foil, over walls; in fact through nearly every trick in the fox's repertoire.

Struggling to find and pass through gateways the followers and riders were soon left far behind but the hounds coped all too well on their own. As the fox jinked, so the hounds checked, but cleverly they cast themselves forward and back and soon regained the line. On and on we sped for mile after mile. It was more like a stag hunt.

We by-passed a massive plantation and were watching the hounds disappearing into the distance when Terry caught up with us, his horse lathered in sweat. He explained that the hounds had in fact killed near the plantation but had immediately found again and were hunting another. He was ebullient because an eyewitness had told him that the fox had been bowled over in the open and had been heard squealing as it fought the hopeless fight with the leading hounds.

The hounds locked on to their third fox of the day and with the scent excellent the end was virtually a foregone conclusion. When exhausted this fox went to ground and was dug out and killed. 'Home' was blown. The horses were totally exhausted.

Completing the week with the Dulverton West on Friday 21st the hounds met at Lower Fyldon, again at the Barnstaple end of their country. Scent once more was excellent. Despite embarking on a most ambitious circle the first fox, unable to elude hounds, was forced to ground and killed. The most memorable feature of the dig-out was that when the fox was shot it was so totally entombed in mud that no man could pull it out. After much trying the full pack were unleashed to complete the task. They managed with ease.

My last day with the Dulverton West was some two months later on March 28th when the meet, though advertised at Twitchen was changed to Withypool Cross. I accepted a lift with the three terriermen, Stan, Roy and Dave. Hunting was brisk in the morning with several foxes about, one of whom was soon marked to ground.

By that time in my hunting career, after the mink hunting episodes, my cover was wearing exceedingly thin so it was an unpleasant surprise to encounter Barry Evans, a stalwart supporter of the Three Counties Minkhounds also following these hounds. He was immediately suspicious of me and voiced his doubts to other hunters but my cover here was long-established and no-one challenged me directly.

However the warnings were there. I knew I had to be extremely careful. Extensive digging was undertaken where the hounds had first marked but, with no sign of the fox, the hounds were taken on. They

Dulverton West Foxhounds, October 19th 1981. The exhausted fox sought sanctuary in an earth, was trapped by a terrier, dug out, shot, then (below) his body is thrown to the hounds.

Left: after a hunt this fox sought sanctuary below ground but was dug to and grabbed.

Dulverton West Foxhounds, October 30th 1981.
There are no quick kills in digging out.
Above: the trapped fox is goaded before being shot.

Right: the hunt terrier bloodied by his underground battle with the cornered fox.

Dulverton West Foxhounds,
October 30th 1981.

Right: a terrierman displays a
fox that was dug out and killed.

Right: one of the hunt terriers.

Bottom: two foxes were dug
out from this badger sett and
killed.

Right: Kennel Huntsman, Terry Beeney, points his gun.

Dulverton West Foxhounds, November 27th 1981.

The digging party hard at work. One fox was dug out, shot and his body thrown for the hounds. Whilst the hounds were distracted a second fox was dug out then thrown alive into the bracken for the hounds to chase. That fox, though injured, escaped when darkness fell.

Dulverton West Foxhounds, February 26th 1982. Two pregnant vixens were hunted to ground then dug out. One was shot. For the second, at another site, the gun was accidentally left in the Land Rover so she was thrown live to the hounds. Bottom: hunt terrier in travelling box.

Tetcott Foxhounds, October 5th 1982.
A hunted fox is dug out from a large badger sett and killed. The hounds tussle over his body.

Dulverton West Foxhounds, October 8th 1982.
Top left: Kennel Huntsman, Terry Beeney, helps with the digging out of the fox.
Top right: the digging party on the hillside. Above right: the dead fox was thrown down the hillside for the hounds to fight over.
Bottom: the dead fox with brush taken as a trophy.

Dulverton West Foxhounds. Top left: August 27th 1982, Terry Beeney cubhunting from a 4pm meet. Top right: January 17th 1983, Kennel Huntsman, Terry Beeney, digs watched by terrierman, Stan Richards.

Right: Hunting Festival, Tetcott Foxhounds, October 2nd 1982. At the meet a young child introduces a hound to her cuddly toy.

Left: Dulverton West Foxhounds, January 19th 1983, Terry Beeney searches for fox below ground, assisted by terrierman, Dave.

Above and right:
Dulverton West
Foxhounds,
October 27th 1982.
Some watch, some
chat.

Right: Fernie
Foxhounds,
December 15th
1982. At the meet.

Top: Eggesford Foxhounds, October 28th 1982. Huntsman cutting the brush off a dead fox.

Bottom: Worcestershire Foxhounds, March 5th 1983. Wherever the fox goes hounds will try to follow, sometimes causing great danger to themselves and others. This does not happen in drag hunting because in this humane sport the lines are never laid over roads or railway lines nor into gardens nor amongst farm livestock.

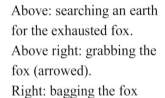

Above: searching an earth
for the exhausted fox.
Above right: grabbing the
fox (arrowed).
Right: bagging the fox

Dulverton West Foxhounds, January 3rd 1983.

Below: the bleeding, urine soaked fox is released from the bag to
continue the hunt, with the hounds some 50 yards away.

South Tetcott Foxhounds, February 12th 1983.
A tired fox sought sanctuary in a long field drain.
The fox (arrowed) was bolted from the drain by a terrier. The fox (below) tries to jump a small stream but falls in the water. He scrambles to get out but fails. As the pack closed in he turned to face them then was engulfed and killed. Bottom right: hounds tussle over the remains of this fox.

Berkeley Foxhounds, March 9th 1983.

Top: the exhausted fox is bolted (arrowed) and the hounds are released immediately.

Above right: Huntsman, Chris Maiden, with hounds waiting at the dig out.

Left: Whipper-in, Patrick Martin, in close pursuit of the fox.

Waterloo Cup 1983. Top: greyhound runs off with live hare, March 2nd 1983. Below : greyhounds close on hare, final day at the Withins, March 3rd 1983.

Left and right: the trophies are awarded, March 3rd 1983

Left: Wyre Forest Beagles, December 29th 1982. Master, Roger Colver, cuts a trophy from the torn carcass of a dead hare.

Right: Wyre Forest Beagles meet at Kinnersley Church, January 8th 1983.

Leadon Vale Bassethounds, February 5th 1983.

Above: Master, David Mann, hounds and hare (arrowed).

Below: hounds rip the hare apart. The hound at top left chews on a large bloody chunk — possibly the head of the hare.

marked a second time in woodland and again the enthusiastic diggers went to work, led by Mr Evans, but again there was no sign of the fox.

When a third mark late in the afternoon produced exactly the same non-result the hunters began to suspect that their hounds regarded it all as a game.

The technical pundits hypothesised on the possible manoeuvres of the fox. The best suggestion seemed to me to be that our vulpine friend simply looked in each hole then ran on. Others more versed in the ways of hounds preferred the theory that the pack had learnt that if they barked at a hole for long enough Terry would spend half an hour with his head stuck down it!

That last meet completed my two year undercover surveillance of the Dulverton West Foxhounds.

The only other fox hunts where I entered the inner sanctum were the Tetcott and South Tetcott (thanks to my local connections). At all the others I was confined to the role of a casual observer, never able to follow for long enough to gain the trust of the terriermen and Huntsmen. It was important though for me to try and find out what the other packs were up to and it certainly helped my cover to have the widest possible experience in hunting.

December 4th 1982 found me in hunting country a world apart from the West Country, namely with the Ashford Valley Foxhounds meeting at *The Royal Oak*, Iden Green, Kent. This was reckoned to be one of the best hunts in the South-East.

There was a veritable gaggle of riders at the meet, nearly all more interested in the glamorous and social side of hunting. If the West Country brings out the killer instinct in hunting man, the South East of England nurtures the razzmatazz element.

The hounds were, as always, friendly and bouncy — innocent participants. Taken to draw south from the meet they soon had a fox on the move. When other foxes intervened the pack split in all directions, with enthusiastic holloaing and shouting from hunt followers adding to the confusion. The casual observer could have been forgiven for thinking that every hunt saboteur in the country had arrived on the scene!

With a field of at least 100 riders all milling about, jostling as they queued to pass through gateways, progress was slow and damage to the fields tremendous. The pack did eventually settle to hunt but there was so much chattering and gossiping amongst the riders that it was impossible to hear the hounds. It might as well have been a point-to-point event.

Hounds were running and horses were galloping in every direction so I was quite astonished when, in the late afternoon, they did manage to run a fox to ground. As I expected, it being my first time with this hunt, the terriermen were hostile to me and secretive.

The car followers directed me to where the fox was to ground. I arrived at the wood to find all the riders and hunt staff gathered outside with the hounds. Pushing on through the undergrowth towards the digging site I encountered a motley collection of diggers including a couple of teenage girls, five young boys, five terriers and two larger mongrels.

The fox had sought sanctuary in a large complex earth. His tormentors appeared more intent on larking about and pushing each other into the earth than on despatching him quickly and humanely. Instead of blocking the holes as the West Country terriermen would have done, they put nets outside each exit to catch the fox should he bolt. After fooling about for what seemed an eternity they finally gave up, firmly blocking all the holes before they left.

I had just read the following letter from that noted hunting authority, JNP Watson published in *The Field* (October 27th 1982) so I half expected this to happen:-

"*Hunting Ethics*

From Mr JNP Watson

SIR, May I, at the threshold of the 1982-83 foxhunting season, crave the courtesy of your columns to express concern about certain ethics of the sport?

As a foxhunter who enjoys days with a dozen or more different packs a season in every quarter of Britain I have been impressed by the universal increase in the size of hunt supporters' clubs. Not only do most of these clubs raise substantial amounts of money to present essential equipment and facilities for use in their kennels and stables — as all the hunts so warmly appreciate — but they are also significant of the grass-root support for foxhunting throughout the country.

On the other hand their enthusiasm is often in conflict with moral and sporting principles. Clearly the burgeoning of the clubs has produced a considerable growth in the "terrier-and-spade brigade"; and in many countries, when a fox goes to ground, there is often a race to see who can get their terriers first to the earth. Since the clubs are good to the hunts, many Masters and huntsmen indulge them. The result in most countries, is a great deal more digging. This is very often done in the twilight or by torchlight, when hounds have returned

*to kennels; and it is rarely carried out in accordance with MFHA
guidelines let alone done in a humane way.*

*The increase in size of the hsc has also resulted in a proliferation
of "amateur" earthstoppers, men who are sedulous in blocking up
holes, but who have no intention of unblocking them at the end of the
day; so that one hears stories, not once but time and again, of foxes
shut in and starving to death.*

*Foxhunters used to be a more sporting fraternity. While fully
acknowledging the need to control fox numbers in some instances,
they honoured the "good" fox that got away; they approved of digging
only if there were strong complaints about marauders by local
farmers, or if the fox gave them a very short run; and provided the
dug fox was disposed of as speedily as possible with the humane
killer. Foxhunters used to take pride in "giving Charlie a sporting
chance". Now the motto seems to be "the foot followers must have
their sport, too".*

*It seems to me a great shame that now, when foxhunting has so
many enemies, and we are endeavouring to present an image of
fairplay and humaneness, that there is greater callousness than ever
before.*

*In these days of short Masterships, mostly composed of juntas,
there is **less** authority in the hunting-field at a time when **more** than
ever is required.*

*I know of several young people who have been put off the hunting
field by the sight of excessive digging and indiscriminate
earthstopping. That does not augur well for the future of the sport.
JNP WATSON Horsham, West Sussex."*

[Such honesty did not go down well with his hunting colleagues.
In his autobiography *Blue & Scarlet* published in 1990 JNP Watson
writes of the response to his letter:

*"The vehemence of the response was quite extraordinary. The
chairman of the British Field Sports Society wrote me the most
vitriolic letter I have ever received in my life, while the chairman of
the Masters of Foxhounds Association demanded to see me
immediately. If I had any complaints to make, he said, I was to make
them through him. Let those who follow me be warned: the fact that
you are set up as a spokesman for hunting does not mean you have the
liberty of free speech!"*]

I left ahead of the diggers but circled back and unblocked the two
main entrances.

It may be harsh to judge after a single visit but I was unimpressed
by my day with the Ashford Valley. Far too many of their followers

were ignorant townsfolk who not only knew nothing about country ways or hunting but, even worse, had no intention of learning.

To oppose cruelty it is not necessary to understand all the technicalities of its form, but those who support it do have a responsibility to gain at least a glimmer of understanding of what it entails.

The following week, December 11th, I headed way out west to the meet of the Banwen Miners Foxhounds at Llangennith on the Welsh coast near Swansea. The hunting world always point to the Banwen Miners as being living proof of working class involvement in hunting. Many miners are allegedly involved with this hunt. I was instructed to assess the truth of this claim. I observed this fox hunt both on the 11th and on their Boxing Day meet on the 27th at the Castle Hotel, Neath.

I soon learned that whatever may have happened in the past, today the hunt have little to do with the mining community. One Joint Master was an auctioneer, his colleague a solicitor. At the Boxing Day meet, which is the one time in the hunting year when all supporters may be expected to gather, I specifically asked to photograph a miner riding to hounds but none could be identified.

The Llangennith meet was most picturesque. I gained some typical hunting shots, showing all the glamour and none of the suffering. One of these was published by *Horse and Hound* on February 25th 1983. A fox was killed late in the day but out of my sight.

From the Boxing Day meet I performed my usual trick of giving away photographs to gain the hunt's confidence, then gave one supporter a lift for the day and was rewarded with some valuable information. He confirmed the complete lack of mining involvement and recounted an interesting tale concerning the hunt a few seasons back.

He claimed that the hounds had rioted and attacked sheep near Banwen and, as a result, the pack was put down. He blamed this failure on the hounds not being walked amongst sheep as puppies but said that they had now cured the problem.

Between the two meets of the Banwen Miners I had a couple of days in the very heart of English fox hunting — Leicestershire. My first was with the Fernie Foxhounds at Arnesby on December 15th and the second the following day with the Cottesmore Foxhounds at North Luffenham. The Fernie were seriously affected by the Co-op ban on bloodsports — losing a meet a week and a fifth of their hunting country. Leicestershire hunting is fast, both in terms of lifestyle and riding. The hounds have tremendous drive and the resultant pace makes following on foot a nightmare.

148

On both days high winds made for appalling scenting conditions and in consequence I saw little hunting. The meet at Arnesby was enlivened when an elderly chap sporting a silk topper was thrown from his horse and did a perfect 'flier' to land unharmed on his feet.

Before Christmas 1982 I returned to the West Country and had a couple of days with the Eggesford Foxhounds. Both the 22nd and the 24th were from Morchard Bishop. On both occasions the weather was atrocious but the hunters persevered, battling through flurries of snow and sleet. Scent was understandably poor so the foxes received a fitting Christmas present.

The New Year brought a day I will always remember — January 18th 1983 — when the South Tetcott Foxhounds met on the coast south of Bude at Crackington Haven. This was my first day with these hounds but I was recognised as a follower of the other local packs so was accepted. It was a typical West Country pack — just eight mounted followers, two hunt staff and about six supporters' cars. The hounds drew first along the cliff top which appeared a bit dangerous but fortunately there was no incident. They then drew a large covert inland. I was assured that these hounds excel at drawing but it was very slow work.

It later transpired that one reason for the apparent hunt lethargy was that the owner of the covert had arrived in an irate mood saying that no-one had bothered to phone him for his permission beforehand and that he did not want to see the hunt there again.

This inhibited the staff but eventually their hounds succeeded in putting up a fox and chasing him towards a nearby village. He crossed the valley and circled back towards his original covert. Completing the ring he continued on but the hounds were not fooled and they forced him to ground in the vicinity of the chapel at Flanders. The supporters knew their hounds were marking the fox to ground by their change in tone.

It was about 3.30p.m. as I drove round, parked and dashed down to the earth that was located amid scrubland and brambles, halfway up a hillside. There was a small group of two men and one woman digging frantically. The hounds were being restrained by the staff some distance away. A terrier had been entered and was being tracked with an electronic bleeper.

Gauging by the sounds audible from the tunnel entrance the diggers cheerfully announced that their terrier was battling with the fox, forcing it further and further back. Holes were dug at positions judged as being above the combat but the adversaries always moved further along before the tunnel was exposed. The iron bar was used to probe for the tunnel pattern and another exit was found hidden below dense bracken. I was sitting watching events from beside the first hole when I was startled by a fox tip-toeing out and creeping away into the undergrowth. He was a beautiful sight, his coat dry and immaculate.

He had clearly not been hunted. I said nothing hoping that no-one else would notice but unfortunately the others saw him and called to the hunt staff.

A misunderstanding ensued. One of the diggers, thinking that the Huntsman said to holloa, did so and the whole pack rushed over. Surprisingly the hounds found it impossible to pick up the scent of this fleeing fox and most were still milling about when called back with much whip cracking and horn blowing. Everyone agreed that the hunted fox, the one they wanted, remained deep in the earth, locked in battle with the terrier.

The second terrier had previously been entered to the hole that the fox escaped from but had come out further on with its nose bitten; indicating that the fox must have been hiding in some side passage. Assessing this to be the situation the terrier lady was distraught. She reckoned that the fox must have been bleeding itself and consequently would have produced a good hunt. She was furious that the hounds had not been unleashed.

After further digging, clearing and probing, the nature of the earth was revealed. It was on a split level. When a second hole was dug the terrier was found with its backside facing out, having switched positions with the fox. The dog was pulled clear and the tunnel roof excavated further, taking care to prevent the fox bolting.

This took time and with darkness approaching the staff left to take their hounds home. The enthusiastic terrier team remained. On and on the dig went until the terrified fox was trapped and could be clearly seen, bright eyes peering out from the tunnel. The youngest lad took aim with the small calibre pistol. There was a mighty bang and clouds of smoke but he missed.

Unsure as to whether the fox had even been wounded he reached in to the hole to try and grab him with the badger-tongs but the fox, still full of fight, snapped at them.

Another terrier went in but was bitten and retreated. Then both terriers were tried. The fox couldn't battle both. Whilst his attention was distracted by one dog the other savaged his head and side. By these tactics one of the dogs eventually gained a solid grip on their victim. The terrier was pulled out, the diggers hoping that if he kept his grip he in turn he would pull the fox out. But he lost his hold. The

Huntsman, Richard, then returned to help, having put his hounds away.

The hole was enlarged even more. Whilst digging one of the terriermen questioned me: "*You're not anti-hunt are you?*" to which I inevitably replied, "*Of course not!*" Satisfied, they then deployed Richard on one side of the exposed tunnel and the young lad on the other. One was armed with a pick the other with the iron bar. Both were tasked with clubbing the fox should he bolt. Wisely the fox refused.

Further investigation in the rapidly failing light revealed that the fox had retreated so far that he had squeezed and wormed his way under a large boulder, just one back leg protruded. The terrier lady grabbed this limb with the badger-tongs and tugged and heaved with all her evident weight. The fox squealed and yelped in response but would not budge. From the sounds he emitted the diggers judged him to be male.

Soon the blackness of night enveloped us and we could see nothing. First matches, then gas cigarette lighters, were used to illuminate the eerie scene. The tongs were levered and pushed as the diggers strained to gain a better purchase on the fox but without success. Next the earth was cleared away in an effort to free and remove the large boulder that was shielding the fox but the lighters ran out before this task could be completed.

In complete darkness the digging team were powerless and it seemed certain that the fox would have to be left. However terrier enthusiasts are nothing if not determined. Two of the men volunteered to trek the considerable distance back to the hunt lorry to fetch a torch and did so, leaving Richard, the terrier lady and myself. The fox was held captive in the iron grip of the tongs. Far from gazing in wonder at the beauty of the bright stars above us on this cold winter's night I was consumed with compassion towards this petrified innocent creature, a child of creation, yelping in agony just a few feet from me.

The sounds were two short, one long, two short, one long. This was not morse code but rather the pitiful whimperings: the grunt-grunt-griaow of this trapped fox, a sound that will haunt me forever. Terrier lady revealed the measure of her compassion by saying: "*Shut up! It's your own fault for going there.*"

Eventually after what seemed like eternity to us and must have felt like more for the victim, actually about 20 minutes, the men returned with the torch. With the scene illuminated the Huntsman used the bar to lever against the boulder, trying to extract it. But it was pressed tight against the fox's abdomen. Every time the boulder moved the fox screamed hideously.

It was painstaking work but by ignoring the fox and heaving, pushing and twisting, the stone was eventually removed. The gun was prepared. Devoid of cover the helpless fox was dragged into the torchlight by the tongs still locked onto its back leg. In a last gesture of defiance he turned to face his tormentors.

The quarry was torn and battered, bleeding from deep bites to his head, neck, and flank. The once beautiful coat was now wet, muddied and matted, but the eyes still blazed defiance.

A terrific bang from the gun finally ended the suffering. The shot echoed in the chamber and across the sleepy valley. Richard triumphantly blew the kill on his horn — long haunting notes that hung in the chill, still air. The time was 6.20p.m., nearly three hours after that fox had first sought sanctuary below ground. Three hours of continuous fighting with one or both of the terriers, three hours of sheer agony, yet by no means unusual for a dig.

Hunt supporters always claim that they kill foxes instantly.

The brush was taken and the shattered carcass returned to the hole from whence it had so reluctantly been extracted and buried.

That was January 18th. The following month I returned to the same pack, on the 12th, for their meet at Boyton. It was a freezing cold day and there were just 7 riders and 15 cars with supporters following. The first fox ran a large circle and tried to break off from this route and escape but his ruse was foiled when watchers gave his game away. The hounds were lifted from the circle and put on the right line.

With scent absent this fox managed to elude hounds but a second one was hunted to exhaustion and marked to ground in a drain in the early afternoon. It was a long field drain ending at a small stream. The smallest terrier was entered some 50 yards into the field and the hounds held back. The hunters hoped to bolt the fox from out of the end overlooking the stream. The fox fairly flew out, swinging towards the onlookers lining the river bank.

Headed by these he swerved towards the river and driven by fear he tried to jump it. The hounds were released in pursuit. They and the hunt followers were in full cry. Despite making a prodigious leap across the river the fox fell just short of the far bank and plunged into the water. From the bank I saw him scrabbling at the bank, trying to climb out as the cry of the approaching pack grew louder. Again and again he jumped up clawing at the overhanging brambles but with nothing to grip on he slipped back into the river.

The full pack was baying from the bank and the fox, helpless in mid-stream, turned to face them. The hounds surged forward for the kill. As their leaders went in the fox twisted and bit the first one. There was a brief melee, a maelstrom of threshing and tumbling in the water and it was all over.

The Huntsman joined the fray, wading into the river to recover the carcass. As the hounds, victors of the one-sided fight, came out I saw that one was bleeding badly from his ear. Hunters describe such an injury as a 'wound of honour'. They view it as a sign of a good hound — one that is at the front of the action.

The next month, March, I followed no less than six different packs of foxhounds as I sought to broaden my hunting experience. One, the Dulverton West meeting at Withypool Cross on the 28th, has already been mentioned. With the exception of this hunt and the South Tetcott on the 29th I was only in the role of casual observer. I lacked the necessary time to gain the confidence of my hunting companions.

On the 5th the Worcestershire Foxhounds met at *The Chequers*, Crowle. This is one hunt that was regularly opposed by an efficient hunt saboteur group and I was interested to see how they would react to strangers.

At the meet I soon ascertained that the supporters were similar in kind to those of the Ashford Valley — the gloss and glamour brigade. As with the Ashford Valley these hounds have a tremendous reputation but I saw little to justify it.

From the first draw a fox was quickly afoot. As happens often, the car followers, by organising the supporters, ensured that he was not headed and was able to cross the main road which he did. When I questioned the wisdom of this, saying that it was risking injury to their hounds, particularly any stragglers, no-one seemed bothered. The fox circled right-handed and crossed the nearby railway line, seconds before a train passed. I expected the hounds to be held back but instead of being checked the hunt staff urged the pack over in pursuit.

A while later I was standing in an open field photographing the Huntsman, John Creed, approaching me on foot with his hounds. I took these photographs as wholly innocuous hunting images of the type so common in country magazines but when John reached me he went completely berserk. He screamed abuse at me, challenging my right to photograph him and threatening me with every form of court action. Fortunately his anger overrode his intellect. I was able to evade and explain away potentially difficult questions as to who I was and what I was doing

When he left I had a word with some supporters and terriermen standing smiling nearby. They laughed and apologised for his outburst saying: "*Don't worry mate, John's been a bit funny in the head since the antis started bothering him!*"

Doubtless after hearing false holloas and false horn calls Huntsmen begin seeing antis behind every tree. The irony was of course that in my case he was exactly right! I left this hunt soon afterwards. It was abundantly clear that even if they did hunt a fox to ground I would not be allowed to photograph anything.

Four days later, on March 9th, my day with the Berkeley Foxhounds at Nympsfield, near Stroud was very interesting. At the meet the school opposite must have come to a complete halt as the nuns marshalled their infant charges out to see the hounds. It was a pity that after witnessing this undoubtedly glamorous side of hunting they were not also shown the true fate of the quarry — a creature that children pay homage to as they sing "*All things bright and beautiful.*"

The first fox hunted went to ground almost immediately and when it proved impossible to dislodge him they simply blocked him in and moved on. In due course when the opportunity arose I returned to unblock the earth. The second victim went away in a large circle with the hounds pressing him very hard. This pack has great drive and the scent was evidently good that day. This tiring fox returned to complete his circle and then also went to ground, but only just in time.

The terriers were entered to the hole. After some digging and probing whilst the hounds watched intently the fox bolted. According to hunting custom it is 'sporting' in these circumstances to give the fox a short start known as 'law'. This ensures that the tired fox is not killed immediately, prolongs the hunt and gives following hunters more fun.

One would certainly have expected a prestigious hunt such as the Berkeley, of whom Prince Charles was a regular supporter, to conform to hunting tradition but they did not. The pack was released immediately and I gained a rare photograph of hounds and fox in the same frame. The fox dashed for only some 200 yards more before going to ground again.

Lengthy excavations ensued in the course of which the young Whipper-in, Patrick Martin, displayed great enthusiasm by disappearing into the hole up to his ankles. The end was almost inevitable — the fox was dug out and shot.

That was Wednesday. On Saturday March 12th I was back in the same area with the elite Duke of Beaufort's Foxhounds, meeting at the Monument, Hawkesbury Upton. Rather than observation of hunting this was mainly to take photographs of the following field. In particular of the Duke himself and his staff, whose comments have done so much to aid the anti-hunting cause. It was the Honorary Secretary Major Ronnie Dallas who confirmed that foxes are encouraged for hunting by his comment: *"If it were not for us building artificial lairs and keeping the foxes alive to hunt, they would become extinct and the whole balance of nature would be thrown out."*

There was also this mention in the most authoritative text of all about fox hunting:-

"In countries where earths are scarce it is sometimes found necessary to make artificial earths, to provide somewhere for local foxes to have their cubs: in other words, for breeding purposes. Another advantage of artificial earths is that in grass countries where the coverts tend to be small and scattered it is useful to have snug earths judiciously placed at regular intervals, thus persuading foxes to take a good line. An additional advantage is that if an artificial earth is left open, it will only take a few minutes to bolt a fox. Also if it is a blank day, one knows where to go with some certainty of finding a fox.........In this book I only wish to touch on the subject, and to tell you what my grandfather had to say.

He felt that artificial earths should be primarily intended as breeding establishments, and so among the chief points to be borne in mind should be the aspect, position, soil, drainage and materials used for their construction." (*Fox-Hunting*. The Duke of Beaufort. Pub. David & Charles. 1980. Page 141)

Apart from some stock portraits of hunt followers that were easy enough for me to take at the meet the hunt was a complete fiasco. It was almost impossible to keep in touch with the hounds. Cars and Land Rovers headed in every direction and no-one knew what was happening.

By the time of the South Tetcott meet at Hornacott Chapel on March 29th, near to their previous meet at Boyton, the ring of suspicion was beginning to close in one me. The two-legged hounds from within the hunting world had locked on to me so that, like the fox, I was being hunted. I knew that I had to be cautious.

The first fox found was probably saved by the intervention of two hares, one of which the pack chased. By the time the hounds settled to hunt another fox it had started to pour with rain.

I was near the village of Alvacott when I heard the hounds in full cry as they ran down the hillside beside a hedgerow. I peered over just in time to see the last hound disappearing out through a gap in the left hand corner of the hedge across the field. Almost immediately I heard the scampering of muddy feet and leaning further over saw the fox running down the slope on the other side of the hedge from me!

Protracted hunting then ensued between Eastcott and Bradridge woods with blankets of dense fog periodically descending to confuse matters. The pack had a field day. Not surprisingly they split and were soon running all over the place. Foxes were numerous and when one passed near the group of hunters that I was with a terrierman blew his whistle to summon the pack.

Regrouped, the hounds settled to hunt this fox. They pushed him on and marked him to ground amid the pine trees of Bradridge wood at about 5.00p.m. There was only one main hole and the terriers soon bayed this fox. But the cornered creature was tenacious. The first terrier to be entered to the hole came out bitten deeply on the nose.

The fox was moving in a circular tunnel and it needed several holes being dug into the tunnel to trap him. When I talked of taking a picture one of the men asked me, "*You're not an anti are you?*" I denied my true allegiance but was even more wary thereafter.

The terriers were pulled out and the hole enlarged until the fox's brush was exposed. The Whipper-in then grabbed it and pulled the fox backwards. One of his colleagues grabbed the fox's body with the badger-tongs. The fox was struggling as best he could. The Whipper-in fired his pistol at him, at point-blank range but missed completely.

The petrified creature, still twisting and writhing, was further restrained by a hand on the scruff of its neck. So tight was this grip that the fox was soon gasping and gurgling for air. The victim was then stunned by a couple of light taps to his skull with the butt of a crop. A solid blow with the crop, the pick or the spade or, more obviously, a second shot would have brought a merciful death, but no such coup-de-grace was delivered.

The fox was still twitching and struggling when the Whip dragged him away by his brush. He was taken out of the wood through what appeared to be a dried up canal and down towards some marshland where the hounds were waiting. Without further ceremony he was thrown to their waiting jaws.

My last day of fox hunting was with the Eggesford Foxhounds at Lower Sutton Farm near Exeter on March 30th. Peter Goulding a journalist from the *Shooting Times* was at the meet so I was on my guard. With few foxes about the hunting was extremely slow and wide ranging. There are even fewer foxes now as one was killed near Morchard Bishop at about 4.00p.m. although I failed to see the end.

CHAPTER NINE
Hare hunting and hare coursing
"In hunting, whether it be of fox or hare, every follower should identify himself with hounds' aims and give his entire sympathy to them. If he allows himself to sympathise with the hare, his pleasure in the chase will be neutralised and he might as well go home at once." (*The Art Of Beagling*. Captain J. Otho Paget. Pub. H.F. & G. Witherby. 1931. Page 217)

"It is probably better to have a good hunt of an hour or 90 minutes, rather than over match the hare and pull her down in 20 min." (*Horse and Hound*. November 7, 1980)

In the autumn of 1982, after spending the summer observing the mink hunting 'exploits' of two of my antagonists in the letters columns of many local papers — Ian Coghill of the Three Counties Minkhounds and Arlin Rickard of the Devon and Cornwall Minkhounds — I switched my undercover work to beagling. This is the hunting of hares by a pack of beagles with the followers running along behind. It is a sport I had always regarded as particularly cruel as the hare is such a timid and inoffensive creature.

On October 16th 1982 I attended the opening meet of the Surrey and North Sussex Beagles at *The Red Barn*, Blindley Heath, north of East Grinstead at 12.30p.m. Beagle meets differ from other forms of hunting in that they usually start in the early afternoon.

After experiences as an active hunt saboteur I knew that such hunting was a prime target for saboteurs because huntsmen and followers are all on foot. Everyone is on the same level. As I had expected saboteurs were in attendance but they found it difficult to get close to the hunters who kept to private land well away from roads and footpaths.

There were very few hares about. The hounds drew on and on cast in an open fan across the fields whilst the followers trailed in their wake. The hunt supporters became increasingly disconsolate as the rain poured down making for a bitterly cold afternoon.

Then a hare was found and the calm was shattered. The hounds had been shuffling along, nose down, sniffing intently. Suddenly a hare shot away like the proverbial bullet. She had remained crouched, ears flattened, hidden until the last moment, as hounds approached. The startled hounds responded with ecstatic cries and swerved in hot pursuit. The hare, nature's perfect running machine, was soon out of sight. The pack settled down to hunt her scent. This is where the calculated cruelty comes in. All hounds are purpose bred for stamina rather than speed and, as mentioned in the quote above, it is calculated that a well-bred pack of beagles will take 90 minutes to run a hare to exhaustion before killing her. Dogs such as lurchers that are bred with more pace would kill quicker but beagling is designed to delay the kill, enabling followers to have a good run behind and see the hounds work out the line of scent.

On this occasion fortune favoured the hare. The scent was patchy and intermittent. The hunt saboteurs, hearing the hounds in cry, were holloaing and blowing their hunting horns from the road, distracting the hounds, but always taking care not to attract them to danger.

This hunt finally ended when the tiring hare ran through cattle foil, leaving the hounds baffled by the smell.

Soon after this welcome intervention I trod on an upright nail when climbing railed fencing. It ripped right through the sole of my boot, leaving me limping for the rest of the day. A second hare was found and hunted but once again was lost because of poor scenting conditions. The hunt staff persevered in pursuit, braving a torrential downpour, but by 4.30p.m. when they found a field of mushrooms, it proved too much of a temptation. The Huntsman blew to end the day and the hunters consoled themselves by filling their hats with free fungi.

The following week, October 23rd, I returned to the same hunt for their meet at Marsh Green, near Edenbridge. This meet had not been publicly advertised so I had to phone the hunt kennels to try and learn the location. They would not tell me the meet and I feared pushing it too far in case they asked to phone me back (I was on my home number). Instead they gave me a Reigate phone number to try. I dialled it, but again was thwarted by a solid wall. The lady answering my call was most suspicious. She would not tell me the whereabouts of the meet and despite my best efforts to describe the day when I accompanied the hunt just the previous week was adamant that she did not remember me.

I played my last card by asking her for the number of the Huntsman, Rodney Cooper, saying that I was sure that he would vouch for me. I had made a point the previous week of chatting to Rodney, outlining my interest in taking 'sporting' pictures. Sure enough when I called him he remembered and gave me the location of the meet.

That day the hounds inflicted two lengthy, punishing, hunts on hares, but there was no kill. Days with hare hunts as a hunt saboteur had taught me that hunted hares typically seek escape by running in circles, either clockwise or anti-clockwise. My time undercover with hare hunters refined this knowledge and I was able to witness that to start with, the circle will be large in diameter but, as the hare tires, so the circles gets smaller until eventually, when totally exhausted, she will break off the ring and run in panic in a straight line.

For the first hunt this day the scent was a bit patchy, particularly over the ploughed fields. However there were plenty of hunt followers dotted about the fields all eager to betray the whereabouts of the fleeing hare. They did so simply by holding their caps or handkerchiefs in the air and pointing.

The hunted hare completed her first circle and began her second, but she was visibly tiring. A fresh hare popped up and briefly led the hounds away, but the staff were quick to whip their hounds off this fresh hare and put them back on the line of the hunted hare. By then this first found hare had disappeared. Rodney took his pack into a farm and cast them to sniff around the outhouses but there was no sign of any hare seeking sanctuary there. He even waded into an overgrown pond with them, thinking that she might be hiding in the reeds on the margins. Eventually, some two hours after she was first found, she was given best.

The next hare waited, as hares often do, until the hounds almost tripped over her in the open field before bolting. When she did run it was with a stunning burst of speed. She had cleared two fields before the pack was even out of the first. The pursuit lasted an hour before she eventually eluded the hounds and the day ended with everyone exhausted at 5.15p.m.

That was October 23rd. A fortnight later I was back with the same pack for their meet at *The Bull*, Chelsham, on the southern outskirts of London. I arrived some ten minutes after the 12.30p.m. meet and was immediately suspicious. There were no hunters in sight but there were a couple of car-loads of hunt saboteurs parked beside the green. I went into the pub to enquire about the hunt but the barman, clearly thinking I was a saboteur, said brusquely: "*They've cancelled.*"

I returned to my car and waited. Soon two more hunt supporters drove up. I asked them what was happening but neither knew. However, one said that he had heard that the hounds were due to set off from nearby Warren Farm. After asking directions for this farm we set off towards it. As we passed the saboteurs they slipped into convoy behind us.

With my hunt saboteur friends for life (but 'opponents' for the day) tailing us we reached the farm and learned that the meet had been changed to *The Fox and Hounds*, Tilburstow Hill. The saboteurs were parked and waiting to follow us. I was worried. My cover within hunting was under great strain at that time for, despite all my pleadings, a short sequence of me talking about the 'Smoking Beagles' rescue operation had been shown in *The Animals Film* broadcast on Channel 4 just the previous Thursday. This excellent film contains some dramatic sequences of hunting and so was likely to be watched by hunters. If any hunter saw it and recognised me my undercover work would be over. I judged it just too risky to lead two car-loads of saboteurs to this hunt. I knew I had to either lose them or find a way of communicating with them to direct them to innocently 'find us' later.

Turning to my hunting companions I suggested we split up and whoever was unfortunate enough to be followed by the saboteurs would have to sacrifice his hunting by leading them elsewhere.

I indicated discreetly to the saboteurs to follow me but they were clearly and rightly suspicious of some strange guy in hunting gear trying to direct them. Even though I drove as suspiciously as possible still they followed another hunter. Had they followed me I could have stopped in a convenient location and explained the situation. As it was, they followed another fellow to a DIY store in Reigate, missed the hunt and ended up cursing.

When I caught up with the hunt the staff were delighted to learn that we had led the saboteurs astray. Far from being weakened my cover was in fact strengthened considerably but I was irritated that (long before the era of mobile phones) I had been unable to communicate with my real friends. Hounds had already put a brace of hares up from some woodland but once again the scent was bad.

There were more hares here and hounds gleefully chased them in all directions. At one point I heard frantic squealing coming from a hedgerow. I dashed down to the source of the sounds fearing it was perhaps a hound hung up in barbed wire, but one of the Whippers-in beat me to the scene and emerged joking: "*Just another bloody rabbit killed!*" Hare hunts kill a lot of rabbits — particularly those afflicted with the dreadful disease myxomatosis.

Apparently this hunt had only killed one hare since they returned from their hunting festival in the Lake District. The light faded as an evening autumn mist came down and home was blown at 4.30p.m. with just the unfortunate rabbit added to the tally.

I was anxious to see what really happens when hounds do catch a hare so the following week, November 13th, I opted to change hunts, following the Pevensey Marsh Beagles meeting at the Rother Valley Hotel, Northiam, north-west of Rye at 11.30a.m. It proved to be a poor choice. The hounds drew over the flat marshes, through the crops, up and down the hillsides, along the hedgerows and through the coverts, but there was not a single sniff of a hare let alone a sighting. It was a complete and utter blank and left me wondering how beaglers convince any landowners that they require access to their land in order to kill hares as a pest control service.

Saturday November 20th was completely different. It was an invitation meet of the Surrey and North Sussex in Pevensey Marsh country, at *The Bulls Head*, Boreham Street.

I arrived to find that there were hunt saboteurs about. Knowing that they would have come from the Brighton/Hastings area and might recognise me I was apprehensive. On this occasion there were plenty of public footpaths so the hunters could not keep the saboteurs off the fields; but they did try. I opted to stay near to the hounds as much as possible. One saboteur, eyeing my camera, asked who I was working for. Knowing that hunters were listening, I explained that I was freelancing with publication in *Shooting Times* in mind and that I was particularly interested to record any violence caused by the saboteurs — a comment which pleased the hunters enormously.

In the event the only pictures I acquired were of hunters pushing and jostling the antis. One saboteur realised what I was actually photographing and shouted across: "*That's a good photograph for Shooting Times — that really shows hunt violence!*" I stopped taking any more pictures lest the hunters became suspicious as to my real motives.

The hunt continued but most of the followers missed seeing their 'sport' as they spent the whole time bullying the saboteurs to keep to the footpaths.

There were hares about and the scent was good. Clearly a recent climatic change had occurred in favour of the hounds. The previous Tuesday the same hunt had killed one hare outright and chased another until, terrified and exhausted, she opted to swim a river and was drowned. They had also killed the previous Saturday.

The hounds ran well and locked on to the scent of one hare. This hare looked to be in trouble but at a point beside a canal the saboteurs were able to intervene effectively to save her. They distracted and confused the hounds by making so much noise that Rodney's shouted instructions were inaudible. There was plenty of banter and verbal exchanges between the two opposing sides but no real violence as the saboteurs outnumbered the hunters four to one.

Hounds then set off after a fresh hare running in another large circle. I cut across the diagonal with other followers and had just reached the brow of a hill, with the hounds in full cry on the other side, when the baying stopped abruptly. Rodney blew the kill. I sprinted forward to record what had happened. The hare had been killed in a field of young cabbages. The hounds were milling about, scrapping over her remains. The triumphant supporters, flocking to see, trampled a large area of the crop — the perfect irony, considering that the prime reason for killing this hare in the first place is that she eats the occasional cultivated plant.

I tried to photograph the dead hare but there was precious little left to see: only splintered bones, blood and fur remained. Learning that I was at my first hare kill (I obviously couldn't tell them that I had seen a kill years before when I was a hunt saboteur), the supporters searched around, found the torn off tail of the hare (scut) and awarded it to me as a trophy. I guess I was lucky that they did not try to 'blood' me. To preserve this scut and keep it as a souvenir for life I was instructed to soak it in methylated spirits for at least three weeks. In fact, at the first opportunity, I buried it.

Hounds were then taken to where another hare had been viewed by followers. They quickly picked up her line and ran away at speed in pursuit. I opted to follow Ian Cunningham, the Pevensey Marsh Huntsman, trusting in his knowledge of his own hunting country.

The hounds circled a hill and were returning towards us when they killed again. The hare had crossed a canal, was coursed down the other side and then caught. Proud of their two successes home was blown at 4.00p.m.

On the long walk back to our cars we were accosted by an angry bunch of saboteurs standing by their van and two cars. Some hunt supporters had let down six of their tyres and stolen the valves to prevent them being re-inflated.

One of the sabs tackled me: "*If you want a picture for Shooting Times, take a picture of this damage and put it in your bloody rag!*" Sadly it was too dark for me to even try.

Rodney and Ian then offered to lend the saboteurs a pump having first driven them to get some new valves. I offered to help as well, but they had it all in hand. Apparently the Pevensey Marsh hunters have an agreement with the sabs not to cause this kind of damage to each other's vehicles (a wise agreement for the hunt to make as their vehicles are the most vulnerable, the most numerous and the most expensive).

A week later, November 27th, I was back with the Surrey and North Sussex Beagles for a meet in their own country, at the appropriately named *Hare and Hounds* pub at Lingfield. Once again hunt saboteurs — this time from Surrey University — were at the meet and in attendance throughout the day. They were led by the determined and dedicated Colin Skilton. I had been so often linked with the appearance of sabs that when Rodney first saw me he asked: *"You're not bringing these antis with you, are you?"* I could only laugh and shrug the comment off. Fortunately I was able to repair the damage done to my cover by this chance linking by telling him that I had left a photograph with one of his staff that I had taken of him earlier in the season at Marsh Green. He was delighted.

One very fit young saboteur ran with the hounds all day but said nothing to reveal his true feelings and caused no trouble. I assumed that as I also had done many years before he was simply on observation to understand what happens. Hunters challenged him, bullied him and ordered him to keep off private land, but he replied that he had paid his 'cap' and produced the little cardboard fob to prove it. This baffled the hunters as they then felt morally bound to let him through and did so, but reminded him that he had to obey their hunt rules.

As we followed the hounds in a fan across the fields a hare popped up right in front of them. She ran away so fast that I was unable to take a picture. She took a big circle and then returned. I was trailing in the wake when I saw her dart through a gateway moments before hunt saboteurs endeavouring to save her life reached the spot. It was a perfect chance for me to judge the effectiveness of sabotage as the hounds were streaming in full cry only seconds behind. The sabs sprayed to cover the line of scent and whistled and shouted to distract the pack.

However, a pack running at full speed has tremendous forward momentum. Though they checked briefly, perhaps for five seconds, they soon cast themselves forward, picked up the line and carried on. Clearly saboteurs intent on saving the quarry need to leave a thick zone of foil to conceal the scent. For many hares such a brief respite as I witnessed may not be enough to save them. Mercifully for this one it was.

I ran and ran to keep up. The fleeing hare crossed a stream. When the hounds piled across after her just seconds behind I thought the kill was imminent. Then a fresh hare intervened and the pack split. Some tried to stay in pursuit of the exhausted hare, others set off after the fresh one. Rodney had to quickly decide which part of his pack was right and he chose wrongly. He stopped the hounds that were actually right. He gathered his pack together and set off to hunt the newly found hare — leaving one very tired hare to escape.

163

Rodney did in time realise his mistake but by the time he re-directed his pack to draw for the original hare it was too late. As the afternoon wore on a cold mist descended. Hounds were entered to one large covert from where immediately sounds of shooting were heard.

In the resulting mayhem the pack split. Some hounds set off with their Huntsman, others with the Whippers-in. The Huntsman returned to the main group of hunt followers. The Whippers-in followed soon after beaming with delight. They claimed their hounds had killed — that they had chopped down a baby leveret. But hares breed in the spring. Either the victim was not that small a hare, or it was not a hare at all. Although these hunters only recovered a tiny ball of fur they were certain their victim was a hare rather than a rabbit. They explained that the hounds had worried it, whereas when they catch a rabbit they merely kill it and leave it.

The following month, December, I ranged right across the country and the 18th found me out with the Warwickshire Beagles for their meet at *The Three Horseshoes*, Wixford near Redditch.

This was the hunt of which Ian Coghill had been Huntsman until he had unleashed a particularly vicious stream of invective on two committee members who, not surprisingly, failed to vote for him as Huntsman next time round! Nevertheless, I had been told that he still followed them and I hoped to meet up with him to watch how he behaved when beagling. I also knew that I would encounter other followers of the Three Counties Minkhounds and would have to be careful.

At the meet I saw that well-known, elderly and affable, hunting character — Loppylugs. I had met him whilst mink hunting. He rushed up to me shouting, "*I'm going to murder you!*" I gulped, fearing that he had recognised me on *The Animals Film*. But it was an innocent joke by him. He simply clutched a terrible photograph of himself hunting to show me and he feared it might prove fatal to my sensitive photographic tastes.

From the first draw a hare bolted almost immediately and the hounds piled after her straight into a field of sheep. The hunters cursed, knowing that they had been banned from that land. None of the uniformed staff dared to go on to whip the hounds out. All they could do was stand on the field margins trying to call the pack out. I watched one and he looked like a man trying to discourage his big bouncy dog from rolling in his neighbours flower beds. The beagles thought it was all great fun but eventually they were coaxed out without the landowner being any the wiser.

As the day wore on large numbers of hares were chased in all directions, but fortunately all escaped. Though able to lock on to the scent left by individual hares the pack seemed to lack the drive to push selected victims hard enough — a failing the hares doubtless appreciated. Late in the afternoon, at about 4.00p.m., an amazing incident occurred.

The hounds were drawing the top end of a grass field when they put their quarry up. She shot away from the hounds and ourselves towards the hedgerow at the far end of the field then stopped. In full cry the pack hurtled towards her. I watched as this hare sat up, ears erect and looked about. She then ran not away but straight back towards the approaching hounds. Attaining her full speed in an instant she hit the approaching wedge of canine venom head on. Darting to her left she missed the lead hound, swerved inside the second, accelerated back from the third, side-stepped and so on. Relying only on her speed and sublime agility she carved her way through the entire pack. They snapped at her fleeing form but without success. Through the whole pack she ran and then was away and out of sight leaving the hounds in complete disarray as their leaders swerved about and were bowled over by those following.

The supporters scratched their heads, looked questioningly at their hip flasks and put it down to the hare being a 'suicide jockey'. I wondered whether, less anthropomorphically, she had leverets beyond the hedgerow, because apart from the first instant, she certainly led the pack away from it. The hunt drew on and on, in near total darkness. They were casting their hounds by the light of the moon but they found no hare. She had vanished.

After Christmas I switched to follow another hare hunt not far from the Warwickshire, the Wyre Forest Beagles, meeting at Coddington Cross, near Worcester on December 29th. Loppylugs was at the meet doling out half a bottle of sherry to the supporters. He gleefully informed me that this is one of the hunt's best meets.

From the first draw we soon found that there were very few hares about. When a rabbit was disturbed the hounds chased it eagerly and were only stopped with difficulty.

I took the opportunity to chat with the hunt followers to learn more about hunting practices. They told me that hounds are first entered to the pack at about 18 months old and that the oldest in their pack was seven years old. After seven, they are destroyed. I calculated that to mean an awful lot of perfectly healthy beagles killed each year — it is not only the hares that suffer.

Eventually a supporter sighted a fleeing hare and holloaed. The pack set off in pursuit in a wide right-handed circle. On and on the hunt went until the hare returned to her starting point. Then, as if in a relay race, a second hare popped up, ran on and took the hounds on for a second circuit. I watched as the tired hare swerved inside, coming off her previous track on a much tighter line. The hounds were fooled and gaily set off for their second lap. This second hare ran the same circle but when she returned there was no other hare to help her. She was visibly tiring and the hounds were gaining on her.

She set off on a second circuit, but in a much tighter circle. High up on a ploughed hillside she was held up by a fence of chicken mesh. By the time she found a way through the pack was only yards behind. At the scene I heard a supporter who had witnessed her terrified, frantic efforts to get through the wire express sympathy for her. Returning to her starting point for a second time again there was no other hare to help. She was on her own.

She broke off from the circle and ran straight. Supporters were holloaing and shrieking in near ecstasy, just as hunters do on a stag hunt. I knew the end was near. She was coursed along the sides of two hedgerows and she then dashed across a bare field towards a brook with the hounds inexorably gaining. I whipped up my camera to record the final act. She reached the brook, went in but never came out. The hounds piled in. There was a brief penetrating squeal and it was over. The remains of the hare were retrieved in triumph and I took some photographs of the Master, Roger Colver, cutting the scut off. The time was 3.15p.m. They drew on and had a brief hunt on a second hare but she escaped.

That was December 29th. In the New Year I was back with the Wyre Forest for their meet at Kinnersley Church on January 8th. On this occasion I missed seeing the kill. When the tiring hare ran round the left-hand side of a farm, instead of following, I tried to be clever and ran round the other side to lie in wait and photograph her approaching me head on. Fine in theory but she never reached me. She was headed by supporters early on in her circle and changed direction.

Scorning a dense pine covert that might have saved her, she darted towards some buildings and in words recounted to me by a smiling eyewitness was caught "*under a cottage gate.*" My informant told how the staff had frantically bundled the hounds out of the private garden, cleared up the remains of the hare and departed before anyone saw them. As he put it: "*It really is better if the hares are killed in the open country, away from public view.*"

The hunt soon found a second hare and with scenting conditions good the hounds hunted her closely. However, just when it appeared that they would kill this hare, again near buildings, the pack rioted and killed a rabbit.

In the course of that hunt I heard an interesting tale from the hunt Treasurer, a lady who wrote hunting reports under the pseudonym of 'Elfin'. The previous Wednesday, their hounds had hunted a hare and marked at a hole in the base of a tree. It is always reckoned that hare hounds do not mark to earths, drains or hollows in trees because hares just do not seek sanctuary in such places. They live or die in the open or in scrub cover. Though cast in all directions from this tree there was no scent leading away. Then blood was noticed on one of the hounds. Looking into the hole the terrified hare was seen wedged in the topmost part, bleeding but still alive. The hounds had been able to reach and chew her hindquarters but she clung on desperately. No-one could reach her and hare hunts do not have followers armed with terriers. This injured hare might have escaped but eventually one of the smallest hounds squeezed in and dragged her out, killing her. In Elfin's opinion, they did not like killing hares that way, as it was "*not very sporting.*"

That was the 8th. On January 22nd I was back with the Warwickshire Beagles for their meet at *The Bell*, Cropthorne. I saw Peter Cooper, a Joint Master of the Three Counties Minkhounds at the meet and he was a bit chilly towards me to say the least.

Later, walking around the fields I learned why. He tackled me brusquely, "*Have you changed your address*?" I could only say "*No*" with an air of puzzled innocence. He added: "*Well Ian* (Coghill) *wrote to you wanting some pictures and had his letter returned by the Post Office marked 'Not known at this address'.*" I mentally cursed the Post Office as they were paid to forward my mail. My only escape was to explain that Ian must have written my address wrongly in some way. To add credibility I was able to truthfully say that Arlin Rickard had done the same but as an explanation it was still a bit thin. I had a distinct cloud of suspicion over me.

That day several hares were hunted to the brink of exhaustion but all escaped.

Peter's girlfriend, Rachel, kindly invited me back for tea but, knowing I was vulnerable to close questioning about my address, I declined, even though by doing so I raised further doubts as to my sincerity as a genuine hunt supporter.

The following week, January 29th, I attended my last beagle meet in the area with the Wyre Forest at *The Bridge*, Tenbury. This meet was the day after their Hunt Ball so they were all a bit jaded. In the crowded bar, I gave Roger Colver a photograph of himself that I had taken earlier in the month with his hounds outside Kinnersley Church. He was well pleased.

Leaving the pub the hunt vanned on to Whitton Farm. From 'Elfin' I learned that Loppylugs had been in his usual form at the Ball, saying to her: "*I can tell you are a woman when I'm dancing with you, but not when I see you out beagling!*"

There were plenty of hares about that day and the hounds ran with fervour in all directions. Eventually they settled to follow the scent of one with distinctive pure white hindquarters. I learned that she was the descendant of an all-white hare that had lived in the area some seven years previously. This hunt had clearly had previous fruitless encounters with this distinctive hare. Roger made it quite clear that he was determined to catch her. With scent reasonable the hounds pushed her hard; then momentarily they lost her. The landowner put them right but only reluctantly. Talking to supporters it transpired that he did not really want to see her caught. He feared that killing her would, in some way, bring him bad luck.

At that, most followers felt that in deference to his wishes the hunt should stop their pursuit but Roger persisted. The chase only ended when the pack rioted after a rabbit and in consequence lost the scent of their original quarry. The usually so willing hunt supporters lacked any real enthusiasm to help their hounds find this hare again. To compound their problems the pace of the hunt had been so fast that the hounds were well split. There were small contingents of the pack dotted here there and everywhere. After much searching they were all found bar one. With no kill made 'home' was blown and the whole pack taken to look for this miscreant.

On the way back to their cars the supporters chatted and joked about the white hare. They sought suggestions as to where she had gone. I opined that she was probably taking off her white trunks to pass to the next hare that is hunted. Picking up the theme another supporter laughed and said that if the antis really wanted to succeed they should spray all the hares white!

My last beagling meet was some two months later. I followed the Surrey and North Sussex meeting at *The Plough*, Lower Beeding, south-east of Horsham on Saturday March 19th 1983 to finish their season. This was some months before the general election that was held on June 9th 1983 — and won decisively by the Conservatives under Margaret Thatcher. The Labour leader, Michael Foot was due to speak at a nearby public meeting the following Saturday so, just before they set off, the Master exhorted his followers to go along to this meeting to heckle him.

With a number of hares about the hounds were soon running. They locked on to the scent of one and pursued her into a small wood. The wood was promptly surrounded by a ring of supporters all eager to see the action.

However, their very presence outside the covert deterred the hare from bolting out. In a furious temper hunt staff stormed up and ordered these supporters to move out of the way. It was pointed out firmly that if they did not move the hare would be 'chopped down' in the wood thereby denying them any 'sport'.

Recognising their error these followers obliged; the hare duly bolted and the hunt continued. But the scent must have been intermittent because the pack never again got on terms with their quarry. They changed hares frequently and eventually, as darkness approached, at about 6.00p.m. 'home' was blown with no kill recorded.

BASSET HOUNDS

Before I followed them the idea of basset hounds successfully hunting anything seemed to me to be ludicrous. With their short legs and long ears, I could picture them scraping their low undercarriage on any deep plough. It is another form of hare hunting in which supporters follow on foot.

I attended my first meet, with the Leadon Vale Basset Hounds at Church Farm, Hardwicke, near Gloucester on February 5th expecting it to be really interesting. I had met two of the keenest followers of this hunt at the AGM of the Three Counties Minkhounds the previous Tuesday and they willingly vouched for me as a genuine hunt supporter.

At the meet I was surprised to see in attendance two gentlemen from the Church wearing dog collars. They were a little perturbed when I took their pictures and notably absent when the action started — doubtless appreciating that it would be poor form to be recorded rejoicing over the tormenting and killing of God's creatures.

The hounds, with a small field of about 10 followers, set off to draw. In the first half hour alone there were no less than eight hares running relays with the hounds. I still could not believe that given their build these hounds would catch any of the fleet-footed hares, but the Honorary Secretary of the hunt, Dave Philpotts, assured me that their hounds had tremendous stamina and that would tell later in the day.

The hunt worked with the definite aim of scaring most of the hares away, so that, left with just a few, the hounds could push selected ones really hard. Round and round the estate we whizzed. Of all the pack hounds I had met these appeared to be the most self-contained and single minded. They simply locked on to a scent and were then oblivious to anything else. Dave recounted to me how on one occasion a basset had been left out overnight after a hunt. When the hunters searched for him the following morning the dedicated and determined soul was found still plodding round and round in circles looking for his hare.

At this hunt I took a rare photograph. By pure chance it showed the Master, David Mann, running with his hounds to a holloa just as another hare jumped up right in front of the pack. It is very unusual to get the hunted, the hounds and the hunter all in one frame.

Early in the afternoon the first hare hunted was chopped down just out of my sight. I only knew that hounds had killed when I saw the pack returning daubed liberally with blood. I learned from supporters that with the pack gaining rapidly the exhausted hare had sought cover in a hedge. A fresh hare bolted, taking the hounds away, but the tired hare made the mistake of backtracking too soon and she ran straight into the jaws of four hounds straggling along behind the main pack.

The hunt drew on anew. Soon we were running in circles again. Locking on to hunt another victim the hounds pursued her in a left-handed circle. She then tracked along the side of the Sharpness - Gloucester ship canal, headed slowly back over a field and with the hounds gaining, made for the protection of a deep bramble shrouded ditch. I arrived to find Dave Philpotts and other supporters running up and down beside this ditch holloaing and screaming with glee.

The exhausted creature desperately sought sanctuary, crawling in the muddy water that lined the bottom of the ditch. The hounds pounced and fell on top of her. There was the briefest of squeals and she was torn to shreds. That particular hunt had been quite short, so the hunters assumed that she must have been tired, having been 'rattled' by one of the earlier hunts in the morning.

The hunters drew on over the fields looking for their third kill of the day. I had been so very wrong in my early assessment of basset hounds as ineffective hunters. The hunt followers however, unlike their hounds, were extremely tired and welcomed 'home' being blown at about 4.00p.m.

A fortnight later, February 19th, I was back with this same pack when they met at *The Horseshoe*, Brooms Green, south of Ledbury. The ground appeared hard after frost but was soft underneath. Hares were about and great circular hunts after them soon developed. The day more or less ended though when the hounds and followers, in the enthusiasm of the chase, bolted a herd of young bullocks out of their field.

Some of the hunt followers were all for carrying on, saying that the farmer should have put up stronger gates, but, to their credit, the staff stopped proceedings and organised a team of hunters to drive the bullocks back to safety. The following month, March 26th, I was back with the same pack for a repeat meet at Church Farm, Hardwick. This was their last meet that season. It was very late in the year to be hunting hares. I had to be very careful as these hunters were extremely suspicious of me and my true motives, particularly those who also followed the Three Counties Minkhounds.

I arrived after the start, to learn that the hounds had killed in their very first field, chopping down one of a brace of hares that popped up right in front of them. That brought their tally for the 1982-83 season to nine brace (18 hares). Hounds soon found again and in the hunt that followed I took the opportunity to question some mink hunting supporters about Ian Coghill reporting the throwing of a live mink to hounds but, for reasons that will become apparent, they became very suspicious of me. One left in a great hurry saying he had to phone his wife. Suspecting that he might actually be phoning some far from friendly mates and organising a 'farewell party' of the painful kind for me, I took it as my cue, made an excuse and I also left.

HARE COURSING

As previously described, my days as a hunt saboteur had taught me that hare coursing is a particularly cold and clinical way of killing hares. The Blue Riband event in the hare coursing calendar, coursing's equivalent of the FA Cup final, was the 64-dog stake Waterloo Cup which took place on wide open wind-swept fields at Altcar near Liverpool every year in the spring.

The Waterloo Cup was the largest hare coursing event and it required a lot of hares. To boost the local stock these timid creatures were caught by being driven into fine nets in other parts of the country, particularly East Anglia, transported in small wooden crates and released on to the coursing fields around Altcar sometime before the event. The Waterloo Cup Report and Accounts for 1982 showed a sundry expense listed for "*Hare re-stocking*" of £363.

One can but speculate as to the eventual fate that awaited the hares that survived the coursing only to exist in a small area unnaturally highly stocked.

171

Hare coursing was seldom if ever justified on the grounds of 'pest control'. The lead arguments put forward by hare coursers were that they killed few hares, those that were killed were killed 'instantly' and finally coursing enthusiasts claimed that they looked after and protected the hares on their land (so that they would have hares to torment and kill at the appropriate time). Fortunately there are plenty of farmers and landowners who are more genuinely benevolent towards wildlife.

Female hares (does) would most likely be pregnant and some even nursing at the time the Waterloo Cup — and other Spring hare coursing events — took place.

The 1983 Waterloo Cup was scheduled for March 2nd-4th and I decided to attend not as a saboteur this time (as I had in 1976 and 1977) but with a more subtle form of sabotage in mind — to try and take some pictures — as Raymond Rowley had done for the League many years before. Knowing there are strict rules preventing photography I thought it wise to phone beforehand to get permission.

I phoned the BFSS with my cover story. They said I was probably too late (it was March 1st) and referred me to a northern based vet, James MacWilliam, the Honorary Secretary of the Waterloo Cup Committee. At this point I felt that I was getting too personally involved and therefore was noticeable. I decided to just turn up at the event as an anonymous punter.

I travelled north on the night of March 1st and chose to stay at a bed and breakfast hotel at Southport, well out of the zone where a combination of my using a LACS credit card to pay the bill whilst driving a car adorned with BFSS stickers might arouse interest.

I heard that hunt saboteurs planned a big demonstration for the first day against the cruelty of coursing, so I expected the coursing supporters to be even more jittery than usual. As it was, they had ducked the demonstration by bringing their start forward by one day. On Tuesday 1st March they had successfully completed a total of sixty six courses. By this unannounced early start they had avoided any trouble on the day when they need to complete the most courses, but by doing so in such secrecy they lost many casual supporters.

It was pouring with rain when I drove up on Wednesday 2nd, to learn that the event had been switched from the scheduled Withins to nearby Lydiate field. The first day is always staged at the Withins, the second at Lydiate and for the finals on the third day the event moves back to the Withins. I drove around to the new site to join a long queue of cars to enter the arena.

Some coursers either parked in nearby villages to avoid using the official car park (where it was easy to get stuck in the mud) or they reached the area by public transport. Either way many faced a long hike from the road to the coursing field so passing some of these walkers I offered a lift to one of the young lads. He eagerly accepted, as did his two mates. They turned out to be beaters from the North Yorkshire Coursing Club. With my car full of coursers I prayed that my routine check of the car to remove all LACS material had been sound. As the queue slowed and finally stopped my car gradually steamed up.

I glanced in my wing mirror and was mortified to see a group of friends wearing hunt saboteur T-shirts approaching from the rear! They were likely to recognise the car, but would they recognise my role and see that I had company — company of the distinctly 'heavy' kind? If my compassionate colleagues were to give me a hearty welcome in all their 'sabs' outfits that would be the end of my undercover project. I breathed again when they passed us by without comment. When it came to paying the £5 entrance fee the beaters said who they were so we all got in free. Giving a lift to these beaters also gave me the perfect cover

After parking I went to have a look at the coursing, but without my camera. I soon saw others in the crowd taking pictures so I judged that it would be safe for me to do likewise and returned for mine. I returned just in time to see a hare jinking away in front of the two greyhounds before she eventually escaped.

I stood amid a crowd of supporters on a long side of the coursing rectangle. A light, misty rain was falling — which proved a bit of a problem for me — a photographer wearing glasses. The set up was that hares were being beaten in across the fields to our left. The lines of beaters were co-ordinated to coax a single hare to run on to the coursing field past the slipper — the man restraining the two greyhounds who at this premier event lurked concealed behind a well-made green lean-to structure.

Four more hares were driven in, of which only two escaped. Often, when being herded forwards they would nearly reach the field, only to veer away at the last minute. They would then run off back from whence they came, meet the lines of beaters and be funnelled back again. The net effect was that some unfortunate hares had done a few circuits in the beating funnel before they even reached the coursing field.

When these hares hit the grass they were already tiring. As individuals passed the slipper he was supposed to judge whether they

173

were fit to be coursed and if they were give them the necessary 80 yards start before unleashing the greyhounds. Hares that are sickly or weak are supposed to be left. The only ones I saw left in the two days of my observations were judged to be leverets.

In practice, as soon as a hare passed the slipper the crowd bayed like mad for the greyhounds to be released. Beer swigging supporters shouted: "*Let the bloody dogs go! What's the bastard up to? Can't he see the f...... hare?*"

Hares might be fast but these greyhounds are bred to be faster. When the greyhounds were released they quickly overhauled their quarry whose only escape was to jink sharply to the left or right. In one course a dog bowled the hare over. Over and over she tumbled, with fur flying off her. She regained her feet and darted off to escape.

Time and again I confirmed what I had first learned as a hunt saboteur with an interest in hare coursing: that for the hare, surviving the first few turns was vital, as the dogs soon tired. Unlike pack hounds that are bred for stamina greyhounds are bred for pure speed — to outpace their quarry — but they cannot sustain full speed for long. The first kill happened over the other side of the field from me so I and the bulk of supporters saw little.

The second kill was different. Jinking and twisting the hare approached the solid crowd. There was no way through for her as the spectators roared the dogs on. She swerved away and was caught. The crowd cheered. One dog grabbed hold of her shoulders the other her back feet. She squeaked and squealed. The dogs tussled for possession and, in an instant, one dog won. As the mounted judge and pickers-up approached this dog ran off triumphantly, still clutching her by the shoulder. Still she squealed and still the crowd cheered and jeered.

The dog circled around, nimbly avoiding the pickers-up. As he approached me, I captured the hare's terror in one quick photograph, before the dog came close to the crowd and was trapped. Firm hands wrestled the hare from its grasp. A picker-up soon put her out of her agony with a chop to her neck. The dog's owner ran up to congratulate his charge.

These five courses were the last that morning as a large group of hunt saboteurs swept across the field in front of the beaters and refused to move. At that time I estimated there to be about three hundred and fifty sabs to seven hundred coursers.

The police were reluctant to remove the sabs from their peaceful protest but the coursers were itching to get at them. Individuals passed amongst the coursing crowd exhorting them to violence: "*Let's teach these student scum a lesson. Stand up and fight for your sport.*"

174

This intense whipping up of anger paid dividends. Some coursers did eventually react and charged towards the saboteurs, only pausing to rip out some fence posts on their way to use as weapons.

I thought that a repeat of the Border Counties Otterhounds incident at Llandinam was in the offing and moved across, camera at the ready. The thin blue line of four police officers saved the day by halting the coursers' charge.

With the two sides in close proximity the coursers baited their opponents. One courser held the body of a hare killed only moments before above his head, shaking it to goad the sabs and swinging it around. The police quickly ordered him to stop.

The saboteurs still refused to move from their position that was so effectively holding up proceedings. The coursers then made it clear to the police that unless they evicted the sabs the coursers would do it themselves. Forced to act the police gathered more personnel and formed a beat line of their own officers intending to sweep the sabs away. The sabs responded by sitting down.

The press, who had been with the coursers, rushed over to take pictures and seizing this opportunity several coursers joined in the stampede, looking for a fight, but the police restrained them.

This running conflict went on all morning. At one point the coursers succeeded in getting amongst the sabs and kicked and punched some to the ground. The police endeavoured to keep the two sides apart and they eventually manoeuvred the sabs back to the road and held them there. The beat line of coursers then walked in as planned but by then there was only one hare left in the funnel. She escaped.

The coursers stopped for lunch to listen to a local radio debate between Richard Course, Executive Director of the LACS and Sir Mark Prescott, famous and successful racehorse trainer and hare coursing addict.

In the afternoon the coursers sent their beat lines out in the opposite direction from that used in the morning. The beaters came in from the right hand side of the field. This time there were plenty of hares. At one point it was announced that there were six in the holding field, just off the coursing field. The trick then for the coursers was to drive those hares just one at a time on to the coursing field.

In that afternoon session I saw about one in three hares coursed escape. I noticed that if they could survive about six turns, they were safe as the greyhounds tired so quickly. On several occasions I watched as the hare ran right off the coursing field pursued by the labouring greyhounds and with their cursing owners plodding along behind. The day ended at 4p.m. after twenty courses had been run. I returned to my accommodation.

Next day, March 3rd, was the day of the finals, held at the Withins. This time no hunt saboteurs attended. Hunt saboteurs have many issues to care about and they had moved off to support a nearby protest against the killing of seal pups in Canada for the fur trade.

At the Withins right from early morning it threatened rain, but surprisingly it held off. The first course started at 9.45a.m. with hares being driven in from the right and escaping through a screen of rhododendron bushes to the left. I soon appreciated that, on this massive field, it was going to be almost impossible to take any significant photographs. I was too far away and needed a far more powerful telephoto lens than I had in my camera bag. At Lydiate we could almost touch the greyhounds; here we were separated by a wide ditch and yards of open space.

A larger percentage of hares were escaping; only about one in five were killed. When I asked a coursing enthusiast why this should be I was informed that it was due to the ground being waterlogged in the middle and the greyhounds slipping and sliding as they turned.

I still saw several kills which included lengthy tugs-of-war. I could hear the hares screaming pitifully, like roughly handled teddy bears, but I was too far away to record their struggles on film.

Eager anticipation amongst the watching crowd built up to the actual finals for the different competitions. I had seen the busy bookies and guessed that a lot of money was at stake. For these finals the supporters roared and cheered the dogs on. In the grand final — for the Waterloo Cup itself — desperately the hare turned every which way she could but when she made an error she was killed.

Afterwards I lingered with other coursers to record the last acts. The final ceremony I photographed was the drunken celebration of it all as Waterloo Cup, Waterloo Purse (for dogs beaten in the first round) and Waterloo Plate (for dogs beaten in the second round) were presented to the winners, whilst the broken remains of the coursed hares — who paid with their lives for this fun — lay forgotten beside the arena.

Left: Devon and Cornwall Minkhounds, April 24th 1982. Master and Huntsman, Arlin Rickard, looks up a drain for a mink.

Devon and Cornwall Minkhounds, May 3rd 1982. Above: Arlin Rickard, taunts his hounds with a live mink.
Below: hunt supporter holds the tiny carcass aloft in triumph.

Devon and Cornwall Minkhounds, May 31st 1982. Above left: moving off from the meet with terrier and spade to hand. Above right: whipper-in , Graham Miles, with remains of mink.

Below left: a dead mink is retrieved. Below right: the remains of the mink are weighed.

Above: Culmstock Minkhounds, June 15th 1982. Master, Norman Bartlett, with his hounds.

Below: Devon and Cornwall Minkhounds, June 26th 1982.

Left: Charlie Harding with remains of dead mink.
Right: Charlie Harding weighs remains of dead mink.

Mink hunting joint week, July 7th 1982. Hunting the River Wye.
Above right: Ian Arnett, Huntsman Four Shires Minkhounds with
dead mink.
Below: a mink is caught by a hound (centre of picture).

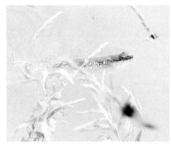

Mink hunting joint week, July 7th 1982.
Top: habitat disturbance.
Above: young mink swims.

Above: Ian Arnett, Huntsman Four Shires Minkhounds taunts hounds with dead mink.

Mink hunting joint week, July 8th 1982. Devon and Cornwall / Three Counties Minkhounds. Left: youth with dead mink. Below: hounds tussle over dead mink.

Mink hunting joint week, July 9th 1982. Devon and Cornwall / Three Counties Minkhounds. Above: mink (arrowed) flees. Right: Whipper-in, Steve Evans, takes a dip.

Mink hunting joint
week, July 10th 1982.

Devon and Cornwall /
Three Counties
Minkhounds.

Top: mink dug out
(left) and bolts (right).

Above: mink swims.

Right: mink bolted
from drain

Mink hunting joint week, July 10th 1982. Devon and Cornwall / Three Counties Minkhounds. Above: supporters stop the exhausted mink escaping. Below: Peter Cooper (Joint Master of Three Counties Minkhounds) holds the dead mink aloft .

Above: mink hunting joint week, July 10th 1982. Devon and Cornwall / Three Counties Minkhounds.

Right: that was a bit close! Three Counties Minkhounds, August 21st 1982.

Left: leading hounds into danger. Three Counties Minkhounds, September 25th 1982.

Three Counties Minkhounds, July 31st 1982. Above left: the two sides — with the author (left) looking slightly uneasy. Above right: Joint Master and Huntsman, Ian Coghill, taunts his hounds with a dead mink.

Right: a supporter carries out some running repairs for Ian Coghill.

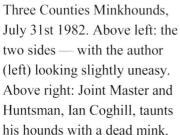

Right: the kill

Three Counties Minkhounds, August 7th 1982.

Top: mink seeks sanctuary in tree. Supporter climbs after him.

Below: Ian Coghill throws the remains of a dead mink to his hounds.

Three Counties / Border Counties Minkhounds, August 25th 1982.
Top: lawn meet at Caradoc House, beside the River Wye.

Bottom: dead mink is retrieved and Ian Coghill cuts the trophies
off.

Three Counties Minkhounds, September 4th 1982. A mink is hunted. He seeks refuge in a riverbank hole. He is then dug out, held alive and thrown up on the bank in front of hounds.

Right: mink (black arrow) in flight.

Below: mink (white arrow) runs but is soon caught.

These pictures are single frames taken from 8mm cine film.

Three Counties Minkhounds, September 8th 1982.
Above right: Jack Charlton assists Peter May in digging for a mink.
Below: filming for *Jack's Game*.

Three Counties Minkhounds, September 11th 1982.

In desperate pursuit of a mink, hunters take a chainsaw to a beautiful old willow tree. The Joint Master and Huntsman, Ian Coghill, was Conservation and Education Officer for the British Field Sports Society.

The three pictures below are single frames from 8mm cine film.

Right: drowning the mink.

Below: clubbing the mink to ensure he was dead.

Below right: pulling the dead mink around in an impromptu drag hunt.

Top left: Ian Coghill at his Three Counties Minkhounds wine and cheese party, September 12th 1982. Top right: Arlin Rickard, Master and Huntsman, Devon and Cornwall Minkhounds, June 12th 1982.

Below: hounds are as innocent as the animals they chase. Three Counties / Devon and Cornwall Minkhounds July 9th 1982.

CHAPTER TEN
Mink hunting

Mink hunting is the summer bloodsport. It replaced otter hunting as the 'sport' that fills the gap between the end of one fox hunting season in April and the start of the next in August/September.

Mink are an introduced species, originally imported to the UK from North America from 1929 onwards to be exploited in ranch farms for their fur. When the fur trade collapsed in the 1940's and 1950's many mink farms went out of business and some owners simply released their mink into the wild expecting them to soon die.

However mink are adaptable creatures; they found a habitat that suited them and soon established themselves. They began filling the riparian habitats that were increasingly vacated by otters.

Both mink and otters are mustelids, both have similar habits and occupy similar habitats. However otters are much larger, they weigh 20 to 30lbs (9 to 13 kg) compared to the 3 to 4lbs (1.4 to 1.8 kg) of a mink. Otters are much better swimmers and are specialised predators.

Otter hunters always struggled to justify their killing of otters on the grounds of alleged damage to fishing interests. Mink pose even less of a threat to fish in open rivers and large lakes so the use of the 'pest control' justification by mink hunters makes even less sense. Mink are a threat to other small mammals and birds but as a pest control measure mink hunting has proved to be worse than useless. Many mink hunted are not caught and those that escape the hounds are often driven far from where they were found. Otter hunting and in turn mink hunting were one of the prime vectors for spreading mink the length and breadth of our countryside.

The marked decline in otter numbers that occurred in the 1970's forced the hunters to search for alternative prey. In much of the country mink were prime candidates. Where they were few in number, as in East Anglia, the coypu, a South American river rat, likewise originally imported to be exploited for its fur, was the selected target. From the 1930s onwards coypu escaped from their fur farms and began to establish themselves in the wild.

For many years, though still claiming the title Otter hunts, the hunts were in facts chasing and killing otters, mink and coypu, dependant on their location. Otter hunters regarded hunting mink or coypu as a poor substitute for otter hunting — they saw it is little better than rat hunting — but for people desperate to follow hounds all year round it was better than nothing.

As outlined on pages 35-41 this continued persecution forced the otter into further decline, with the situation worsening to the point where the species was placed on the protected list from January 1978. It then became illegal to kill otters. Tormenting and killing otters for sport had continued right up until the last hunting opportunity — certainly until the summer of 1977,

However there was a legal anomaly that proved very convenient for hunters. It was only illegal to kill otters not to hunt them. This wording left the summer bloodsports free to continue. All that was required was a change of name and a change of focus to either of the alternative prey — mink or coypu. Some otter hunts that did not switch to hunt these new quarries reverted to the status of hunt clubs. One such club, the Courtenay Tracy Otter Hounds Club, was careful to retain control of their former hunting areas *"pending a possible resumption of otter hunting."* (*Baily's Hunting Directory* 1980-1981)

Otter hunts such as the Dartmoor Otterhounds closed down and new hunts like the Devon and Cornwall Minkhounds were set up to hunt similar areas. It was largely the same people using many of the same hounds to hunt the same rivers from the same meets in very similar fashion.

During the passage of the Wildlife and Countryside Bill in 1982 the Labour MP for Stockport North, Andrew Bennett, proposed an amendment that would have provided full protection for the otter. The powerful hunting lobby recognised the threat to their interests, opposed the amendment and it was defeated.

At the same time the Minister responsible, Hector Monro MP, assured the House of Commons that otter hunting was already illegal. However, a Home Office briefing document, leaked to the League, makes it clear that, at the time, Hector Monro was advised that otter hunting was not completely illegal. Referring to Andrew Bennett's amendment this document says:

"The amendment may also be intended to place a complete ban on otter hunting."

The LACS exposed this confusion that was so convenient for hunters. Soon afterwards Hector Monro MP, a keen supporter of bloodsports, was sacked.

The main threat to otters, through the continuance of mink and coypu hunting, is from the disturbance of the habitat. [Determined efforts by the Ministry of Agriculture, Fisheries and Food (forerunner to the Department for Environment, Food and Rural Affairs) are believed to have killed the last coypu by 1989] This type of hunting entailed many hounds from a mixture of breeds, including reject foxhounds, rampaging through the riverside vegetation. These are accompanied by free-running terriers and any holes that these dogs show interest in are probed and often dug-out by terriermen. To breed successfully otters require peace and freedom from harassment. There is also the more direct threat in the form of the very real risk of hounds rioting and hunting and killing otters in the same way that foxhounds riot and kill cats.

*****

My investigation into mink hunting differed from my other undercover work to expose hunts because I had never even seen a mink hunt as a hunt saboteur. I had only ever sabbed otter hunts. With no previous experiences of mink hunting to talk about I was counting on my by then extensive knowledge of West Country fox and stag hunting to give me the required hunting credentials.

The first mink hunt I attended in my undercover role was on April 24th 1982. I had been following Spring stag hunting in the West Country and, along with many other hunters, I drifted over to see this curious new 'sport'.

The chosen hunt was the Devon and Cornwall Minkhounds. Their young Master, Arlin Rickard, enjoyed a reputation as a rising star in the hunting world. The meet was at *The Claycutters Arms*, Chudleigh Knighton near Bovey Tracey at 11.00a.m.

Sporting the full camouflage of stag hunt and BFSS stickers on my car windscreen and wearing hunting clothing I was made very welcome. As a courtesy I asked permission to take photographs and they were delighted to agree. There soon assembled a motley collection numbering some 20 or more followers, ranging from the roughest looking terriermen to young children.

The hounds were a similar mixture and included what appeared to be pure-bred otterhounds, part otterhounds and pure foxhounds — I learned later that these were rejects from fox hunts. Typical hounds, they were big, bouncy, friendly and, with a mite of encouragement, would readily plant their paws on your shoulders and lick your chin.

Mink hunting, like otter hunting, takes place on foot. When the hunt moved off the hounds drew ahead on either bank and swam the river between. The Whippers-in, one of whom was Arlin's wife Liz, ran ahead to ensure that the hounds did not forage too far forward. The hunt followers split into two groups on either side of the river and immediately engaged in earnest hunting conversations.

Arlin encouraged his hounds, "*Try over, try over.*" He blew his horn and waded backwards and forwards over the river, investigating any likely holes or holts. When wading he took care to use his hunting pole to prod the river-bed ahead to assess its depth. Many a riparian

Huntsman has been known to disappear up to his cap on encountering a hidden underwater gully — to the delight of those watching from the safety of the bank. The hunt terriers, running loose in attendance, were frequently called forward to investigate when hounds sniffed at likely spots.

Aware of very real public concern about their activities mink hunters claim never to hunt where there are any signs of otters. Yet on my very first day I found that there is a world of difference between what hunters claim and the facts. In the very first draw a Whipper-in called Arlin's attention to a fresh otter print found in the mud. Others were found nearby, yet the hunt still continued.

I found that compared to fox or stag hunting, mink hunting proceeds at a very leisurely and sedate pace, most of the time. Some hunts, the Devon and Cornwall being one, even make time to stop for a picnic lunch. There were few mink about that day. When the heat of the sun had passed the hounds did speak briefly to an unknown scent. This produced a surge of expectant excitement amongst the followers but it was short lived as nothing was found. Arlin suggested two reasons for this lack of activity.

Firstly that the water was too cold to hold any scent, secondly that they would only be able to hunt dog mink as the bitches were with young and at such times leave no scent. Having already witnessed pregnant vixens being hunted, marked to ground and thrown live to foxhounds, I was sceptical about the latter point.

The following Saturday, May 1st, the same hounds met at Boyton Bridge near Holsworthy. Here I first met Belmont, a beautiful old rogue of a hound, drafted out of the Snowdon Valley Foxhounds for lack of speed — he had a lopsided gait caused by a deformed foreleg.

I soon realised that Belmont had a playful nature. Though vaunted by the hunt as being their best marking hound — that is, the hound most likely to find hidden mink — he appeared to me to be distinctly mischievous. He seemed to mark at any hole or tree-trunk for the sheer fun of seeing the consequent agitated attempts by hunters to dislodge non-existent mink.

This was a more successful day for the hunt. Early on they found and destroyed a fresh nest containing green grass and rabbit fur. Soon after, the hounds marked to a hole in the bank that Arlin, after close examination, announced was occupied by a bitch mink and her kits.

Oblivious to the supposed lack of scent left by such creatures, the hounds and terriers bayed like mad at the entrance. In the face of much hissing and spitting from within the diggers endeavoured to enlarge the hole but, for all their valiant efforts, it was still too narrow for the terriers to enter. The attack was switched to the tunnel roof. They dug frantically but these efforts were also thwarted when their spade broke. All manner of implements were then directed against the entombed mink but without success.

Arlin then had a hunter's brainwave; cutting a long thin stick from a nearby tree he used his knife to carve the end to a sharp point. Inserting this improvised spear in the hole he rammed it up as if clearing a drain from Dover to Calais. He smiled when he encountered resistance, drew the stick back and rammed it viciously in, again and again, waggling it around just to be sure. When he drew the stick out the end was smeared with blood, fur and flesh. Eagerly other followers rushed to take their turn to have a prod. The hunters did not move on until they were confident that the trapped mother and young mink were all stabbed and ripped to death.

Mink hunting may be a pastime conducted over some of the most beautiful parts of our countryside but it certainly has a dark and unpleasant core.

The first kill in open view that I saw with the Devon and Cornwall occurred the following Monday when they met at *The Maltsters*, Harbertonford, north-east of Dartmouth, at the southern end of their country. Some of the pre-meet conversations in the pub were particularly interesting once the whisky had started flowing. There was much concern that, after two meets, the hounds had yet to kill. One supporter suggested that the new entry of puppies would really benefit if caged mink could be found and released in front of them.

This certainly conformed to the traditional hunt view that inexperienced hounds should be taught to hunt and kill as a unit and thereby enter the pack by being unleashed on the most vulnerable quarry. Such a strategy in mink hunting was clearly inspired by the attempts by the Ministry of Agriculture to check the spread of mink using live cage trapping. These traps were used so that any otters, inadvertently caught, could be released unharmed and any mink killed humanely.

It was certainly never envisaged by the Ministry that they could be used to ensure a steady supply of helpless victims for frustrated huntsmen. Sitting amongst supporters I listened intently to their chatter, absorbing their knowledge and opinions. Following the killing of the bitch and kits there was some discussion as to the merits of waiting until the mink family emerged — instead of killing them in their nest.

Many held that it was a waste to kill a bitch whilst pregnant because it only added one to their tally whereas if they waited for a few weeks until she gave birth she and her offspring could provide 'great sport' on the open river — and as many as five kills might be notched up.

Clearly, in the interests of 'sport', the mink hunters are happy to forget their public claim that, unlike other bloodsports, their sole intention is to eradicate their quarry.

As the drink flowed tongues loosened further and I learned more. I mentioned to Liz Rickard how fortunate it was for their style of hunting that mink are now an established substitute for the otter. She agreed wholeheartedly.

When eventually we set off the hunt drew the river north from the meet with 8½ couple of hounds and an assortment of terriers.

Almost immediately the hounds spoke and the mink was sighted — a point confirmed by rather drunken holloas. The terrified creature swam up a short tributary away from the main river, landed, and ran alongside a hedgerow, darting amid the brambles with the hounds and followers in hot pursuit.

Turning about, he ran beside the tributary back to the main river but was attacked by a terrier just short of his goal. The hiss and spit of battle was clearly audible but, for all the terrier's tenacity, the mink escaped, albeit almost certainly with severe injuries. The mink flopped into the water with the hounds all around, their frantic splashing whipping up a maelstrom.

Arlin waded into the fray together with his Whipper-in Graham Miles. The injured mink was struggling on the surface, incapable of diving. Arlin hooked the crippled creature out with his pole and held it up to bait his hounds. With a flick of its tail the mink twisted off the pole and fell into the waiting jaws. Death came swiftly.

The torn body was recovered and weighed (3½ lbs). I was told that information about each kill was carefully recorded and then passed to the local Naturalists' Trust.

The hunt moved on in high spirits. Suddenly frantic yelps of pain from the hounds betrayed the presence of a live, electric fence. One hound in particular, a big white fluffy creature named Regent, did not like it at all and disappeared in double quick time.

After a picnic lunch a second mink was found near the main A38, a road crowded with holiday traffic. With scenting conditions excellent the hounds ran with fervour. The mink was repeatedly viewed as he darted in and out of the reeds lining the river banks. Occasionally he landed and when he ran he was so fast in the grass that the hounds seemed clumsy in comparison.

Backwards and forwards the quarry went within the short stretch of river that obviously constituted his home range. Soon the scent trail became hopelessly foiled by the hounds and supporters milling about in baffled pursuit.

Arlin called his hounds back to take stock of the situation and perhaps to allow things to settle. He then cast them back. They spoke intermittently as they caught faint whiffs of scent but there were no further sightings.

They were about to call it a day when one of the elderly supporters, Jane Miller, a former Master of the Dartmoor Otterhounds, saw the mink curled about the topmost branches of a tree, gazing down!

Arlin called the pack and hunt followers to the safety of one side and a barrage of stones and mud was thrown at the mink in an effort to dislodge him. Clinging desperately to the branches he sustained a few hits without moving, but eventually a particularly large rock jarred him and he fell into the murky river below. The supporters cheered their success.

The hounds sprang forward into the water and enthusiastic hunt followers waded in their wake. The mink dived. With 17 quadrupeds and many humans milling about, the river-bed was soon whipped up into a frothy morass of murk.

The mink took full advantage of this aquatic smokescreen. Like destroyers searching for submarine contacts the hounds swam in patterns seeking their quarry but there was no sign. In such a confined area though, it was only a matter of time. Soon one of the best hounds, Prospect, marked at a hole in the bank. Arlin enlarged the shelter with his pole and exposed the exhausted mink, huddled against the muddy wall. A terrier grabbed him, the pack burst forward and it was all over. The mink was literally torn apart but, conscious of the need to weigh the carcass, the hunters searched diligently for the remains. The largest portion recovered weighed 3¾ lbs but adding an estimate for the blood and guts that had been ripped out and lost the hunters claimed 4lbs.

That was the beginning of May. At the end of the month, the 29th, I was back with the same hunt for their meet at *The Arundell Arms*, Lifton, near Launceston. Mink hunters claim to be able to distinguish whether hounds are chasing mink or otter according to the length of the drag. For a mink the drag is short, the quarry soon sighted, but for otters that roam over much larger territories the drag is longer. On this occasion the hounds hit a long, long drag in the afternoon, so protracted that many of the followers were convinced that it was an otter; but the hounds were not called off.

The supporters regarded it as great fun. The end of the planned draw brought the end of the hunting day even though the hounds were still willing to drive on after their unseen adversary.

The opening meet for the Devon and Cornwall Minkhounds was two days later on Monday 31st at *The London Inn*, St Neot. The hunt had no sooner commenced than their hounds spoke, a mink was sighted and, after a brief desperate 'game' of hide and seek, a 2½lb bitch was killed. She tried to find sanctuary amid dense brambles but with all the followers about looking and helping the hounds she simply ran out of room to hide. Lunch was taken as a picnic at the East Cornwall Hunt kennels washed down with a liberal dose of Bell's whisky. Suitably fortified the hunt restarted and, after another short chase, killed a 3½lb dog mink. The torn and battered carcass was about the size of a large hairy slipper. That day I first heard glowing tales of the exploits of West Midlands Huntsman Ian Coghill. His hunt, the Three Counties Minkhounds, is reckoned to show the best summer 'sport' of all.

During June 1982 I attended four mink hunts. Following uneventful meets of the Devon and Cornwall at the very picturesque Fingle Bridge, Drewsteignton on the 12th and at Kismeldon Bridge, Bradworthy on the 14th I had my one and only day with the Culmstock Minkhounds at Black Torrington Bridge on the 15th.

This is another hunt with direct connections with otter hunting. The aged Master, Norman Bartlett, was Master of the Culmstock Otterhounds for many years. This pack enjoyed a fearsome reputation for being vicious not only towards their natural quarry but also to anyone who dared to interfere. In 1964 four of its supporters were bound over to keep the peace following an assault in which a hunt saboteur's jaw was broken.

Norman Bartlett is a hunting man to the core. He was Master of the Axe Vale Badger Hounds for many years. This mink hunt may have a cruel heritage but the supporters made an amusing picture, with Norman dressed in old-fashioned hunting garb, complete with bowler hat. After lunch the pack locked on to the scent of a particularly large mink. Try as he might he could not shake them off. He ended up ripped in half.

On Saturday June 26th at *The Bullers Arms*, Marhamchurch south of Bude, I was back with the Devon and Cornwall Minkhounds. During the day I was offered and readily accepted a place on the excursion by Devon and Cornwall hunters to join the Three Counties and Four Shires hunts at a coming Joint Week of mink hunting in the West Midlands. Arlin promised me that I would have every opportunity to take some excellent pictures. Clearly I was fully accepted and trusted as a genuine hunt supporter.

The 26th was most interesting with a lengthy hunt after a very elusive mink. In their enthusiasm to catch him the Whippers-in waded into the water almost up to their necks to dig at likely hiding places in the river banks.

The mink twisted, turned and dived but there was to be no escape — there were simply too many hounds and too many people. When eventually caught, Charlie Harding, son of Norah, the Joint Master and leading light within the Devon and Somerset Staghounds, was proud to display the shattered remains for my camera.

JOINT WEEK

The Joint Week, Monday July 5th to Saturday July 10th 1982, involved three packs of mink hounds — the Three Counties based in the West Midlands and Welsh Borders, the Four Shires who operate just west of London and the Devon and Cornwall.

The idea is simple — a week long bloodsports jamboree with hunting and killing interspersed with much pub fun in the evenings involving liberal drinking, reminiscing about past hunts and the raucous singing of hunting songs. Ian Coghill, the organiser, chose a week early in July because that is when the young mink first leave their nest and are easily found. I was assured that it was marvellous 'sport' watching the hounds chase the struggling youngsters.

The week commenced on the Monday but I arrived with the Devon and Cornwall contingent for the triple meet on Wednesday July 7th at a small pub *The Cottage of Content* near Carey, by the beautiful river Wye. I turned up full of expectation and interest in finally meeting Ian Coghill, my formidable antagonist in the letters columns of many local papers. He was Conservation and Education Officer for the BFSS. I (as Mike Wilkins) was Press Officer for the LACS. But he was not there. His own followers explained with mirth that, unable to swim, he is none too keen on the wide and deep Wye.

The Devon and Cornwall hounds were late due to their Land Rover breaking down, so Ian Arnett, Huntsman of the Four Shires Minkhounds took charge of the combined packs — his own hounds and those of the Three Counties.

It was a scorching hot summer's day with very still air. To start with the hounds drew a small brook beside the pub. They soon spoke excitedly, ran briefly, then marked to ground, with the terriers just as

185

keen. The Three Counties terriermen waded into the fray digging at the earth with great gusto and soon exposed, not a mink, but a quivering, terrified rabbit. The creature was seized and thrust in front of the jaws of one of the terriers that had bayed with such enthusiasm. The dog was clubbed as punishment for his error and the rabbit released.

The hunt returned to the river Wye, drawing upstream first. The river was wide and deep, the water clear. With the river filled with weed flowing lazily with the current and its banks shrouded by a tangled web of vegetation it was ideal mink/otter country.

The hounds quickly spoke and after a short chase killed a mink. Cast again they spoke again ran a bit and killed again. The scenario was repeated. It was slaughter of the youngsters. When I questioned why these young mink were so easily caught one of the women laughingly explained that their fur was still too fluffy to allow them to dive properly. Able only to flop about on the surface it was an aquatic version of coursing. Whenever possible the torn remains were recovered, brought out and held aloft, goading the hounds to jump for their reward.

Around midday the Devon and Cornwall finally arrived and their hounds were added to the canine contingent. Arlin agreed to let Ian continue hunting the combined trio of packs. This veritable hound army, about 60 strong, soon spoke again and raced off upstream in pursuit of their tiny quarry. The pack headed for some islands in midstream and the supporters went to follow. Wading out they soon found and feared the depth of the water, so returned. Finding the scent of another mink the hunt dashed downstream in and out of the lush vegetation. This victim was white and as such an added attraction but, for all their efforts, they could not catch him.

Returning, the hounds again set off for the islands. Anxious not to miss anything the supporters decided to risk the perilous crossing and, linking arms for mutual support and safety they waded over. Though I had been forced by necessity to wade similar but much colder rivers during my expedition to Afghanistan clutching my cameras above my head, I opted not to risk such an action this time. I had the remainder of the week ahead and water does not work wonders in modern cameras.

With other hunt followers I watched from the safety of the river bank. Out on the islands the hounds set about the resident mink families, killing four youngsters very quickly and scattering the remainder. Some passing canoeists out to enjoy genuine sport paddled to the scene, attracted by the baying of dogs and whoops of glee. They gazed in amazement as grown men and women in fancy dress waded chest deep in the river and uttered the most unearthly guttural screams. In time hounds were called back to our side and the ensemble moved downstream with the hunt deliberately split to increase effectiveness. Arlin took charge as Huntsman when the packs were on our bank. Ian Arnett acted as Huntsman when they were on the opposite side.

As the dipping sun brought a welcome coolness a small kit was disturbed from the vegetation on our side. He struck out bravely for the far bank. Mink are poor swimmers at the best of times but, when young, they are hopeless. The full pack left our side in excited pursuit and soon closed the gap. The Wye is wide so the race was potentially a long one. It was soon apparent that some hounds were better swimmers than others — they pulled away. The mink struggled on with two hounds vying to lead close behind. The small creature was caught some 10 yards short of the far bank and soon disappeared as the eager hounds piled in.

Hunting continued on the other bank. In time hounds found and chased another mink back over towards us. This mink was either a better swimmer or had more of a start as he won his race for life and immediately ran to ground under an enormous slate on our bank. The hunt terriers were entered to the entrance but with without success. He just would not budge.

Everyone was cleared from the line of sight of the hole and the covering slate rattled, stamped on and whacked with spades. The resultant din forced the terrified mink to bolt. He promptly dived into the river and swam downstream. Though initially only yards behind the hounds rioted after a rabbit on the bank then lost the scent of their true quarry.

With the winter hound sports darkness usually forces an early end to the day but there is no such relief for wildlife from mink hunting. Here the day ended at 7p.m. with the hunters exhausted but well pleased. Though nine mink had been added to the tally, most of them youngsters, they were confident that plenty of mink remained to be hunted at some future date.

That evening the Four Shires hunt and their supporters returned home. I joined the Devon and Cornwall contingent and retired to the hospitality of *The Black Swan* at Much Dewchurch where we were all staying.

The next few days during which I shared accommodation with enthusiastic hunters were a nightmare for me. We all slept on the floor in the Games Room at the back of the pub. Knowing that I have a

187

habit of talking in my sleep I was afraid to close my eyes in case I made some incriminating reference in my slumbers.

Breakfasts and evening meal times were another minefield to be negotiated. The traditional British breakfasts of bacon, sausage and eggs were proudly thrust in front of us. Dinner saw the traditional British fare of Steak and Kidney Pie and Roast Beef being served. This fare was all greeted with delight by my hearty hunting colleagues, but not by me.

When offered pork pies and sausage rolls at hunt meets I had learned that my best defence was to accept these gifts with relish and gratitude — and then surreptitiously feed them to the hounds. But here there was no such avenue for escape. I could feign stomach cramps to dodge one meal but not meals produced over days. I had no choice but to bite not the bullet — but the body of an animal. It was the first time I had eaten any meat for eight years. After such a long abstinence I found it sweet and sickly and had to fight an urge to vomit. Somehow I managed to look as though I was enjoying it as much as the others.

The meet the following day at Tregare Mill on the River Throssey was between the Devon and Cornwall and the Three Counties. Once again Ian Coghill was absent so Arlin took charge of proceedings. The combined pack drew first a small runner (brook) behind the meet. Mink often frequent such sites. The hounds soon spoke and, after a brief hunt, marked to ground. The terriers and diggers moved in excitedly but, rather than a mink, it was an indignant black cat that bolted! With a lot of horn blowing, shouting and whip cracking the hounds were stopped from any further pursuit. The cat could count that as one of his nine lives lost.

The hunt then turned about and returned past the meet. They paused for drinks to alleviate the thirst caused by the intense heat and then headed on for the main river. Hunting was intermittent as the hounds repeatedly bayed, ran and stopped. Eventually after a considerable walk for followers in the sweltering heat the hounds suddenly marked at an old wood pile in mid-stream.

The hunt supporters moved in and set about destroying this habitat in their efforts to evict their quarry. Under this assault it was not long before the mink bolted and sought sanctuary high in the branches of an adjacent willow. He was clearly visible, peering down at his tormentors. Surrounding the tree the hunters hurled stones and rocks at their victim. They did this without thought at first. It was only when one supporter was nearly knocked out by an overthrow of a stone from another that they saw the wisdom of all standing to one side.

One determined tree climbing hunter then put his talents to work. He scaled to the highest branches and shook the tree vigorously. As the branches whipped to and fro in response the mink clung on for dear life and hissed and spat defiance. After a battle of wits, lasting all of twenty minutes, involving much jockeying for position as the mink sought safety, the creature was eventually dislodged.

Tumbling down from branch to branch he hit the ground with stunning force and stumbled rather than dived into the water. Urged forward the hounds jumped in grabbing whatever they could, including each other's tails which, when black and wet, look distinctly mink-like. A brief squeal was clearly audible before the quarry was torn apart.

The hunt moved on and discovered a nest of kits. Slaughter ensued as three of the youngsters were added to the tally. The assorted remnants of 2½ of the 3 were found and the hunt wits suggested claiming two confirmed kills plus one very seriously injured. I found it difficult to join in the laughter.

Drawing on, the hounds marked at another spot from whence a large bitch and her four offspring were seen to bolt. Pursuing the bitch first, the hounds, surprisingly, lost her. They then turned their attention to her more vulnerable youngsters. One sought sanctuary in a long field drain. The terrier crew moved in but despite desperate digging and poking with iron bars, an assault that cracked most of the drain, this mink was resilient. It could not be bolted so was left.

The other three siblings were not so fortunate. They were quickly found and despatched. The death of one was particularly brutal. Flapping about on the water surface he was first bitten by a terrier most inappropriately named Parson. The bite, though not fatal, was clearly serious. It possibly severed the spinal cord as, streaming blood, the mink struggled on, trying to escape whilst trailing its back legs and emitting plaintive squeaks.

A large chocolate coloured hound named Kingfisher dived in to attack and snapped at the youngster but not hard. I was told by experienced hunters that mink taste distinctly unpleasant to hounds, hence their unwillingness to bite through them with the same relish that they would bite through say a hare. With the arrival of the full pack a melee developed and the infant mink was torn apart. His all too brief life was over.

The hunters viewed this as an excellent day with seven mink killed, again mostly youngsters and good prospects for future 'sport' as at least two mink survived to provide fun another day. The next morning, Friday July 9th, was my first meeting with Ian Coghill.

I was introduced to Ian by Arlin as a keen hunting man and photographer. With Arlin to vouch for me I was accepted without question. The meet was at Trigate Bridge on the river Monnow with Ian Coghill hunting the combined pack of hounds.

The day, overcast and with rain threatening, was a welcome break from the previous heat. The whole hunt went mobile and advanced upstream by vehicle. Their aim was to work their way back and finish at the meet. From the start there was a short excursion even further upstream. Hounds spoke briefly. Both Arlin and I could smell the mink but when in pursuit the hounds invaded an otter haven Ian thought better of it, turned them and headed downstream.

The return trek was blank all the way to a particular bridge where the knowledgeable followers had predicted they would find and sure enough they did. A youngster caught flapping about on the surface was attacked by the pack. He was bitten, but not fatally, so Ian clubbed him with his hunting pole to finish him off.

Sharp-eyed hunt supporters informed Ian that another mink had been viewed swimming downstream so the pack was cast towards him. A young Whipper-in, Steve Evans, impetuous and incautious with youth, waded forwards in the river and promptly slipped into a deep pool. He had to swim for it, managing to retain his cap if not his dignity in the process. Another follower sporting a camera found this mishap hilariously funny and continued to laugh until he too fell in, drenching his camera.

Soon the rain that had threatened arrived. The heavens opened bringing a deluge to soak us all. Hunting continued unabated. The hounds marked to a tree, from whence, despite all the hunters' enthusiasm, the mink simply would not budge. Frustrated at being thwarted they drew on and in a particularly deep stretch of the river killed three more youngsters. I observed that Devon and Cornwall supporters holloa and screamed like dervishes on sighting a mink but the Three Counties followers were far more reserved — emitting only a quiet 'tally-ho'. With the hounds in amongst these mink there were tally-ho's coming from every sector of the bank as the quarry panicked and scattered but to no avail.

A few hundred yards further on the hounds disturbed a really large mink. Far from giving them the good run they expected he promptly evaded the hounds by climbing to the heights of the nearest tree. One of the young girls following volunteered to climb after him. She was very capable and the mink was soon dislodged. He fell to the bank but without injury, as he ran off at high speed and climbed another tree.

Hounds and followers crashed forwards in pursuit. In my haste to keep to the fore I misjudged my footing on the bank and slipped into the river. It was deep, very deep. All that prevented the total immersion of myself and the destruction of my precious camera was Ian Coghill's outstretched crop — the butt of which he offered me and which I gratefully clutched. Ian then pulled me to safety — as I would have done him had the circumstances been reversed.

Shaken from sanctuary in the second tree, the mink ran on then further infuriated the supporters by climbing yet a third tree. This was ancient, with the height to match and, with the mink clinging to the very highest branches, I felt sure he was safe.

However the hunters were determined to see some more fun. A supporter climbed to the precarious heights and dislodged the quarry. The hounds were held in check to give him a chance to run, a bit of hunting 'law', and he did so, but only briefly.

The mink was clearly tiring. If nothing else he had done a lot of climbing. The fourth tree he chose was a small flimsy willow. Shaken from there he jumped for safety but straight at me, head-high. I twisted back and sideways in avoidance and, in doing so, blurred what would have been a useful photograph, recording the creature's terror.

The desperate mink climbed two more trees. On being dislodged from the second instead of as previously breaking his fall on a cushion of low branches or landing in the river the mink landed with a bone crunching thud on the hard ground. Stunned, winded or perhaps even dead he was engulfed by the pack.

What remained of the carcass was retrieved from the hounds and handed to Ian. The supporters gathered around him on the bank and performed a trophy-gathering ceremony. They formed a square box with their hunting poles held horizontally to keep the hounds back. In the safety of the middle Ian cut off the trophies — the mask, four pads, and tail and, after much twisting and tugging, extracted the penis bone. It was always traditional in Otter hunting to cut out the latter from the vanquished and wear it as a tie or neck pin, so I was not in the least surprised to see this ghoulish practice carry over into the replacement 'sport'.

Ian Coghill then blew for home, comparatively early for them, it was only 4.30p.m. The tally was five, again mostly youngsters. Back at the pub, by the meet, we had a long wait for the transport to catch up. As the hounds collapsed exhausted upon each other they were a picture of innocence.

The following morning, Saturday July 10th, the last of this Joint Week the meet was at *The Lamb*, Stoke Prior, near Leominster, on the

191

River Lugg. This time Arlin took charge and hunted the combined Devon and Cornwall and Three Counties packs.

At the meet I was the victim of unfortunate experience that gave much amusement to those watching. I had opted to wear wellingtons in the hope of keeping my feet dry and was busy photographing the hounds when I heard a sniggering from hunt supporters standing near me. Then I felt a spreading warm wet patch just above my knee. I moved sharply sideways and found that one of the hounds had marked me in the usual canine fashion — the product from which was rapidly filling my right wellie. Perhaps that hound had extrasensory perception as to my real sympathies!

In the first draw down the River Arrow to its junction with the River Lugg the hounds were completely silent. They ran and sniffed, played and rolled, but could find nothing. At the junction Devon and Cornwall's Kindly spoke immediately and led the pack in a charge up the Lugg. It was about midday. Kindly is a hound with an immensely sensitive nose, so sensitive that she is often accused of babbling (a serious fault in which the hound speaks when there is no scent at all — the usual remedy is a bullet).

The other hounds spoke only intermittently, heading up the Lugg towards a railway line. Hunt followers scoured the water and vegetation but there was no sighting of the mink. The hunting was virtually all on Kindly's shoulders and most supporters seemed willing to disown her. Certainly the Three Counties supporters were muttering that she must be stupid and should be put down. Why had no other hound picked up this elusive scent? Even Arlin was beginning to have doubts. However, Kindly was right, as just before the entourage reached the railway line, Arlin's Whipper-in Graham holloaed the mink away.

At the railway bridge over the river this mink, a beautiful silvery brown creature, came out of the main river, crossed to a small stream and went to ground under an old, partly exposed, tree root. As always in this Joint Week the Three Counties hunters led the digging party. Ian Coghill rushed to the fore and rooted about under the tree but to no avail. The mink was eventually bolted by the terriers attacking his hiding place from above. Seeking escape he dashed down the tiny stream, dodged the hounds and whooping supporters and went to ground again. This time Ian and fellow Joint Master Peter Cooper went to work with spades. The terrified mink bolted again and, after another short sprint, found sanctuary in a really big earth. At last he appeared to be safe. However these hunters are resolute. Major excavations began, led by the Three Counties twins Peter and Rick May who did the terrier work for their local fox hunts.

Deeper and wider they dug in the baking heat. It was slow and hard work. When half an hour had passed without sign of the mink the hunt moved on and they were left to continue their work. The hounds were taken forwards to try for another mink upstream across the railway line.

Two swans accompanied by three cygnets were viewed swimming in mid-river ahead of the pack. To avoid any riot the hounds were called out and back whilst the supporters moved forwards to scare the swans away with shouting, backed by a barrage of stones.

A breathless runner then caught up with this main part of the hunt with the information that the first mink had showed and was about to bolt. That was a timely intervention. The hunters left the swans and returned back over the railway to the previous dig site. By then the diggers were in a frenzy of excitement as they neared their objective. The mink bolted, leaping out of the earth in full view of all and headed straight for the stream where it was promptly lost again.

A lengthy search ensued, with the supporters wading in and probing the river banks. Eventually this highly elusive mink was again sighted but, after a short dash, he disappeared into a narrow drain beside the railway bridge. With the terriers unable to enter the small hole it appeared that at long last the terrified creature had found a safe sanctuary. But mink hunters are determined and very resourceful.

Ian Coghill searched around and acquired a long length of wire. By feeding it into the other end of the narrow tube he managed to poke and prod the mink until he bolted again. He sprang into the stream, swam along, landed, and went straight to ground yet again. This was far less of a stronghold. He was soon evicted and promptly dived into the main river.

Now the hunt was really on — and this tiring mink was fast running out of escape options. I accompanied Arlin on one bank with the bulk of supporters whilst, on the other side, Ian led his team of Three Counties hunters. He organised these into a line to beat the undergrowth lining the top of the river bank to prevent the mink escaping to the adjacent cornfield. It seemed to me that their priority was not to protect the cornfield, the fringes of which they themselves trampled, but rather to prevent the mink reaching safety.

No longer was it a game of hide and seek; now it was truly a life or death battle of wits. The mink, a beautiful full adult, was one against the many, nature's perfect predator against two of the best hunting packs in the country. This was always an unequal contest but it was not the hounds but rather the vast mob of baying hunt followers who were to finally tip the scales.

To the mink's advantage the river was fast flowing and murky. Thus when it dived, swam from one side to the other and landed to hide in the undergrowth its scent was carried away down on the wash, causing the hounds to overrun the true line.

Against this, the air that is trapped in the mink's coat on diving is gradually expelled forming a chain of bubbles visible on the surface. Just as, in earlier days, such a chain betrayed the whereabouts of many an otter so it does the mink. The supporters lined the banks searching for these tell-tale bubbles and holloaed or shouted 'tally-ho!' whenever they saw them.

Time and again when it seemed the mink had escaped these followers put the hounds right. Mr. Mink crossed the river, diving constantly, backwards and forwards but there was to be no escape. Every time he tried to creep up the bank out of the river and away he was chased back with shrieks of glee.

As the hounds gained, so exhaustion took its toll. It was noticeable that the quarry's dives became of increasingly shorter duration. Many times the mink was swimming on the surface when a hound leapt at it from the bank. The crash-dives in response were only just in time.

Desperately the mink tried to return upstream to the sanctuary of the earths beside the railway but he was thwarted. The struggle moved downstream towards the junction with the River Arrow. Again and again the sequence of dive, hide and find, was repeated until at about 4.00p.m. the mink reached the Arrow, crossed the junction to the far side and went to ground beneath a large willow tree.

The ever-enthusiastic diggers arrived on the scene and commenced massive excavations. Several times the mink was spotted but doubtless exhausted he simply would not bolt. The men dug, dug and dug. Their trench must eventually have been all of 5ft deep before, at about 6.00p.m., excited holloaing and joyful whoops from hunters indicated that their quarry had bolted again.

The hounds were unleashed in frantic chase but then stopped when this fleeing mink was seen to be totally black. The dejected hunters realised that their original quarry was still hiding in the earth. The newly found black mink was allowed to escape to provide 'sport' on another day.

Digging restarted and not long afterwards the silver/brown mink bolted once more. Running out like a bullet from a gun he dived in to the river and disappeared. This agility both surprised and pleased the onlookers. Usually animals that are bolted after a long dig and a long hunt come out very stiff and are all too quickly caught.

Arlin drew the hounds back up the Lugg. I had actually seen Mr. Mink go down the Arrow but nevertheless I assured Arlin that I thought he was right — that the mink had gone up the Lugg. I was playing the best card I had to try and save the life of this courageous mink but my ploy was foiled when there was a holloa from supporters standing in mid-stream down the Arrow. I swiftly excused my error by saying that I must have seen another mink. There were after all several about. The last hunt now commenced with nearly forty hounds all on and in full cry.

The gallant victim again went to ground in a small stick pile but was dislodged by supporters. He made a final dash for the river but was caught by the pack just a yard short. There was a brief skirmish with the mink hissing and spitting as it tumbled over and over with the lead hounds in battle, then it was all over. The time was nearly 7.00p.m. That was some seven hours after Kindly had first spoken at the rivers' confluence.

The torn carcass was brought to our side of the river and held aloft in triumph by Peter Cooper. The mask, pads, tail and penis bone were removed. Months later the mounted mask was presented to Arlin in recognition of his 'great exploits'. The supporters enthused over the day's hunting. Many regarded it as the best they had enjoyed since the 'heady' days of otter hunting.

I suggested to Arlin Rickard that some of my pictures be released for publication in the hunting media. I received the following hand-written reply (to Michael Wright) dated July 14th 1982:-

"Dear Michael,

I have spoken with Ian Coghill and mentioned that there ought to be some pictures we can release to the Shooting Times or Field.

Although he was pleased that there were some pictures taken (I'm sure he'll be glad to receive some) he expressed concern about the wording of the story to cover the pictures. Names, dates etc., as you know they are anti-orientated.

I therefore suggested that you would forward him such photos as you thought particularly suitable for release and ask him to supply story and send them to the magazines himself.

Hope you are well. It was a really great week in mink hunting history.

Yours
Arlin"

HUNTING WITH IAN COGHILL

Having been successfully introduced to the Three Counties Minkhounds and Ian Coghill I switched focus and keenly followed that pack. On July 31st I attended their meet at Pandy north of Abergavenny on the River Monnow. Five young mink were killed, most in the morning. Whenever possible the remains were recovered and Ian used them to bait his hounds. The idea is for the hounds to jump and jump again for the body so that when it is eventually thrown to them they will fight for it.

During the hunt one mink was so petrified that it completely lost its bearings in the shallow stream. I was standing ankle deep with a mob of followers when the mink swam directly towards me with the hounds in hot pursuit. I tried to focus my camera as this mink by-passed me to nestle between the boots of a uniformed hunt follower beside me. He tally-ho'd but only in a whisper and pointed to the fugitive hiding between his legs. The hounds swung over in our direction, the mink darted out, there was a brief melee and another was added to the tally.

Late in the afternoon the hounds had some fun chasing cattle on the river bank. Sadly the bullocks failed to appreciate the frolicsome nature of the pack. In their panic two burst through their enclosure and ran into the river ahead. Ian was furious as the hunt was held up whilst they were herded back to safety.

In the pub afterwards the drink flowed freely as I joined hunters to reminisce about their previous hunting experiences. This is where it is important to have a depth of hunting knowledge to exchange. I learned that the Three Counties hounds riot frequently and that the new hounds Rockdove and Ringlet had killed a duck. The young Whipper-in, Steve Evans, mentioned this to me. When he did everyone else hushed him saying: "*That's not the sort of thing we talk about.*"

The following Saturday, August 7th, the Three Counties met at Upleadon Mill beside the River Leadon, north-east of Newent. The hounds drew first a small brook away from the main river. Two mink were found and quickly killed despite the fact that each sought sanctuary in a variety of trees. Hunting then came to an abrupt halt when an irate farmer stormed across the fields complaining that the pack had chased cattle into nearby cornfields. The hunt followers appearing more amused than contrite did little to calm his temper.

Eventually Ian placated him by saying that they would take their hounds out, to allow him to bring the cattle back and that the hunt would pay for any damage caused. Like schoolchildren caught scrumping apples, the hunt trooped sheepishly back to the road to await events. A report came through that 19 cattle had trampled over two cornfields and caused a lot of damage.

Fearful of the financial implications most of the supporters said that it was the farmer's own fault — that he should have had more secure fencing.

Ian reassured them that his hunt was covered by insurance against just such an event and, accordingly, they had no worries. In his view the insurance company would fight it out with the farmer and he was confident that the latter would win nothing.

The hunt returned to the main river by the mill in high spirits. A third mink was found and, after a short chase, killed. The hounds chased many others, but the quarry kept scampering up trees. One good sized mink was hunted for some time. He tried many manoeuvres but could not escape. Eventually I observed the end as I saw hounds biting him, holding on briefly and then dropping him in the water. He bobbed his head up briefly then sank from sight.

The terriermen were convinced that he had crash-dived and swum underwater to find sanctuary in a hole in the river bank. They frantically dug at any likely spot, but could find nothing. Ian cast the hounds upstream and downstream, but there was no sign and no scent. His whereabouts were a mystery. Some onlookers speculated that this mink had been killed by the hounds and his body carried downstream, but Ian thought not saying: "*There is not a one in a million chance of a mink being killed by one bite from the hounds.*"

That view certainly tied in with the visual evidence I had recorded. Many mink are snapped at by the hounds then released to struggle on wounded. This in no way tallied with the usual mink hunters claims to the public that hunted mink are killed instantly when caught.

Backwards and forwards swept the hunt dragnet searching for this missing mink but eventually they had to concede defeat. The official record for the day was five mink found and three killed. The one that was severely bitten but escaped was not added to the tally.

The following Saturday, August 14th, was a scorching hot day. I travelled to Worcestershire to join the meet of the Three Counties Minkhounds at *The Mason's Arms*, Wichenford. The river was a small, twisting brook of swift flowing muddy water, encompassed by a mass of tangled vegetation. It was ideal mink country. The first two mink found escaped because the hunt supporters could not track them through this veritable jungle.

In mink hunting, perhaps more than in any other hound sports, the followers play a vital role. Their observation of where the mink lands and scuttles off to hide, or the chain of bubbles rising as he swims underwater, is necessary for most kills.

In the afternoon a third mink was found on a more open stretch of water. As usual he darted up a tree to escape but was soon dislodged and pursued up and down the brook by the hounds. He made the best use of available cover but, after a protracted chase, was finally cornered in a nettle bed. The supporters gathered, eagerly linking arms around the bed, in a manner akin to holding-up coverts in cub hunting; the hounds were put in. The mink ran to and fro and a sharp fight ensued, evidenced by much hissing and spitting, squeaking and squealing. One hound was badly bitten on his nose.

Amazingly this mink escaped from this melee and dived back into the water but the pack was all around. In a desperate bid for life the mink jumped out, clambered up and ran over a hound's back and was caught. The field waded in and the shattered body was recovered and brought to the bank in triumph. Ian cut off the pads as trophies before tossing the remains to the pack.

On the 21st the hunt arrived at the Temeside Hotel, Little Hereford, south-east of Ludlow with expectations of enjoying an excellent day. I was told that at the meet there the previous year, though only travelling across three fields, they had found six mink and killed three, leaving a further three for breeding.

However, unbeknown to the hunters their plans for 'sport' had been ruined. Other country folk had responded to their well-publicised scare stories concerning mink and were trapping the species. The hounds set off but only found a sniff or two. They half-heartedly marked at various drains but there were no definite sightings of mink. For the supporters trailing along behind it was a boring morning, enlightened only by passage through a private garden and orchard where some lingered to fill their pockets with apples.

On and on they drew. At one point hunters clambered up the bank and over a railway line. They just cleared the line moments before a train hurtled by. Crossing a dual carriageway the hunt encountered a river bank populated by fishermen from the Birmingham Angling Association (BAA) engaged in an angling contest.

In the old days of otter hunting, when hunting held sway, they would have trampled forward and any angler who protested would have been given an early bath — but times have changed. The very survival of hunting is now dependent on the support of anglers. To please the latter, the hunters simply packed up and returned home.

On the return to the meet, the senior staff engaged in earnest conversation concerning the way the previous year someone had apparently ruined the BAA's competitions by putting "*Cancelled*" stickers on their advertisements.

In Ian Coghill's view the more of this kind of sabotage that occurred the better. He said that if anglers could be drawn into a war with the antis they would be more likely to support hunting — many of his followers understood his far from subtle hint!

The following Wednesday, August 25th, I joined the same hunt for their lawn meet at Caradoc House near Sellack, beside the River Wye. Such meets were a great tradition of otter hunting. The hounds certainly made a very picturesque sight gathered in front of the palatial mansion. This was a joint meet with the Border Counties Minkhounds (the name that strikes fear in the heart of some old hunt saboteurs). For me the wheel had turned half circle. Only a few years earlier I had opposed the forerunner of this hunt, now I was welcomed as a 'trusted supporter'!

The hounds drew downstream first then reversed to head upstream towards Hoarwithy. As with the triple meet in July, on this wide river the hunters split their forces into two. The Border Counties staff hunted hounds when they were on the far bank and Ian Coghill took charge when they were on our side. The first mink was uncovered on the Border Counties side, lodged beneath a rotting tree stump. Dislodged, the creature struck out bravely towards us and dived. Mink are not very aquatic and find prolonged dives exhausting. When this mink surfaced he could only flail around but, with the hounds lagging far behind, he had time to take a breather. He then found sanctuary under some rocks at the water's edge on our side.

Eagerly the hunt servants moved in with iron bars and spades and destroyed this boulder bunker. Bolted, the mink swam upstream close in; from the bank we could see his tiny feet paddling furiously. Some hounds swam and some ran in pursuit. One runner leapt from the bank at the quarry, missing him only by the barest whisker as he dived. Surfacing, the mink was surrounded by hounds and caught. The carcass was retrieved and brought to the bank, where hunt supporters eagerly formed the familiar box of hunting poles for trophy retrieval. Thus shielded from hounds, in the centre Ian cut off the pads, tail and head for trophies, distributing the pads and tail to supporters. He carefully tucked the bloodied head into his trouser pocket. The few remains were thrown to the pack.

Finding a second mink on the far bank, a swimming hunt (such a common feature when hunting the wide and deep Wye) then ensued. The mink was coursed across the surface in circles and figures of eight. As the pack closed in, he promptly dived, leaving the hounds totally bemused. The mink then surfaced a few yards away and the process was repeated. It all gave great amusement to the followers who cheered the hounds on from the banks. In time, the dives were of shorter and shorter duration until the mink, exhausted, could dive no more and drifted helplessly until he was caught.

A third mink swam powerfully backwards and forwards across the river and when tired found sanctuary in a drain on the far side. Whilst swimming from one bank to the other some hounds were distracted on our bank, ran riot and killed a rabbit. As for the cornered mink for a considerable time the hunters dug and dug at the drain but without success. The mink was safely lodged so was left.

MORE GENERAL MINK HUNTING

Following this mid-week meet I headed to the West Country to observe some summer stag and fox hunting as described previously. I then returned to observe more mink hunting.

On Saturday, August 28th, I attended the meet of the Devon and Cornwall Minkhounds at *The New Inn*, Moreleigh west of Dartmouth. Their first draw was downstream where the hounds perceived a whiff of scent but there was no clear sighting. Proceedings came to an abrupt halt when the hunt entered land where, to say the least, they were unwelcome. The owner came out cursing and swearing, unleashing his guard dogs on us — the supporters turned back recounting in humorous, irreverent detail previous confrontations with this gentleman.

Returning upstream we paused at Gara Bridge for a scenic picnic lunch. From the restart the hounds spoke quickly and were soon hunting a mink in amongst some domesticated ducks quacking about on the river. Given that Arlin Rickard is so concerned over his public hunting image I expected him to stop this, pull his hounds out and by-pass the ducks, but he did not. Instead the six feathered friends were terrified; in panic they scattered.

Speaking to the scent of the fleeing mink the hounds marked first at a hole in the bank then, driving on again, in some bushes in a dried up stream feeding the main river. Despite a diligent search no sign of this mink could be found. I was with other supporters watching this prolonged search when a large, black, woolly hound appropriately named Satan brushed past me clutching a brown and very dead duck in his jaws. He had lingered for some alternative mischievous 'sport'.

Arlin was amused but immediately sought to hide the duck. He wanted to bury it or hide it in the undergrowth but one of his supporters begged him to let her take it home to cook. Finally Arlin relented and gave it to her, but with strict instructions to hide the body adding, "*I cannot stress that enough.*" She stuffed the bloodied victim up her shirt out of sight but when a friend arrived he took it and concealed it in the poachers pocket in his shooting jacket.

Hounds drew again upstream, speaking to an intermittent scent, before they made a definite find on our side. The eager terrier crew rushed to assist and with great gusto smashed down a dead tree, forcing the mink to bolt. He dived, swam the river, surfaced on the far side, darted up beside a small stream and then returned to find sanctuary in a drain.

The hunters, crossing the river by an adjacent bridge, put their terriers in. One dog battled with the mink and soon gained a grip. We could hear growls and grunts interspersed with hissing and spitting.

When the terrier was drawn out by his hind feet, he in turn pulled the mink out also. However, one Whipper-in (a young lad) foolishly gave a holloa far too soon. Before the adversaries could be separated the whole pack piled in on top of both terrier and mink. In the ensuing chaotic melee in the muddy water the hounds understandably bit at anything and everything. A terrier was badly bitten and had to be taken away for immediate veterinary treatment. Arlin waded in to recover the carcass for trophies but there was little remaining.

That was Saturday August 28th. The following Monday the Devon and Cornwall Minkhounds met at *The Fox and Hounds*, Eggesford, a famous hunting pub. From the very start, Arlin acknowledged that they had little chance of finding any mink in the nearby river. It was the classic case of hunters falling victim to their own inaccurate propaganda as the salmon fishing there is much valued and the fishermen, having regard for the scare stories concerning mink put about by mink hunters, trap or shoot every mink they can. Mink, being poor swimmers pose little threat to salmon. It was a repeat story of the blank day endured by the Three Counties Minkhounds when they met at the Temeside Hotel, Little Hereford on August 21st.

Optimistically the hunt set off, determined to make the best of it. There was no drag found on the upstream draw, but going downstream hounds did find the faintest smell. Once again Satan snatched another duck — emerging from the river looking well pleased with himself. But as he opened his mouth to adjust his grip the duck promptly flew off with much indignant quacking.

In the absence of mink the hounds understandably became bored. When the lead hounds disturbed some fox cubs resting by the water's edge the whole pack rioted in hot pursuit. They flew on, swinging away from the river, high up into the tree shrouded hillsides, in full cry. On most fox hunts the staff are mounted and can keep up with their hounds, even if they cannot control them; being a leisurely mink hunt, everyone was on foot and it was in the full humid heat of summer.

The Whippers-in raged as they struggled to battle through the hillside vegetation in the wake of their recalcitrant charges. There was an abundance of shouting, swearing and cracking of whips, but it was only when the scent from the fleeing foxes was lost and the hounds tired, that they returned looking sheepish.

Heavy rain arrived late in the afternoon, boosting the humidity and the day ended at about 4.30p.m. It was a near complete blank. At *The Fox and Hounds* afterwards I joined the hunters for a social gathering — a photographic evening. My contribution was to show a selection of my slides taken during the Joint Week in July.

MORE HUNTING WITH IAN COGHILL

At the end of that week, Saturday September 4th, I was back with the Three Counties Minkhounds meeting at Ketford Bridge on the River Leadon. This proved to be the most significant day in all my time observing mink hunts. Ian Coghill was present so took charge. Hounds drew upstream first. They made some brief contacts near some aged willows and spoke occasionally but there was no confirmed view of a mink. The end of the upstream draw was reached in sweltering heat and the hunt turned about.

Persevering through difficult conditions they drew on and on for some four and a half miles with just the occasional sniff of mink to excite the followers but no actual sighting.

Just before Upleadon Bridge there was a short frantic burst of action after a mink that disappeared. The hounds were cast but for all their efforts could not find this mink. The hunters returned to the bridge that marked the end of the draw, at 4.00p.m.

It was deemed too early to finish and the followers seemed extremely frustrated after a day with neither 'sport' nor a kill. To appease them Ian took his hounds back upstream for a last try to find a mink.

With other supporters I paused at the bridge waiting to see what would happen. I was soon moved into action by an outburst of raucous holloaing.

Running forwards I quickly learned that a mink had been sighted but was proving extremely elusive as it ran and swam up and down a stream. It was a situation similar to that of the seven hour marathon hunt at the joint meet with the Devon and Cornwall at Stoke Prior. To the mink's advantage the river was fast-flowing and muddy and his scent was almost non-existent.

To the hunt's advantage the river bank was open, giving the massed ranks of hunt followers good observation points from which to help their hounds — they could not have been more enthusiastic.

Just when it seemed the mink had won the hounds marked him to ground. Bolted from his sanctuary, he swam downstream, ducking and weaving amid the rushes with the pack only yards behind. In their wake, the followers whooped and holloaed with delight at this turn of events. Crossing the river, the quarry just made it to the safety of a hole in the river bank with the leading hounds only inches from his tail. The pack bayed frantically at the spot.

One of the Whippers-in, Peter May, who also does the terrier work for the Croome and West Warwickshire Foxhounds and is a close friend of Ian Coghill's, reached the scene. He put a terrier into the hole. Hissing and growling ensued as canine and mustelid fought in the narrow tunnel. Ian Coghill waded across the stream and stood with a small group of Whippers-in and terriermen immediately above the hole holding his hounds in check.

Peering into the hole, Peter said that he could pull the terrier out and, on Ian's advice, did so. As the two foes had locked jaws when the terrier was dragged out by his hind feet he in turn drew the mink out. Peter thrust the pair of them underwater to force them to break their grip. Grabbing the mink immediately behind the head with his right hand, he held it triumphantly aloft for all to see. Struggle as he might, the victim could neither escape nor twist sufficiently to bite the hand that held him. The hounds bayed with feverish excitement on the bank.

Peter called: "*It's still alive Ian, what shall I do?*"

To which Ian replied: "*Throw it up on the bank behind the hounds.*"

Peter complied with these instructions, hurling the mink up in a high arc to land on the grass behind the pack. Despite hitting the ground hard, the mink was immediately up and running for his life but the hounds caught him before he had travelled five yards. The mink was torn limb from limb and Ian blew the 'kill' triumphantly.

The hunt returned to Upleadon Bridge and Mill. Whilst waiting for the hound van there was much laughing and joking amongst supporters about the 'flying mink' and Ian made a point of asking me if I had recorded the incident on film. After my experience of losing valuable images on previous occasions I was naturally evasive saying that I wasn't sure.

Keeping my own counsel I resolved that one day the cruel abuse of that mink, that had indeed been clearly recorded, would be exposed to a very large audience.

The meet of the Three Counties at Newnham Bridge on the River Teme the following Wednesday, September 8th, was an interesting event enlivened by a visit from a television film crew. They were there to film hunting enthusiast — and renowned footballer — Jack Charlton for the mink hunting episode of his TV series, "*Jack's Game*".

Knowing Jack Charlton's idea of 'sport' I was not in the least surprised to see him out mink hunting. He went on record on a Tyne-Tees TV programme saying publicly in regard to football: "*I have a little book with two players in it, and if I get a chance to do them I will. I will make them suffer before I pack this game in.*" Clearly it was small wild animals that were now in his 'little book' as he was doing his best to "*do*" them!

I soon learned that this hunt was to be a stage-managed event for the benefit of the camera. Word was passed amongst supporters from the Master that the hunt would be quite happy to catch nothing, thus ensuring there would be no embarrassing revelations of the truth which might be filmed.

We were ordered to be very careful about holloaing any mink we might see. It was clear that no live mink would be thrown: everything was to be by the book. This was doubtless a welcome relief for the local wildlife.

The cameraman, with his expensive equipment, was loaded precariously aboard a canoe and the whole charade proceeded. The hounds spoke occasionally and performed for low level camera shots. Eventually they hit a strong drag and, after a short hunt, marked a mink at a large tree.

Ian Coghill and his team were fearful lest this mink should bolt and be torn apart in midstream in front of the camera. They need not have worried. When he did bolt he ran just a few yards before disappearing to ground again in a larger more complex earth.

The ever enthusiastic terrierman, Peter May, moved in armed with spade and dog and, to the delight of the film crew, Jack Charlton rushed over to assist. Effusive swearing interrupted proceedings as the sound recordist stumbled and came to grief in mid-stream, soaking his expensive equipment.

After an enthusiastic but conveniently fruitless dig this mink was given best and the hunt carried on to draw again, but without success. At that point some of the hounds ran riot and one named Ranger killed a rabbit. Ian was not unduly bothered as this happened out of camera shot. The day ended at 4.30p.m. with no other kill, much to the relief of the hunt staff.

Three days later on Saturday September 11th, the Three Counties meet at *The White Hart*, Maismore near Gloucester was to be another revealing day.

After the meet hounds were taken by van to the main river but the first draw was along a small brook leading away from it. There were several mink about as the pack, after being cast ahead, spoke almost immediately. They raced back towards us, circled and then streaked away into the distance with the exuberance so typical of hounds when they are first unboxed. Believing them to be at fault Ian stopped them and brought them back.

He was right. They spoke excitedly and this time marked at the base of a tree that just happened to contain a hornet's nest. I was rather hoping the hornets might wreak vengeance for the animal kingdom on the hunters, but it was a futile fantasy.

The mink was sighted curled up in the topmost branches of a thorn bush. With the hounds held in check, the bush was shaken, prodded and poked until the mink was dislodged. Tumbling down through the branches he soon recovered and darted into a short drain. He was soon bolted again only to seek sanctuary in a beautiful old willow tree.

Higher and higher he climbed. Eventually so high that I thought he must be safe. But no, a fanatical supporter climbed after him. This gallant gentleman shook the branches ever so vigorously but still the mink clung on. A long, thin stick was passed up and by using it rather like a billiard cue the hunter was able to pot the mink off the branch.

Bouncing down from branch to branch he was fortunately caught in a tangle of vegetation just above the ground but beyond the reach of the hounds. Evading them, he ran along a lower branch and disappeared into a hole in the trunk of another willow. Sensing an imminent kill the hunters moved in eagerly. They tried every conceivable tactic to dislodge this terrified mink from his sanctuary. The hounds, powerless to help, watched and waited impatiently.

Peter Cooper tried to poke the mink out from above with a stick whilst Rick and Peter May assaulted his refuge from below. The terriers were put in at every angle and one hunt follower lent assistance by thumping the trunk with the flat of a shovel. Even when Rick May hacked at the tree with his hatchet the mink stubbornly stayed put.

The followers rapidly became bored with waiting so Ian Coghill took his hounds off in search of another victim, leaving Peter Cooper, and Peter and Rick May under strict instructions to do whatever was necessary to bolt the mink.

These three hunting 'conservationists' then brought in the heavy equipment in the shape of a chainsaw and a tractor — a formidable array of weapons to pit against a creature weighing less than four pounds!

A burly follower grabbed the chainsaw and started it. It burst into life with a mechanical roar that shattered the peace of the countryside. Amid clouds of exhaust smoke the hunter set to work digesting the base of the willow. This is soft wood so, like using a cheese-wire on butter, the saw sliced into the ancient tree but in doing so produced such vibrations that eventually, before the tree was felled, the petrified mink fled.

A breathless runner arrived to tell us that the hunt had run another mink to ground downstream and they wanted to have some 'sport' with that first. They were unsuccessful though and returned to join us, albeit after a brief diversion along the route when the pack rioted after a fox.

Our mink was by then high in another tree from which he was soon dislodged, only to run up a thorn tree. Now the trap was closing. The hole where he had remained hidden for so long previously was now blocked and there were supporters at every vantage point to drive him back should he make a break for the river.

Shaken from his perilous haven the mink ran along the bank above a stagnant slimy pool. Peter May, standing knee deep in the pool, made a grab, aiming to snatch the small fugitive just behind his head. Peter was too slow though and instead caught the mink halfway down the body. Given a chance to bite the mink promptly twisted and sank his teeth into Peter's hand.

By this time the hounds were milling all around the two combatants. Ian waded into the slime clubbing them back with the butt of his crop. Peter thrust his hand along with the struggling mink under the water and held it there. After a good few minutes he confirmed that the creature felt limp and asked Ian what he should do.

On Ian's instructions the mink was laid on the bank, clubbed a few times with a crop to ensure he was dead and his body tied to the thong of a long whip. Whilst the hounds were held back, Peter Cooper ran off dragging this carcass behind him around the perimeter of the adjacent field.

Ian's idea was to give his hounds some excitement in the form of a mini drag hunt. The body was towed back towards the river and hidden in some bushes. Once released, the pack ran the course well but went too far. When they could not find the body they were stopped and encouraged to cast for the scent. They eventually found their prize.

My filming of both the drowning of the mink and this curious drama played out with the body clearly aroused the suspicions of one supporter. He seemed to spend the rest of the day warning followers about me. However Ian must have dismissed his doubts as no one directly questioned me.

Another couple of mink were found but both escaped; one, on a railway embankment, the other beneath some massive boulders. The hunters were happy to leave them for a future day.

That night, Peter Cooper made me very welcome at his home in preparation for the hunt's Wine and Cheese party at Cropthorne the next day. We drank fine whisky way into the night. Peter reminisced over what for him were the glorious and exciting days of otter hunting. He regarded mink hunting as a poor substitute — but better than nothing.

I heard that the previous year's Wine and Cheese party had been a very drunken affair. I always tried to attend such functions in the hope of picking up some loose talk, soaking up knowledge rather than alcohol but in this regard I was disappointed. The party of 1982 was a very sober affair and I left at 5.00p.m.

A HUNTING FESTIVAL

Mink hunters introduced me to that great hunting attraction — the hunting festival. This is when three different packs meet at a venue, or area, to hunt three separate species on a single, long, day.

Diehard hunting fanatics follow various hound sports according to the seasons. For a few short weeks the sports overlap and, by tradition, at such times the dedicated hunting type will follow as many different 'sports' as possible, ideally all in one day.

Old hunters regarded it as perfection to kill a fox cub in the morning, a hare at lunchtime and an otter in the evening — nowadays the latter is replaced by a mink.

These three styles of hunting overlap in September-October when the fox and hare hunting season is underway and the more aquatic bloodsports are about to end.

With the decline in otter hunting, festivals also declined but in the autumn of 1979 they re-emerged when *Shooting Times* proudly announced that the county of Warwickshire was going to "*Ring to the sound of a hunting festival.*"

Three packs of hounds — The Croome and West Warwickshire Foxhounds, Three Counties Minkhounds and the Warwickshire Beagles — had met at T*he Coventry Arms* near Worcester at various times during the day.

The local hunt saboteurs had turned up in force and, with the Three Counties Minkhounds largely made up of former followers of the Border Counties Otterhounds, the result could have been predicted. The sabs were attacked. Three needed hospital treatment for head and eye injuries, one was admitted to hospital for three days' observation. To add insult (and criminal damage) to injury, the hunters overturned a sab's mini bus and severed the brake pipes.

So it was with some interest, and no little trepidation, that I decided to visit hunting festivals as part of my undercover work. I attended two festivals in 1982.

The first, on September 18th took place, again in the vicinity of *The Coventry Arms*. The day commenced early with a meet of the Croome and West Warwickshire Foxhounds at Caddicroft Farm, near Worcester at 7.00a.m. Travelling from London I always expected to be slightly late but I was further delayed by fog along my route. I arrived to find the hunt drawing a particularly large area of woodland near the meet.

It was soon clear that there were plenty of foxes about but, with the temperature steadily rising, the scent declined and there was no kill.

I left in time to attend the meet of the Three Counties Minkhounds near Peopleton at 11.00a.m. By then it was a scorcher of a day.

At the meet we learned that hunt saboteurs had been out with the foxhounds and that we could expect them to descend on us at any time. As we meandered up the brook towards Crowle reports filtered back that there were sabs on the bridge ahead. I strolled over to chat with Dick Whitlock, a keen supporter of the Border Counties Otterhounds, to discover his attitude to the situation.

Clearly relishing the prospect of a good punch-up he whispered to me: "*We haven't given them a good sticking for years.*"

Innocently, I enquired, "*When was that then?*"

He replied: "*Down at Llandinam. We were expecting them and we had hunt people come from all over the country. On John Bridge's (the Huntsman) instructions the hunt staff took off their coats and really sorted them out. They had broken noses and broken jaws.*"

With a little encouragement from me he told me more and more of the story I had waited six years to hear. The hunt had drafted in a sizeable contingent of rough-necks from the Blencathra Foxhounds —

John Peel country — and a team of terriermen from Manchester, described by Dick Whitlock as, *"Right tidy with their fists."*

He confided that he had acted as decoy to lead the sabs away from the hunt by driving the hound van up into the mountains. Now, six years later, he and other followers eagerly anticipated renewing combat.

We reached the next bridge to find that it stank of antimate. This is the harmless spray designed for use on bitches in season that hunt saboteurs use to mask the scent of fleeing quarry. There were six young saboteurs there. Many of the hunters wanted to have a go at them but they were restrained by other hunt followers. Leaving the saboteurs behind the hunt drew on and on in the sweltering heat but it was not until the end of the draw, near *The Coventry Arms*, that the hounds hit a drag. After a brief sortie upstream the mink was viewed escaping in the opposite direction under the bridge.

I dashed back to look. I finished one film but, before I could reload another film into my camera there was a frantic burst of holloaing from upstream. I ran up to the road towards this and was just in time to see a tiny mink darting across a grass field with the pack in hot pursuit.

Hounds snapped at him, bowling him over, then lost him in the long grass. The mink ran on but was hopelessly beaten for speed and, as the pack converged, turned to face them.

Truly at bay, this courageous creature reared up on his hind legs, spitting defiance. As the lead hound, Candle, thrust forward he was bitten on the side of his nose. It was the last gesture of defiance. The pack descended and the mink was ripped to pieces and so completely devoured that nothing remained as a trophy.

This hunt then vanned on to another brook, while I left to go on to my third hunt of the day — the meet of the Wyre Forest Beagles at Crowle at 4.00p.m. I arrived late to find the hounds already out in the fields drawing. Hares were running all over the place but, with scenting conditions poor, the pack was not very effective.

These late afternoon meets for such hare hunts are a kind of pre-season training to get the hounds in trim. They are the beaglers' equivalent to cub hunting.

Hounds changed hares frequently and did not catch while I was present. Hunt supporters were disconsolate. They complained that their hounds were bred to be short in the leg, beyond the point of benefiting the 'sport', simply so that their Huntsman, Roger Colver, could keep up.

MY LAST MINK HUNTS

My last day's hunting with the Three Counties in the 1982 season was from their meet at *The Black Swan*, Much Dewchurch on Saturday, September 25th. From the meet the hunt vanned to Wormbridge and set off, drawing downstream.

Turning about and hunting back towards Wormbridge they found in a ditch close to the bridge on the main Abergavenny road and the hunt was on. The mink was sighted several times but clearly there was little scent. The hunt staff had great difficulty keeping their hounds off the road that was busy with holiday traffic.

Sally Whittall, a reporter with *Farmer's Guardian*, was following this hunt to do a feature on mink hunting. When she asked me to do some pictures for her ("*Nothing too gory*") I agreed. But some hunt followers were suspicious of her. One warned me: "*She's wearing a BFSS badge, but so could anyone. You have to be careful.*" I agreed wholeheartedly.

The hunted mink was lost near the bridge, so the hounds pressed on searching towards Much Dewchurch. They crossed the railway line twice but couldn't find any scent of mink. The day ended on reaching the pub at Much Dewchurch at 6.00p.m. Chatting to supporters here I learned that their total tally of mink up till then was 75.

I attended a second hunting festival a week later on October 2nd in the West Country. All three packs met at *The Bullers Arms*, Marhamchurch, near Bude. The first hunt out, the Tetcott Foxhounds, killed a fox cub. The second, the Marhamchurch Beagles, killed nothing and neither did the last pack, the Devon and Cornwall Minkhounds.

I attended only two mink hunts in 1983. By then my cover had virtually been blown and I had to be extremely careful.

In the early days of my career as an undercover agent, caution on my part was all important as I compiled the dossier of evidence against the hunts. By April 1983, after some two years of successful work, with others taking my place, both I and the League felt that the time was drawing near when I could reveal my findings. People working undercover often find it difficult to call the right time to end their project. It takes a lot of time and effort to reach the point where you are fully trusted by your opponents so why and when should you give it up? There is a fine balance to be struck between staying undercover in the hope of gathering more evidence versus declaring your role and using the evidence you have already gathered before it is degraded in some way by being dated.

Richard Course and I agreed that my undercover role was nearing an end and I began to take risks I would not have contemplated taking in the earlier phases. For nearly two years I had been swapping written punches with an unsuspecting Ian Coghill in the letters pages of national and local newspapers.

In my capacity as Mike Wilkins, Press Officer of the LACS, I tirelessly attacked hunting in my letters. As Conservation and Education Officer of the British Field Sports Society, Ian Coghill denied any accusations that I made against hunting. He responded that all hunting was necessary and humane. Little did he realise that whilst hunting his own hounds he was rubbing shoulders with his main antagonist, drinking with him at the bar and allowing him to film incriminating sequences of the kill.

Knowing that discovery of my undercover role was only a matter of time, my accusations in the press began to be more pointed, naming dates and incidents. The following exchange of letters appeared in the *Northern Echo*:

My letter published January 12th, 1983:

"Sir,

Your correspondent, and hunt apologist, Ian Coghill has spent most of his adult life hunting otters, so it is hardly unexpected that he has little knowledge of fox hunting.

Foxes most certainly are thrown live to hounds, are released in front of hounds and on occasion are crippled prior to release to reduce their chances of escape.

Even with the latest bloodsports craze — mink hunting — we receive reports of mink being thrown live to hounds.

If by way of New Year's Resolution hunting people made some attempt to understand the biology of their quarry we could hopefully look forward to all hunting being ended before the end of this year!

If Mr Coghill knew anything about fox biology he would know not to make the fatuous claim that fox hunting grants foxes a close season. Vixens give birth during March-April, and yet fox hunting continues well into April and in some areas even into May!"

Ian Coghill replied as follows on February 1st, 1983:

"Sir,

Mr Wilkins of the League Against Cruel Sports (January 12th) knows full well that live mink and foxes are not thrown to hounds, and it is disgraceful that he should attempt to mislead the public.

It would be splendid if I could use the columns of a newspaper as widely respected as the Echo to ask Mr Wilkins to name Masters of

211

fox and minkhounds who he alleged have thrown live foxes and mink to their hounds.

Unlike most other animal users and controllers, the hunting world has to operate in public and it is impossible that such behaviour would go unseen.

I challenge Mr Wilkins to name the Masters so that these serious allegations can be properly investigated. Let us not have a lot of historical nonsense, let's hear about people who are running hunts in 1983."

This debate was followed closely by the readers, but suddenly Ian Coghill dropped out of the issue. At that point he must have known that somehow the LACS really did have information about the mink throwing incident.

It came further to a head when Ian appeared at a public debate in Worcester about bloodsports on Tuesday February 15th 1983. Representing the League, Richard Course, asked him if he had ever known of an animal being thrown live to hounds.

Ian Coghill replied, "*No.*"

Richard pressed the point: "*Have you ever known of a live mink thrown to hounds?*"

Again, Coghill denied it, but by then he must have been really worried as to what had leaked out. I calculated that he would soon recall who had filmed the live mink being thrown. But did that label me a spy or merely a careless and talkative fool — perhaps with untrustworthy friends?

I endeavoured to stay as close to this hunt as possible to try and pick up any information available. The League had to know the extent to which BFSS Officers were prepared to lie to cover up such incidents as the mink throwing one.

After I had shown a suitably selected set of slides at the Three Counties AGM on February 1st 1983 (ironically the very day when Ian Coghill's reply in the *Northern Echo* was published) I was invited back to their Keepers Evening at Defford near Pershore on March 11th to show some of my movie film.

On that very morning I learned from *Horse and Hound* that the Three Counties Minkhounds had 'sacked' their terrierman Peter May. Clearly the hunters had held a 'kangaroo court'. They had 'sacked' Peter May for what they described as a mistake when, in reality, it was Ian Coghill who had given the instructions who was responsible. *Horse and Hound* claimed that Peter May was the hunt's professional terrierman yet the hunt's own accounts show that no terrierman was paid. It was all rather strange.

I deliberated at length as to whether or not to attend that evening but realised that if I did not it would be an admission of my guilt and the end of my project. There was still valuable evidence to gather as to the true feelings of these hunters regarding this issue so I had to continue my project for a little while longer if at all possible.

In my experience as an undercover operative if someone doubts you or suspects you, moving away from them does not help at all, it only serves to confirm their suspicions. The best course of action, albeit difficult, is to move towards those who are suspicious of you.

The evening was a very tense affair for me. Ian Coghill's manner was distinctly cool. He asked me if I had the film of the mink being thrown and I replied that it was elsewhere but that I would bring it at the earliest opportunity.

Obviously I was under close investigation. I knew it was only a matter of time before my true identity was uncovered. I was being hunted hard.

So it was that I only followed two more mink hunts. The first was on April 30th, with the Devon and Cornwall Minkhounds from their meet at North Tamerton, a small village just along from Boyton Bridge where I had followed them the previous year.

I was apprehensive at first, thinking that Ian Coghill would surely have passed on some warning about me to his hunting colleagues, but my fears were groundless.

The hounds drew towards Boyton first and soon encountered some strong drag. Working up to this the pack marked at one end of a long field drain. It was too narrow to enter a terrier at the river end and the terriermen were equally unsuccessful when they tried at the other end further up the field.

On occasion the cornered mink would peer out of the exit overlooking the river. The hounds found it tantalising enough but the watching supporters were beside themselves with frustration. One astute hunter then noticed a steady flow of water out of the drain and had the idea of temporarily blocking the other end.

Hunt supporters set about building a miniature dam with rocks and polythene. By doing this and thereby stopping the water escaping down the pipe a veritable lake of water built up. Their idea was that when released the surge of water would sweep the mink out from his refuge.

Good in theory for the hunters but poor in practice. The idea failed because unbeknown to them when they started their construction work there was a break halfway along the drain. When released the water simply surged from this break out to form a large puddle in the field.

Other ideas, like thumping the ground with spades and digging behind the bank, were tried but to no avail. Arlin was soon bored and took his pack on to try for another mink. One Whipper-in, Graham, stayed behind to try his luck.

He lay flat on the bank overlooking the hole and began to 'talk' to the mink. If I had not seen it for myself I would not have believed it. There he lay, chattering, hissing and spitting like a mink down the drain until, to everyone's amazement, the mink bolted into the water.

The hounds were holloaed back and were soon in hot pursuit. After a long, long dive, when he was clearly visible in the crystal clear water of the stream, the mink emerged exhausted. The hounds jumped for him and there was an almighty melee. In their enthusiasm the hounds snapped at the mink and anything that looked like a mink — including the tails of other hounds.

Some of their bites were accurate. The mink was crippled. He struggled on the surface for a short time then disappeared beneath thrashing canine jaws. He might have sunk from sight but Arlin hooked him out with his pole. The small carcass was hoisted up onto the bank where Arlin hacked off the trophies.

A picnic lunch was taken back at the meet. The hounds were then cast in the other direction but without much success. I left before the end, fearful that if I lingered too long I could be asked some pointed questions.

My last hunt, the end of this phase of my undercover work, was with the Three Counties Minkhounds from their meet at Longtown near Hereford, on Saturday May 7th 1983. Heavy rain beforehand had produced swollen rivers. This caused the hunt to switch location from their planned meet at Much Dewchurch.

I had arranged for hunt saboteurs to attend in force. I had to put in an appearance myself if only to prove to my anti-hunt colleagues that the League are truly active in the fight against bloodsports.

A clammy silence descended over the crowded pub at Longtown when I entered. With difficulty some of the hunters tried to appear friendly towards me as I threaded my way through the crowd and up to the bar, but they were poor actors. I had no doubt that they were certain that I was the spy in their midst.

Inwardly quaking, I ordered a whisky and used all my control to keep my hand steady as I drank it. I remembered all the violence from hunters towards conservationists at that Border Counties Otterhounds meet years previously — and feared that I might be in line for some.

Loppylugs, the elderly and amiable supporter who had told me of the change of meet was rebuked by Ian Coghill for doing so. The rebuke was pointed. Loppylugs had been my constant source of information during my mink hunting and hare hunting days. He was terrified that I might reveal his indiscretions to his hunting friends.

When the hounds moved off I followed them with other hunt supporters but within ten minutes some hundred or more hunt saboteurs arrived, piling out of a convoy of transit vans.

Ian stopped the hunt and summoned me to the front. I braced myself expecting a confrontation. Instead he directed me, for my own safety, to go ahead and photograph the saboteurs. Clearly he recognised that violence could easily break out, would do no-one any good and was something to be avoided. I was grateful to him.

Later, in the face of such a large contingent of saboteurs, he was forced to abandon hunting altogether and return to the pub.

In the early afternoon the police arrived and the hunt moved elsewhere. The saboteurs followed. Linked by C.B. radios they were able to keep in touch despite the police intervening to stop and search as many of their vehicles as possible.

Although that day was completely ruined for the hunt, their subsequent report in *Shooting Times* claimed that they had suffered little inconvenience and that they had even killed a mink.

Whatever the truth, that day's hunting brought stage one of my undercover work to a close.

In the interests of fairness I will detail some of what Ian Coghill said in response after my work became public.

The *Observer* August 7th 1983 printed a report under the heading: "*Blood-sport spy film was a set-up, says hunter.*" Ian Coghill was then reported as saying that I had 'set up' incidents in order to take incriminating pictures and further that on one occasion I had unsuccessfully proposed that a boy should be 'blooded'. My response is that I was never any more than an observer to these hunting events. I was always on the side of the hunted animal — and I always did whatever I could to ensure that quarry escaped. I never asked nor suggested that hunters do anything other than pose for pictures in situations that they had already contrived. I did not suggest that anyone have blood smeared on their face.

EPILOGUE

Towards the end of May 1983, Richard Course, Executive Director of the LACS, received a call at his London office from the *Sunday Telegraph*'s features department. They asked if he knew that Mike Wilkins, whom the League employed as Press Officer, was really Mike Huskisson who had a criminal record and that furthermore he masqueraded at hunts as Michael Wright.

The call came just at the start of the general election campaign, an election in which the League was known to be supporting the Labour Party because of their fine manifesto pledge to ban all hunting with dogs. Any smear campaign against the League at that vital time may possibly have affected the Labour Party. Thinking quickly, Richard parried the question. When the journalist pressed for a definite yes or no Richard simply said: "*If you believe the story go ahead and print.*" The story never appeared. The general election was held on June 9th and the Conservatives won a decisive victory.

Knowing this information in the possession of the traditionally pro-hunt *Telegraph* would surface again, the League acted swiftly. Information and evidence was supplied to the *Times*, *Daily Mirror* and *News of the World* and in August 1983 film of one mink being thrown live and another drowned was released and shown on ITN News and other television programmes. The pro-hunting lobby condemned my claims as, "*ludicrous, exaggerated and lying.*" (*Daily Mirror* August 4th 1983). Mr Stephen Hastings, chairman of the BFSS accused me of 'trickery' adding: "*Hunts are open to allcomers and it is absurd to say they have been 'infiltrated.'*" (*Observer* August 7th 1983).

Some 5,000 negatives and transparencies and nearly 2,000ft of movie film remains in stock as supporting evidence for this book. This was offered to the hunting authorities in early August 1983 — in case they needed it for any disciplinary enquiries. To date (September 2015) they have shown no interest.

Most campaigners are resolute in their beliefs but occasionally people, for a variety of reasons, change sides. Some even change back again. People are courted and rewarded with cash.

For example here is the text of a proposal sent to the hunting fraternity at the end of 1983, just before *Outfoxed* was published, by former League undercover investigator Mike O'Reilly who switched sides. I have corrected some spelling errors. This letter was acquired by the League by good fortune — and honesty.

The BFSS referred to was the British Field Sports Society that later changed its name to the Countryside Alliance. Dave Wetton, a former Secretary of the Hunt Saboteurs Association, was at the time a member of the Executive Committee of the LACS.

Here is the text:-

"PROPOSED CONTINUATION OF CURRENT PROJECT INCLUDING TERMS AND PROJECTION OF EVENTS LEADING UP TO 1987/8 GENERAL ELECTION

As is already known I am quite prepared to continue my current work for a further period of between two and five years providing the terms of agreement are acceptable to both parties. I say a period of between two and five years as I am of the opinion that to expect sweeping success overnight would be at best unreasonable and at least very difficult. If we agree to continue this work I would suggest a re-valuation of the project in two years time to assess its significance both in terms of finance and information/documents obtained. If after this re-valuation it is considered viable to continue then so be it. It should be remembered that in order to achieve a good position within the League Against Cruel Sports at the time of the next General Election foundations have to be laid and I can think of no better time to start than the present (subject to agreement) as I am in particular favour with Mr. R. Course and many members of the League Executive Committee & staff at headquarters. I am also making inroads with the Hunt Saboteurs Association.

L.A.C.S. and HSA Committee elections

Next summer I shall be taking the necessary action to stand for both the League & HSA Executive Committees. With the H.S.A. I can see no problem with standing for election. As mentioned above I am currently "well in" with Course etc. so shall stand for election to the L.A.C.S. Executive Committee next Summer. Two things could then happen. Firstly Mr Course could give his seal of approval and not interfere or alternatively he may ask me not to stand and choose instead to offer a full or part time employment with the League, no doubt as a mole against hunts/field officer with Mike Huskisson. This if I were to accept would give access to all kinds of League documents/Committee minutes and other activities on a daily basis. If on the other hand I were to be elected on to the full Executive Committee, minutes and daily/weekly reports would be forwarded to me by post.

I understand from Nick that you wish to prove a connection between the League & HSA in view of all the recent violence between Hunt Saboteurs and Hunt followers at the recent Opening Meets. This can only be achieved over a period of time, and then I can give no

217

absolute promise of total success. What I can say however [is] that if we come to an agreement & decide to proceed then I shall "bend over backwards" to achieve good results in the defence of fieldsports. I do believe however that our goal should be the next General Election.

TERMS OF AGREEMENT – TO BE REVIEWED AFTER TWO YEARS

That a sum of £3000 be paid to me on an annual basis. This sum would be broken down into twelve (12) consecutive monthly payments after a figure of approx. £1200 is made available for a suitable vehicle for the duration of the project.

I further propose that the vehicle should not exceed a cost of £4,500 (i.e. good x or y reg. vehicle) including deposit (approx.. £1200) and that the balance of the account of the said vehicle be paid off on a H.P. basis at the end of each calendar month over a period of 2 years. Also, as a precautionary measure, the vehicle be solely registered in my name, thus avoiding any direct link between us.

[There then followed detailed financial breakdowns that have been omitted here]

Current League activities
OUTFOXED – MIKE HUSKISSON

The book is currently at the printers and Dave Wetton informed me on Sunday (20th November) that it should be out in the next three weeks. I'll get a copy early & will pass it on to you. Wetton also told me that Huskisson has approached W.H. Smith and Sons. with a view to them selling it. W.H. Smith's told Huskisson that their legal department would need to see a copy first. Perhaps W.H. Smith's legal dept. should be approached & informed of Huskisson's past record of grave desecration etc. It can be seen from the enclosed leaflet that there is no proof whatsoever that the chap photographed "dropping a bagged fox" did so on a hunting day. Mr. Hugh Clayton went so far as to say that the man in the photograph could even be Richard Course himself dropping the fox. Looking at the photograph itself there is no way it could be said to have been taken on the Dulverton West Foxhounds. A line of defence could be for the terrier man to claim the dropping of the fox occurred on a Sunday afternoon & that Huskisson was with him when the animal was released, hence the photograph.

Mike Huskisson – FUTURE PLANS

Huskisson has every intention of carrying on his moling activities against hunts. He hopes to be able to unearth more damaging material in preparation for the next General Election.

218

Huskisson is certainly a man to keep an eye on. It may be an idea, as I have said before, to publish his photograph in both Horse and Hound and Shooting Times in say a year or so's time. The reason behind this could be a "flash back" to the year before.

League to produce two new films – Fox hunting and Hare Coursing
Dick Course has informed me that the League are in the process of producing two new films, one on fox hunting (no doubt using material I obtained against Chris Wood & West Percy Foxhounds & additional material obtained by Huskisson. i.e. the bagged fox episode & films/photographs of kills etc.) and the other on coursing. Here I understand Huskisson has provided much of the footage, such as three Greyhounds coursing a single hare (one had slipped its leash).

H.S.A. telephone liaison system – A central telephone number
Mr. Dave Wetton has informed me that following all the recent violence at the Opening Meets this season, and the fact that the B.F.S.S. were quick to issue press releases giving their side of events, and the H.S.A. have been extremely slow in providing its Executive Committee with their interpretation of events, which has consequently resulted in a delay in the H.S.A. issuing a press release, it will be discussed at the next H.S.A. Executive Committee Meeting for a Central telephone number to be available for all groups to report acts of violence on the evening of the event. In this way a single person will be able to collate all information & consequently be in a better position to deal with the media."

Armed with this document Richard Course and I fed misleading information to this double-agent and through him to his handlers. At the appropriate time we confronted him and ended his sad attempts to harm the interests of his former colleagues.

After *Outfoxed* was published in November 1983 I carried on working for the LACS. However, it troubled me that the cruelty that I had exposed within hunting was more than matched by the cruelty in vivisection. But there was a problem exposing this cruelty. Vivisection takes place behind closed and well-guarded doors. To go undercover you cannot simply turn up at a research laboratory and ask to watch — as I had made initial contacts by attending hunt meets

Some animal rights groups formed in the early 1980s that explored new ways of exposing the grim secrets of vivisection. These were the Animal Liberation Leagues that specialised in mass trespass in daylight using the new weapon for animal rights campaigners — the videocamera. In August 1984 I joined one of these groups — the formidable South East Animal Liberation League — as a photographer on their mass invasion of the research premises of the Royal College of Surgeons (RCS) at Downe in Kent.

I went to the wrong laboratory unit and in the confusion of the day ended up taking away documents passed to me that revealed the cruel mistreatment of monkeys at the establishment. I passed all these to lawyers for the British Union for the Abolition of Vivisection (BUAV) and subsequently gave evidence for the BUAV in their 1985 prosecution of the RCS for cruelty. The RCS were convicted and fined. They appealed and their conviction was upheld but later they were acquitted on a legal technicality after Judicial Review. Following my admission in court of my involvement in another illegal act Richard Course had little choice and sacked me from the LACS.

I met Sue in the summer of 1984 and we married the following year. In September 1986 at Maidstone Crown Court I was jailed for 18 months for my role in removing papers from the RCS. Our first child was born 3 weeks later. I was released after 6 months and set about using my lengthy experience coupled with the latest equipment to work lawfully to investigate and expose cruelty to animals.

From January 1989 I worked again for the LACS, as a self-employed consultant — on the strict understanding that I only operate within the law. In June 1989 I set up my own investigation group — the Animal Cruelty Investigation Group (ACIG). Funded by supporters and aided by many colleagues, particularly Melody MacDonald, Ed Maynard, Mike Michalak, Lawrie Payne and Les Ward, I then used the latest video equipment to carry out successful investigations into bloodsports and vivisection that will be the subject of a future book. I am nondescript and I could still work undercover within hunting. In 1995 I created the Animal Welfare Information Service to publicise the information uncovered by the ACIG.

Just as my undercover work for the LACS to expose hunting followed that by Mike O'Reilly and Raymond Rowley so was my work followed in turn by others, in particular Kevin Hill and Paul Tillsley. When they were no longer able to work undercover they, along with Joe Hashman, Andrew Wasley, Peter White, Jim Wickens and many others, achieved considerable success with open and covert investigations and monitoring of hunting. This work continues.

In 2000 I was an observer (along with Graham Sirl) for the Campaign for the Protection of Hunted Animals at some of the visits made by the Lord Burns Hunting Inquiry team that were tasked by Parliament to see and report on fox and hare hunting and hare coursing and their humane alternatives — drag hunting and drag coursing. The Inquiry team were not asked to evaluate whether such hunting was cruel. The inherent cruelty in these pastimes is obvious but it was for MPs to decide whether the measure of that cruelty was acceptable in the modern world. They decided it was not.

In November 2004, after many hours deliberation, the UK Parliament passed the Hunting Act 2004. This banned the hunting and coursing of wild animals as described in this book. Hunting itself was not banned in order to allow the humane alternatives to continue and avoid the slaughter of hounds and horses. Before the Hunting Act was passed some 40,000 hunt supporters signed a declaration vowing to ignore it. Many said they would go to prison rather than obey it. There are far too many loopholes in the law that hunters have exploited to the full. Many hunts end up 'accidentally' hunting live quarry. Some hunters simply ignore the law — and do so with impunity.

There are now increasing demands for the Hunting Act to be strengthened by Parliament. The police should also enforce it better. No-one should be above the law. As ever people can help our police but whilst the public should be encouraged to watch over our wildlife — perhaps through a Countryside or Wildlife Watch to match Neighbourhood Watch — they should not be forced into the role of enforcing wildlife law. Too often we see courageous hunt saboteurs and hunt monitors (particularly Associates of the group Protect Our Wild Animals) out in the fields facing aggression, criminal damage and violence from hunters as they observe and record hunting. Penny Little and Judy Gilbert are examples of particularly successful hunt monitors — their video evidence helped secure the landmark 2012 conviction of the Heythrop Foxhounds for illegal hunting. The Heythrop Hunt Ltd, a Master and the Huntsman all pleaded guilty in a case brought at great expense by the RSPCA.

Hunt saboteurs, all volunteers, sometimes find themselves having to take action as necessary to protect wildlife from illegal hunting. The public should not have to do the very jobs that they already pay our police so well to do. Furthermore, it is surely wrong that charities such as the RSPCA should feel obliged to take the considerable financial burden of prosecuting all wildlife crimes.

The legal issues around hunting could all be resolved if only hunting people would look closely at their own pastimes — see the inherent cruelty — and take positive steps to walk away from it. They do not have to flout the Hunting Act just because they can. Most hunt riders are only there for the thrill of a cross-country gallop. For them the pursuit of an artificial scent as in drag hunting is the answer.

Since August 1984 — soon after I met my wife to be — I have campaigned entirely lawfully for better animal protection laws. I now work closely with various animal welfare and animal rights groups and the police to see the Hunting Act 2004 strengthened and enforced.

I also strive with colleagues and other like-minded groups to extend the umbrella of animal protection legislation. Given my history I am particularly keen to help educate the next generation of campaigners to help them avoid the many mistakes I have made. To this end I offer some words of advice to young people entering the animal protection movement and eager to make an effective contribution. I have seen every phase of the struggle to protect animals — from collecting money and signed petition forms to Durham jail — yet my most significant contribution to help our cause was entirely lawful. This was to work undercover and both see, and record for the world in turn to see, the reality of hunt cruelty. This is one area of campaigning work where individuals really can make a difference. We must strive to ensure that everyone obeys the law — and if anyone has to go to prison it is only the animal abusers — not the animal protectors.

We also need to change minds so that more people view all our wildlife as valuable assets to be cherished. Animals must no longer be seen as mere toys to be used, abused and destroyed on a whim. Life is precious. Every creature has a valuable role to play in our ecosystems.

I should also make clear who really is responsible for the violence in the hunting fields. It cannot be a surprise that those whose 'sport' depends on hurting helpless creatures will also inflict violence on people trying to stop them. History proves that hunt saboteurs are routinely battered and bruised by hunters. Some hunt saboteurs have been crippled for life and some even killed as they tried to protect animals. The animal welfare side endured countless disappointments in Parliament without violence. It was the hunting fraternity who fought with police as hunt supporters tried to batter their way into the Houses of Parliament during the passage of the Hunting Act.

I will always remember the many courageous people around the world who have given their lives to protect animals from cruelty. Every news bulletin produced by the ACIG includes the following **IN MEMORIAM** section:-

"Tragically, far too many people working for animals have suffered appallingly at the hands of the abusers. Several have paid the ultimate price. They must never be forgotten. The memory of their sacrifice should inspire us all to do much more for the causes that we know to be just. ALL who give their lives for animals are remembered but we do particularly recall the following whose lives were taken by our opponents:-

James Piper, RSPCA Inspector: Died in 1838 after sustaining
severe injuries tackling cockfighters at Hanworth, Middlesex.
William Sweet, LACS member: Murdered 6/1/1976 after altercation
with man shooting birds. Assailant was jailed for life but has long
been released.
Fernando Pereira, Greenpeace photographer: Murdered 10/7/1985
by the French Secret Service when the vessel "Rainbow Warrior"
was sunk by two explosions, Auckland Harbour, New Zealand.
Michael Hill, Hunt Saboteur: Killed 9/2/1991 protesting against
hare hunting at the Cheshire Beagles.
Thomas Worby, Hunt Saboteur: Killed 3/4/1993 protesting against
fox hunting at the Cambridgeshire Foxhounds.
Jill Phipps, Animal Rights Activist: Killed 1/2/1995 protesting
against live exports of farm animals, Coventry Airport.
Paola Quartini, animal activist for LIPU (Italian League for Bird
Protection - UK) from Genoa, Italy and Elvio Fichera, a volunteer
for the Association of Abandoned Animals: Both were murdered
12/5/2010 whilst trying, with police, to serve a warrant on Renzo
Castagnola for cruelty to animals. Renzo Castagnola shot them
dead, then injured his wife, then killed himself."

Some good news for our wildlife since the original *Outfoxed* was published has been the recovery of the otter in our waterways. In 1983 the species faced imminent extinction. However, thanks to dedicated work by people like the late Philip Wayre (1921-2014) and his Otter Trust formerly based in Earsham, Norfolk and the constant pressure against mink hunting by hunt saboteurs, otters have now recovered to the point where they can be found in most rivers across the UK.

In conclusion, the hunting of wildlife with packs of hounds is a pastime that is cruel by design and cruel by calculation. The hounds used are bred not for the speed that might produce a quick kill but rather for the stamina that guarantees the lengthy hunts the followers seek. Such cruelty has no place in the UK today.

For further information about the Animal Cruelty Investigation Group and the Animal Welfare Information Service please write to:
ACIG/AWIS, PO Box 8, Halesworth, Suffolk IP19 0JL.
Alternatively you can check out their web site at:
www.acigawis.org.uk
You can also find some of the film clips referred to in this text and other relevant later video clips, taken by the ACIG and other groups, on their YouTube channel at: **www.youtube.com/user/AWISACIG**

Here are other campaigning groups that you might like to contact:-

Fox Project: A charity dedicated to the protection, rescue, and advocacy for the wild fox. Also offers advice about foxes including treatments and deterrents.
Contact: Fox Project, The Lodge/Kings Toll Road, Tunbridge Wells, Kent, TN2 4BE.
Web site: www.foxproject.org.uk

Hounds Off: Is the hunt still riding roughshod around your neighbourhood despite the ban? Are you worried about hunt trespass? Now you can protect your property, pets and livestock. Hounds Off will show you how with our range of no-nonsense online resources developed specifically to keep the hunters and their hounds in check.
Contact: Hounds Off, PO Box 162, Shaftesbury, Dorset, SP7 7AZ
Web site: www.houndsoff.co.uk

Hunt Saboteurs Association: The only organisation that works directly in the field to protect wildlife from the hunter. Hunt saboteurs are all volunteers. They are the thin line of compassion that stands between the animal abusers and their victims.
Contact: BM HSA, London, UK, WC1N 3XX
Web site: www.huntsabs.org.uk
Facebook: www.facebook.com/HuntSaboteursAssociation

League Against Cruel Sports: The leading UK charity helping to prevent cruelty to animals associated with sports such as fox hunting, game bird shooting and wildlife crime.
Contact: League Against Cruel Sports, New Sparling House, Holloway Hill, Godalming, Surrey, GU7 1QZ
Web site: www.league.org.uk

Protect Our Wild Animals: Campaigns for a complete, effective and enforceable ban on the hunting of wild animals with dogs in England and Wales. A number of POWA Associates are independent hunt monitors who keep a close watch on many hunts.
Web site: www.powa.org.uk

Animals are increasingly vulnerable in our modern world. They need our help.

GLOSSARY OF SOME HUNTING TERMS

Account for: Kill.

Artificial earth: This is a fox den constructed by hunt supporters with the object of encouraging foxes to breed. Major Gundry, Joint Master of the Duke of Beaufort's Foxhounds stated: "*Without artificial earths a number of hunts would have to disband*". Hunt supporters also commonly feed foxes around artificial earths.

At bay: Said of a stag that, exhausted, has turned to face the hounds.

At fault: Hounds which have lost a scent.

Bagman, or Bagged-fox: A fox released when required for a hunt. The fox is taken in a sack or box and may be released into a covert, an earth, a drain or an open field. This may be done days before the hunt, hours before, or even with the hounds in the near vicinity.

Bay: Hounds bay when marking a fox to ground. An exhausted stag facing the pack is at bay and the hounds that bark at him are said to be baying him. A terrier facing a fox, badger or mink underground and giving tongue is also said to be baying.

Blank: A covert is blank when it does not hold any quarry. A blank day is one on which no quarry is found.

Blood: To daub with the blood of the dead quarry the cheek of a new recruit to hunting (usually an infant) after his or her first kill. The person blooded may be told not to wash the blood off. It also means giving young hounds their first taste of their quarry. A pack which is 'out of blood' is one that has not killed for some time; while one that is 'in blood' has recently killed several times in quick succession.

Bolt: To force the quarry out of the drain or earth where it has sought refuge with the aid of a terrier, stick, or any other means.

Brace: Pair (of foxes).

Break up: A pack of hounds break up their dead quarry.

Brush: The tail of a fox.

Cap: Uniform for foot followers of hunting. Also a money collection made at the meet from those who are not subscribers to the hunt.

Cast: Hounds spreading out in search of a scent; hounds may cast themselves or be cast by their Huntsman.

Charlie: Name given to the fox by hunt supporters, derives from Charles James Fox the eighteenth-century politician.

Check: An interruption in the hunt when hounds lose the scent (are unable to own the line).

Chop: The quarry is chopped if it is killed by the hounds without giving the supporters any fun, i.e. before it had had the chance to run.

Country: The area hunted by a particular pack of hounds.

Couple: A pair of hounds. A pack is counted according to the number of couples, thus 35 hounds = 17½ couple.

Course: Hounds course their quarry when they pursue them in full view; also the matching of two greyhounds against one hare.

Covert: Any patch of wood, gorse or thicket where the quarry may lie for shelter (pronounced cover).

Cry: The sound, or music, hounds make when running. Hence: in full cry.

Drag: The scent left by the quarry on its nocturnal wanderings. Hounds 'drag' up to their quarry when they work out this stale line until they find him.

Drag hunt: A humane sport in which hounds pursue an artificial scent. This can be dripped from tanks either side of a saddle, on a rag towed behind a horse, or may be the 'clean-boot' of a running man.

Draw: To search for the quarry with hounds.

Earth: The lair, burrow or den of a fox.

Earth stopper: An employee of the hunt who blocks an earth entrance with tree stumps, filled sacks, or anything to hand, while the fox is out hunting and thus prevents the fox seeking refuge there.

Enter: To enter a hound is to start it on its hunting career.

Field: The followers of a hunt.

Foil: To obscure the scent of the quarry with some other scent. This may be caused by cattle or sheep running over the line or by horses, hounds and spectators milling about.

Gone Away!: This is the hunting cry shouted when the fox or other quarry is seen leaving the covert.

Gone to ground: The hunted fox is said to have gone to ground when he has escaped hounds by finding refuge in his earth, an artificial earth, a badger sett, down a drain or in a similar place of refuge.

Harbourer: A stag hunting term. One who advises the hunters as to the whereabouts and condition of suitable stags for hunting.

Head: To head the quarry is to divert it from its original course.

Heel: The reverse line of a scent to that taken, i.e. where the quarry has been rather than where he is going.

Hold up: To hold up a covert is to surround it with riders and foot followers so that cubs cannot escape during cub hunting.

Holloa: A loud, high scream or screech given by hunt followers to attract the attention of the Huntsman when the quarry is viewed (pronounced holler).

Law: Of hare coursing, the start given to the hare before the greyhounds are slipped, usually 60 to 80 yards. The start given to any quarry when bolted to ensure that it is not killed too quickly.

Lay on: To put the main pack of hounds on the trail of a stag after the tufters have driven him out from covert.

Line: The scent trail left by the quarry.

Mark: When hounds bay outside the earth, or drain in which the exhausted fox or mink has sought refuge, or in which it is lying.

Mixed pack: This is a pack of hounds containing both sexes.

Music: The cry that hounds make when they are running.

Own the line: Hounds which speak on a line are said to 'own the line'.

Pad: The foot of a fox or mink. It is sometimes given to followers as a trophy.

Riot: When hounds hunt anything that moves other than their proper quarry.

Run to earth/ground: To chase the quarry into some kind of hole or drain.

Scut: The tail of a hare.

Sinking: The quarry is described as sinking when it is running out of strength and weakening.

Slipper: The official in hare coursing whose job is to let the greyhounds go when each has fairly sighted the hare and the hare has been given a suitable start.

Slot: The foot of a deer, the track of a deer, or to track a deer by its footprints.

Speak: Hounds speak or give tongue when they are on the scent or have struck the line.

Stern: The tail of a hound.

Take: Stags that are killed are 'taken'.

Tally-ho!: A hunting cry that means 'I have seen the quarry'.

Trail hunting: Common since the Hunting Act took effect in February 2005. It involves using hounds to hunt a trail dragged behind a horse or by a quad-bike that is a scent based on the traditional quarry — so former fox packs may hunt a scent based on fox urine.

Tufters: In stag hunting refers to the small number of selected and steady hounds put into a covert to separate a stag from the rest of the herd and to drive him out from the covert for the full pack to hunt.

Velvet: The soft skin well supplied with arteries that covers the growing horns of a stag. It is very tender and bleeds easily if knocked.

To view: To see the quarry.

Walk: To walk a hound puppy is to take one into a farm or rural house after weaning and to rear it until it is ready to join the pack.

Whipper-in: Assistant to the Huntsman. Generally two, known as first whipper-in and second whipper-in. Usually shortened to 'whip'.

Worry: Of hounds, to kill their quarry and tear apart the carcass.

DIARY OF UNDERCOVER INVESTIGATIONS

Hunts attended by the author from 1981 to 1983:

1981

April 28th: Devon and Somerset Staghounds, Bicknor Bridge
April 30th: Devon and Somerset Staghounds, Aldermans Barrow
August 19th: Quantock Staghounds, Volis Cross
August 20th: Devon and Somerset Staghounds, Potter's Cross
August 22nd: Devon and Somerset Staghounds, Mounsey Hill Gate
August 24th: Dulverton West Foxhounds, Mockham Down Gate
August 25th: Devon and Somerset Staghounds, Wheddon Cross
October 3rd: Devon and Somerset Staghounds, Cuzzicombe
October 5th: Dulverton West Foxhounds, Burcombe Hill
October 6th: Devon and Somerset Staghounds, West Buckland
October 7th: Quantock Staghounds, Seven Milestone
October 8th: Devon and Somerset Staghounds, Webber's Post
October 10th: Devon and Somerset Staghounds, Morebath
October 17th: Devon and Somerset Staghounds, Brendon Two Gates
October 17th: Tiverton Staghounds, King's Nympton
October 19th: Dulverton West Foxhounds, West Buckland
October 20th: Devon and Somerset Staghounds, *Black Cock*, Molland
October 21st: Tiverton Staghounds, Van Post
October 22nd: Devon and Somerset Staghounds, Pitcombe Head
October 23rd: Dulverton West Foxhounds, *Royal Oak*, Withypool
October 24th: Devon and Somerset Staghounds, Comers Gate
October 26th: Stevenstone Foxhounds, Duerdon Cross
October 27th: Devon and Somerset Staghounds, *Culbone Stables*
October 28th: Tiverton Staghounds, Knowstone Moor Cross
October 29th: Devon and Somerset Staghounds, Bratton Fleming
October 30th: Dulverton West Foxhounds, Burcombe Hill
October 31st: Tiverton Staghounds, Chulmleigh Beacon
November 14th: Devon and Somerset Staghounds, Twitchen
November 16th: Dulverton West Foxhounds, Stoke Rivers
November 17th: Devon and Somerset Staghounds, Nutscale Drive
November 18th: Tiverton Staghounds, Edgiford Cross
November 19th: Devon and Somerset Staghounds, Bury
November 26th: Devon and Somerset Staghounds, Wheddon Cross
November 27th: Dulverton West Foxhounds, Tarr Steps Post
November 30th: Quantock Staghounds, Dead Woman's Ditch
December 1st: Devon and Somerset Staghounds, Scob Hill Gate
December 2nd: Tiverton Staghounds, Chain Bridge
December 3rd: Devon and Somerset Staghounds, Morebath
December 5th: Devon and Somerset Staghounds, Aldermans Barrow

1982

January 20th: Tiverton Staghounds, Chawleigh
January 21st: Devon and Somerset Staghounds, Horner
January 22nd: Dulverton West Foxhounds, Newtown Bridge
January 23rd: Devon and Somerset Staghounds, Mounsey Hill Gate
February 24th: Tiverton Staghounds, Rackenford
February 25th: Quantock Staghounds, Dead Woman's Ditch
February 26th: Dulverton West Foxhounds, Hawkridge
February 27th: Devon and Somerset Staghounds, Brendon Two Gates
February 27th: Tiverton Staghounds, *Black Cock,* Molland
March 16th: Devon and Somerset Staghounds, Wheddon Cross
March 17th: Tiverton Staghounds, Swineham Hill
March 18th: Devon and Somerset Staghounds, Haddon Hill
March 19th: Quantock Staghounds *Ship Inn*, Porlock
March 20th: Tiverton Staghounds, Chittlehampton
April 10th: Tiverton Staghounds, Holmingham Farm
April 24th: Devon and Cornwall Minkhounds, Chudleigh Knighton
April 26th: Quantock Staghounds: *Blue Ball*
April 27th: Devon and Somerset Staghounds, *Black Cock*, Molland
April 30th: Quantock Staghounds, *Carew Arms*
May 1st: Devon and Cornwall Minkhounds, Boyton Bridge
May 3rd: Devon and Cornwall Minkhounds, Harbertonford
May 29th: Devon and Cornwall Minkhounds, Lifton
May 31st: Devon and Cornwall Minkhounds, St. Neot
June 12th: Devon and Cornwall Minkhounds, Drewsteignton
June 14th: Devon and Cornwall Minkhounds, Kismeldon Bridge
June 15th: Culmstock Minkhounds, Black Torrington Bridge
June 26th: Devon and Cornwall Minkhounds, Marhamchurch
July 7th: Three Counties, Four Shires and Devon and Cornwall Minkhounds, *Cottage of Content*, Carey
July 8th: Three Counties and Devon and Cornwall Minkhounds, Tregare Mill
July 9th: Three Counties and Devon and Cornwall Minkhounds, Trigate Bridge
July 10th: Three Counties and Devon and Cornwall Minkhounds, *Lamb*, Stoke Prior
July 31st: Three Counties Minkhounds, Pandy
August 7th: Three Counties Minkhounds, Upleadon Mill
August 14th: Three Counties Minkhounds, Wichenford
August 21st: Three Counties Minkhounds, Little Hereford
August 25th: Three Counties Minkhounds, Caradoc House, Sellack

August 26th: Devon and Somerset Staghounds, *Froude Arms*, Anstey
August 27th: Dulverton West Foxhounds, Worth Farm
August 28th: Devon and Cornwall Minkhounds, Moreleigh
August 30th: Devon and Cornwall Minkhounds, Eggesford
August 31st: Devon and Somerset Staghounds, Mounsey Hill Gate
September 4th: Three Counties Minkhounds, Ketford Bridge
September 8th: Three Counties Minkhounds, Newnham Bridge
September 11th: Three Counties Minkhounds, Maisemore
September 12th: Three Counties Minkhounds, Wine and Cheese Party at Cropthorne
September 18th: Hunting Festival: Croome and West Warwickshire Foxhounds, Caddicroft Farm; Three Counties Minkhounds, Peopleton; Wyre Forest Beagles, Crowle
September 25th: Three Counties Minkhounds, *Black Swan*, Much Dewchurch
October 2nd: Hunting Festival: Tetcott Foxhounds, then Marhamchurch Beagles then Devon and Cornwall Minkhounds all at *Bullers Arms*, Marhamchurch
October 4th: Tiverton Foxhounds, Queen Dart Cross
October 5th: Tetcott Foxhounds, Wainhouse Corner
October 6th: Tiverton Staghounds, Witheridge Moor
October 7th: Tetcott Foxhounds, Morwenstow
October 8th: Dulverton West Foxhounds, Willingford Bridge
October 9th: Tiverton Staghounds, Chittlehamholt
October 16th: Surrey and North Sussex Beagles, Blindley Heath
October 23rd: Surrey and North Sussex Beagles, Marsh Green
October 27th: Dulverton West Foxhounds, Croyde
October 28th: Eggesford Foxhounds, Chulmleigh
October 29th: Dulverton West Foxhounds, Cuzzicombe Post
October 30th: Tiverton Staghounds, Stoodleigh
November 1st: Dulverton West Foxhounds, Yarde Down
November 2nd: Mid Devon Foxhounds, Caddiford Cross
November 6th: Surrey and North Sussex Beagles, *Bull*, Chelsham
November 13th: Pevensey Marsh Beagles, Northiam
November 20th: Surrey and North Sussex Beagles, Boreham Street
November 27th: Surrey and North Sussex Beagles, *Hare and Hounds*, Lingfield
December 4th: Ashford Valley Foxhounds, *Royal Oak*, Iden Green
December 11th: Banwen Miners Foxhounds, *King's Head*, Llangennith
December 15th: Fernie Foxhounds, Arnesby

December 16th: Cottesmore Foxhounds, Pasture House, North Luffenham

December 18th: Warwickshire Beagles, *Three Horseshoes*, Wixford

December 22nd: Eggesford Foxhounds, Venn, Morchard Bishop

December 24th: Eggesford Foxhounds, Mear, Morchard Bishop

December 27th: Banwen Miners Foxhounds, Castle Hotel, Neath

December 29th: Wyre Forest Beagles, Coddington Cross

December 31st: Dulverton West Foxhounds, West Molland

1983

January 1st: Tiverton Staghounds, *Fortescue Arms*, King's Nympton

January 3rd: Dulverton West Foxhounds, Gunn

January 8th: North Ledbury Foxhounds, *Wheatsheaf*, Fromes Hill

January 8th: Wyre Forest Beagles, Kinnersley Church

January 15th: Tiverton Staghounds, Spurway Moor Gate

January 17th: Dulverton West Foxhounds, Hunstone Cross

January 18th: South Tetcott Foxhounds, Crackington Haven

January 19th: Dulverton West Foxhounds, West Down

January 20th: Quantock Staghounds, Warm Corner

January 21st: Dulverton West Foxhounds, Lower Fyldon

January 22nd: Warwickshire Beagles, *Bell*, Cropthorne

January 29th: Wyre Forest Beagles, Tenbury

February 1st: Three Counties Minkhounds A.G.M., *Mason's Arms*, Wichenford

February 5th: Leadon Vale Basset Hounds, Church Farm, Hardwicke

February 12th: South Tetcott Foxhounds, Boyton

February 15th: Devon and Somerset Staghounds, *Culbone Stables* — Deer Drive

February 19th: Leadon Vale Basset Hounds, *Horseshoe*, Brooms Green

February 22nd: Devon and Somerset Staghounds, Court Place, Porlock — Deer Drive

February 24th: Devon and Somerset Staghounds, Horner — Cancelled

February 26th: Tiverton Staghounds, Benley Cross

March 2nd: Waterloo Cup hare coursing, Lydiate

March 3rd: Waterloo Cup hare coursing, The Withins

March 5th: Worcestershire Foxhounds, *Chequers*, Crowle

March 9th: Berkeley Foxhounds, Nympsfield

March 11th: Three Counties Minkhounds Keepers Evening, Defford near Pershore

March 12th: Duke of Beaufort's Foxhounds, Monument, Hawkesbury Upton

231

March 19th: Surrey and North Sussex Beagles, *Plough*, Lower Beeding

March 26th: Leadon Vale Basset Hounds, Church Farm, Hardwicke

March 28th: Dulverton West Foxhounds, Withypool Cross

March 29th: South Tetcott Foxhounds, Hornacott Chapel

March 30th: Eggesford Foxhounds, Lower Sutton Farm

April 30th: Devon and Cornwall Minkhounds, North Tamerton

May 7th: Three Counties Minkhounds, Longtown

INDEX

A

Adams, Anthony (Kennel-Huntsman, Exmoor Foxhounds) 135
Animal Liberation Front (ALF) 16, 17, 61, 62, 73, 82
Animals Film, The 160, 164
Arnett, Ian (Huntsman, Four Shires Minkhounds) 185, 187
Art of Beagling, The by Captain J. Otho Paget 157
Artificial earth 11, 52, 155
Ashford Valley Foxhounds 145, 147, 153
Asplin, Tim (Joint Master, Essex Union Foxhounds) 51
Atkins MP, Humphrey 29
August, Bob 74
Axe Vale Badger Hounds 184

B

Baily's Hunting Directory 178
Band of Mercy 16, 52-54, 57, 60
Banwen Miners Foxhounds 148
Barrington, James (Jim) 74, 114
Barter, Gwen 75
Bartlett, Norman (Master, Culmstock Minkhounds) 184
Beeney, Terry (Huntsman, Dulverton West Foxhounds) 121, 124, 128, 129, 132, 137-144
Beith, Mary (journalist) 54
Belstone Fox, The 42, 43
Bennett MP, Andrew 178
Bentinck, Lord Henry 133
Berkeley Foxhounds 154

Birmingham Angling Association 198, 199
Blencathra Foxhounds 208
Blue & Scarlet by JNP Watson 147
Border Counties Minkhounds 199
Border Counties Otterhounds 39, 40, 87, 175, 208, 214
Boyles, Dennis (Huntsman Devon and Somerset Staghounds) 83, 88, 89, 98, 107
Bridge, John (Huntsman, Border Counties Otterhounds) 208
British Union for the Abolition of Vivisection (BUAV) 98, 220
British Field Sports Society (BFSS) 8, 29, 33, 37, 38, 43, 50, 74, 75, 81, 93, 96, 147, 172, 179, 185, 210-212, 216, 219
   Country Fair 50
Brooks-Ward, Raymond 37
Bryant, John 52, 60
Bucks and Courtenay Tracy Otterhounds 37
Bull-fighting 73
Burns, Lord, Hunting Inquiry 220

C

Caldbeck
   St Kentigern's Church 61-64
Cambridgeshire Foxhounds 13, 14, 17, 19, 25,
Campaign for the Relief of Wildlife 17

Carlile QC, Alex 60
Carlisle Crown Court 64
Charlton, Jack 204
Cheshire Forest Foxhounds 140
Clayton, Hugh (journalist) 218
Coghill, Ian (Huntsman, Three Counties Minkhounds / Conservation and Education Officer, BFSS) 157, 164, 167, 171, 184, 185, 188-193, 195, 196, 199, 202-205, 211-215
Collins, Tony (Kennel-Huntsman, Heythrop Foxhounds) 124
Colver, Roger (Master, Wyre Forest Beagles) 166, 168, 209
Come and Hunt by The Hon. Charles Willoughby 133
Conservative Independent 74
Conservative Party 29, 168
Co-op ban on bloodsports 148
Cooper, Jilly 28
Cooper, Peter (Joint Master, Three Counties Minkhounds) 167, 192, 195, 205-207
Cooper, Rodney (Huntsman, Surrey and North Sussex Beagles) 158
Corner, Charles (Master, Eastern Counties Otterhounds) 41
Cottesmore Foxhounds 148
Countryside Alliance 8, 216
Course, Richard (Dick) 59, 74, 75, 76, 90, 175, 211, 212, 216, 218-220
Courtenay Tracy Otter Hounds Club 178
Coypu 28, 37, 177, 178

Creed, John (Huntsman, Worcestershire Foxhounds) 153
Croome and West Warwickshire Foxhounds 203, 208
Crowder MP, Petre 10
Cullen, Muriel 29
Cumberland News 64
Cunningham, Ian (Huntsman, Pevensey Marsh Beagles) 162
Culmstock Minkhounds 184
Culmstock Otterhounds 184

D
Dallas, Major Ronnie (Honorary Secretary, Duke of Beaufort's Foxhounds) 155
Dartmoor Otterhounds 178, 183
Davies, Mark 16, 76
Deer control 33
Deer Hunting 33-35, 81-116
   Autumn Stag Hunting 84-101
   blooding 89
   'bridge waiting' 92
   carted deer hunting 75
   deer drives 111
   harboured stag 84
   Hind Hunting 101-111
   'hocking' 111
   hounds attacking deer 95, 111
   hunting by torchlight 109
   hunt followers aiding the chase 105, 114
   hunting pregnant deer 102-104
   killing wounded/disabled deer 108, 111

Marsh Bridge 85, 102, 103, 109
  post-kill ritual 88
  slot 83, 89, 91, 104
  Spring Stag Hunting 8-9, 81-84, 111-116
  stabbing to death 110
  stags that will not run 94
  tushes (teeth) 88, 91
  tufters 34, 84, 90, 97
Devon and Cornwall Minkhounds 125, 157, 178-192, 200-202, 210, 213
Devon and Somerset Staghounds 33-35, 81-116, 136
Dewhurst (Judge) 33
Drag Hunt 100, 138, 220, 221
Duke of Beaufort's Foxhounds 154
Dulverton West Foxhounds 118-124, 127-129, 131-145, 153, 218
Durham Jail 11, 65-69, 222

E
Eastern Counties Otterhounds 41
East Essex Foxhounds 22
Edmondson, Judge A.A. 66
Eggesford Foxhounds 130, 134, 149, 156
'Elfin' (Treasurer, Wyre Forest Beagles) 167, 168
Enfield Chace Foxhounds 26
Essex Foxhounds 51
Essex Union Foxhounds 51
Evans, Barry 144, 145
Evans, Steve (Whipper-in, Three Counties Minkhounds) 190, 196
Express, Daily 76, 78

F
Farmer's Guardian 210
Fernie Foxhounds 148
Field, The 146, 195
Foal Farm Animal Sanctuary 78-80
Foot, Michael MP 168
Four Shires Minkhounds 185, 187
Fox and Hare in Leicestershire by Eric Morrison 133
Fox-Hunting by the Duke of Beaufort 119, 155
Fox, self-regulating population 52
Fox Hunting 10,11, 13-28, 50-52, 71,72, 117-156
  artificial earth 11, 52, 155
  badger sett 120, 122, 126, 133
  bagged fox 140-143, 219
  blooding (of foxes) 141
  blooding (of hunt supporters) 89
  Cub Hunting 51, 52, 118-131
    purpose of 119
  digging-out 122-130, 133-144, 146-147, 149-152, 154, 156
    badger-tongs 150-152, 156
    bolting 152, 154
    by torchlight 146, 151
    three hour dig 152
  earth-stopping 121
  'holding up' 120, 131
  holloa 139, 145, 150
    with a whistle 156
  hounds
    breeding 132, 133
    turnover of 118

killing pregnant vixen 136, 137
Main Season 131-156
Pony Club 89, 138
three levels of 117
throwing live fox into hounds 137, 156
trophies 126
'wound of honour' 153
Fur trade 52, 176,177
anti-fur trade t-shirt 71

G
Gabbert, Michael (Editor, *Sunday Independent*) 142
Garfield, Rorke 14
Gilbert, Judy 221
Girling, Colonel Barry (Secretary, Surrey Union Hunt) 24
Goodman, Cliff 53, 54, 60
Goulding, Peter (journalist) 156
Gunn (Devon village) 138, 142, 143

H
Harding, Charlie 185
Harding, Norah (Joint Master, Devon and Somerset Staghounds) 116, 185
Hare Coursing 10, 29-33, 50, 171-176
Anti-Coursing Bill 10
importing hares 171
Private Members Bill to prohibit 29
Waterloo Cup 10, 31-33, 171-176
Hare Hunting
Basset Hounds 28, 169-171
Beagling 28, 29, 157-169

'cap' 163
behaviour of hunted hare 28, 159, 165
hare killed in a tree 167
holloaing a hare 166
hound breeding 165
length of time for ideal hare hunt 157, 158
silent holloa 159
trophy 162, 166
Harris, Claud (Huntsman, Tetcott Foxhounds) 126
Hashman, Joe 33, 220
Hastings, Stephen (Chairman, BFSS) 216
Heath MP, Ted (Prime Minister) 29
Heffer MP, Eric 10
Hertfordshire Hunt 10
Heythrop Foxhounds 124, 135, 221
Heythrop Hunt Ltd., Master and Huntsman plead guilty to illegal hunting 221
Hicks, Jo 78
Hicks, John 78, 79, 88, 114
Hill, Bertie (Joint Master, Dulverton West Foxhounds) 121, 138, 140, 141
Hill, Kevin 220
Hill, Michael 223
Holderness Foxhounds 11
Horan, Frankie 33
Horse and Hound 26, 93, 142, 148, 157, 212, 219
Hunkin, Peter (Master, Tetcott Foxhounds) 125
Hunting Act 2004 75, 81, 221, 222
Hunting and Watching Exmoor Deer by H.P. Hewett 84

Hunting Festival 160, 207-210
Hunt Saboteurs Association
(HSA) 14-19, 25,26, 28-41,
62, 110, 163, 172-176, 214,
217, 219, 223
  antimate spray 209
  banner demonstrations 18,
26, 32, 37, 44
  formation of 14, 75
  HOWL magazine 29, 38, 51
  hunt saboteurs killed at hunts
223
  London group 17, 19
  structure 17
  tactics 17, 19
    beagling 28
    confusion 50
    deer hunting 33-35
    false holloa 17, 21, 28, 34,
38, 154
    fireworks 25, 26
    fox hunting 14-27
    hare coursing 29-33
      Waterloo Cup 32, 33,
171-176
    hunt ball 50
    hunting horn 23-25, 154
    otter hunting 35-41
    ultrasonic devices 26
    undercover 20-22
    wiring gates shut 25
  victims of violence and
intimidation 18, 26, 34, 39, 50,
184, 208, 209, 223

I
Independent, Sunday 142, 143
International Animal Rescue
71, 78

J
Jack's Game (TV programme)
204
James, Ken 33
Joint Otter Group 38
Jones, Trefor Owen (Master,
Vale of Clettwr Foxhounds) 24

K
Kendall, Ena (journalist) 74,
81, 90
Kent Messenger 57
Kenyon, Lord 31
Kimball MP, Marcus 29, 38,
43, 74, 75
Kirkham Open Prison,
Lancashire 69
Knight, Alan 71
Knutsford Crown Court 60

L
Labour Party, manifesto
pledge to ban hunting 216
Lawless, Maureen (journalist)
111, 114
Leadon Vale Basset Hounds
169-171
League Against Cruel Sports
(LACS) 9-11, 14, 16, 29, 34,
35, 74-76, 96, 105, 106, 114,
131, 172, 173, 175, 178, 185,
210-212, 214, 216-220, 223
  member killed by shooter 223
  sanctuaries 34, 75, 85, 88, 90,
97, 105-107, 113,114,
  undercover investigations 10,
11
Lee, Ronnie 16, 53, 54, 60
Little, Penny 221
'Loppylugs' 164, 165, 168,
214, 215

M
MacDonald, Melody 220
MacWilliam, James (Honorary Secretary, Waterloo Cup Committee) 172
Maidstone Crown Court 220
Mann, David (Master, Leadon Vale Basset Hounds) 170
Marhamchurch Beagles 210
Martin, Patrick (Whipper-in, Berkeley Foxhounds) 154
Masters of Fox Hounds Association (MFHA) 147
May, Peter (Terrierman, Three Counties Minkhounds) 193, 203-206, 212
May, Rick (Terrierman, Three Counties Minkhounds) 193, 205, 206
Maynard, Ed 220
McNay, Iain (Press Officer, HSA) 16, 44
Meddows, John (Chairman, HSA) 26
Meads, Jim (hunting photographer) 82
Mendip Farmers Foxhounds 16
Michalak, Mike 220
Mid-Devon Foxhounds 131
Mid-Wales Wildlife Conservation Group 39
Miles, Graham (Whipper-in, Devon and Cornwall Minkhounds) 182
Miller, Jane (Master, Dartmoor Otterhounds) 183
Miller, Loveday (2nd Whipper-in, Tetcott Foxhounds) 126
Mink Hunting 133, 144, 157, 177-215

chain of bubbles 194, 198
damage to agriculture 196, 197
history 177, 178
holloa 182, 192, 202-204, 209
hounds attacking a terrier 201
Joint Week (Three Counties, Four Shires, Devon and Cornwall Minkhounds) 185-195
seven hour hunt 195
stabbing mink with sharp stick 181
throwing live mink in front of hounds 203
tree, evicting mink from 183, 188, 191, 205, 206
trophies 191, 198, 199
wine and cheese party 207
with Ian Coghill 196-200, 202-215
Mirror, Daily 10, 136, 216
Miss 'L' 98
Monro MP, Hector 178
Mujahideen 76-78
Murray-Wells, Simon (Master, Border Counties Otterhounds) 40

N
National Trust, Arlington 97
National Anti-Vivisection Society 55
New Forest Animal Protection Group 33
New Forest Buckhounds 33
New Musical Express 53
News of the World 98, 111, 114, 116, 216

Norrish, John (Whipper-in, Dulverton West Foxhounds) 136
Northern Animal Liberation League 73
Northern Echo 211, 212
North Yorkshire Coursing Club 173

O
Observer, The 74, 77, 81, 90, 215, 216
O'Reilly, Mike 10, 216, 220
Ormskirk Magistrates Court 32
Openshaw (Judge), WH 33
Otter
  decline in numbers 35, 177
  recovery in numbers 223
Otter Hunting 35-41
  Royal approval 41
  trophies 36, 37
Otter Trust 223
Oxford Crown Court 53
Oxfordshire Coursing Club 31, 32

P
Parry, Olive 73
Payne, Lawrie 220
Pedlar, Dr. Kit 54
Pedler, Ian 17
Peel, John 11, 61, 62, 64, 67, 209
Pevensey Marsh Beagles 160-162
Philpotts, Dave (Honorary Secretary, Leadon Vale Basset Hounds) 169, 170
Phipps, Jill 223
Piper, James 223
Prescott, Sir Mark 175

Prestidge, John 14
Preston Crown Court 33
Prince Charles 62, 154
Protect Our Wild Animals 221
Puckeridge Hunt 10

Q
Quantock Staghounds 84, 85, 90, 91, 106, 111-113

R
Rickard, Arlin (Huntsman, Devon and Cornwall Minkhounds) 157, 167, 179-195, 200, 201, 214
Rickard, Liz (Whipper-in, Devon and Cornwall Minkhounds) 179, 182
Rioting, hounds 23-25, 90, 108, 125, 130, 148, 167, 168, 187, 196, 200, 201, 204, 206
Richards, Stan (Terrierman, Dulverton West Foxhounds) 139, 140, 142
Rowley, Raymond 10, 35, 75, 172, 220
Royal Family 9, 37
Royal Windsor Horse Show 37
RSPCA 52, 54, 221, 223
  Inspector dies from injuries inflicted by cockfighters 223

S
Save Our Stags 17
Shooting Times 26, 110, 156, 161, 162, 195, 207, 215, 219
Sirl, Graham 220
Skilton, Colin 163
Smith, Angela 75
Smith, Colin (journalist) 77
Smoking Beagles 11, 54-60, 74, 160

Smythe, Fred (Master, Dulverton West Foxhounds) 122
South East Animal Liberation League 73, 219
South Herts Beagles 28
South Tetcott Foxhounds 118, 145, 149, 153, 155
St. Francis of Assisi 73
Street, Bob (Huntsman, Tiverton Foxhounds) 124
Sun, The 33, 60, 64
Surrey and North Sussex Beagles 157-164, 168, 169
Surrey Union Hunt 24
Sweet, William 223

T
Telegraph, Sunday 24, 216
Terrier work equipment 21
Tetcott Foxhounds 118, 125, 145, 149, 210
Thatcher MP, Margaret (Prime Minister) 29, 74, 168
Tillsley, Paul 220
Times, Sunday 36
Times, The 142, 216
Tiverton Foxhounds 124
The Farming Ladder by George Henderson 117
Three Counties Minkhounds 39, 100, 144, 157, 164, 167, 169, 171, 184-215
Tiverton Staghounds 8, 9, 84, 94, 95, 97-100, 107-111, 114-116, 136

V
Vale of Clettwr Foxhounds 24
Vicars who hunt 47, 49, 169

W
Wallace, Capt. Ronnie (Master, Heythrop Foxhounds then Exmoor Foxhounds) 47, 49, 124
Ward, Les 220
Warwickshire Beagles 164, 167, 208
Warwickshire Foxhounds 135
Wasley, Andrew 220
Waterloo Cup (hare coursing) 10, 31-33, 171-176
Watson, JNP (hunting author) 146, 147
Wayre, Philip 223
Western Mail 25
West Percy Foxhounds 219
Wetton, Dave and Cee 16, 17, 19, 23, 74, 216-219
Whaddon Chase Foxhounds 18
White, Peter 33, 220
Whitelaw MP, Willie 29
Whitlock, Dick 208, 209
Whittall, Sally (journalist) 210
Wickens, Jim 220
Wigton Magistrates Court 64
Williamson, Chris 75
Wildlife Action 33
Wildlife and Countryside Bill 1982 (amendment to fully protect otters) 178
'Wilkins', Mike (Press Officer, League Against Cruel Sports) 9, 185, 211, 212, 216
Wood, Chris 11, 219
Worby, Thomas 223
Worcestershire Foxhounds 153
Wyre Forest Beagles 165-167, 209